HUMAN RIGHTS AND PROBATION SUPERVISION

HUMAN RIGHTS AND PROBATION SUPERVISION

P. Prathapan

KALPAZ

ISBN: 978-93-5128-096-5
Price: ₹ 690

First Published, 2015

Published by

Kalpaz Publications
C-30, Satyawati Nagar,
Delhi-110052
Ph. : 9212142040
E-mail: kalpaz@hotmail.com

Laser Typesetting : Gyan Prints (AB-I), Delhi
Printed at : G. Print Process, Delhi

Contents

GANDHIGRAM RURAL INSTITUTE – DEEMED UNIVERSITY

(Estd.u/s. 3 of the UGC Act. 1956 vide Notification
No. F.9-1/76-U.3/3.81976 of GOI)

Re-Accredited with A Grade by NAAC

DEPARTMENT OF GANDHIAN THOUGHT AND PEACE SCIENCE

Dr. M. William Baskaran

Professor, Dindigul District,
Gandhigram – 624 302

Ph. 0451-2452371 (Off), 9443457098, Fax: 0451-2454466,
E-mail: willkaran@yahoo.co.in, willbas@rediffmail.com

Date: 13-06-2014

Message

Trial and punishment to the offenders are the ultimate destination of the contemporary judiciary in most of the countries, throughout the world. In its midst, probation came into being as an alternative to imprisonment based on the philosophy that there are traces of goodness in every human being, which could be tapped to correct their wrong behaviour. Probation, helps an offender to retrace his old ways and enables him to mend his ways. This is aimed to prevent and nullify the ill effects of imprisonment and persecution.

To monitor and undertake the correctional measures, Probation officers are posted in all districts of India. As per the Probation Offenders Act, the probation officers are expected to use humanistic and creative strategies and techniques to undertake reformative and rehabilitative activities on the probationers, placed under their supervision. Though many voluntary organisations are working in the field of correctional and rehabilitation work, the responsibilities and initiatives taken by the government in this direction are something noteworthy and important. Probation is an effective method of correction. Though, those concerned grossly neglect it. Public awareness and participation are very much required for the furtherance and effective implementation of the probation service in India. This needs systematic and deeper research and proper dissemination of information and knowledge about probation for the acknowledgement and wider acceptance of the public.

Dr. P. Prathapan has made an in-depth research and analysis on the status and impact on probation work in southern states of India. This is an authentic and pioneering work in the field of jail reform. He started his career as a Probation Officer and later rose to higher position in the department of social welfare in the state of Kerala. His study and efforts in the field of correctional work were genuine and sincere.

With these qualifications and background, he has worked on this book with selected areas from the reports of various Prison Reforms Committees constituted by the Government of India and studies relating to probation in India and in other countries for the benefit of the policy makers and probation officers. This book deals with different aspects of probation in a scientific and systematic manner. Some of the key aspects of probation like origin, objectives and advantages of probation, legal status including court decisions, contents of presentence inquiry reports, need of probationers, personal qualities of probation officers, techniques of correction, problems in probation service and role of voluntary organisations in probation supervision are covered in an elaborate manner. It provides a comprehensive and panoramic view of probation.

I express my sincere wishes and appreciation to his pioneering work.

M. William Baskaran

Preface

Probation is accepted world over as method of treatment of offenders, it is conditional suspension of sentence and it involves supervision and treatment of the offender. Probation is the non-institutional treatment of the offenders in community settings; and it gives a chance to mend the ways of offenders. Thus, Probation Service which occupies an important place in the Criminal Justice System, is implemented mainly through the Probation Officer as per the Probation of Offenders Act 1958.

More than 50 per cent of the prisoners in India are remand prisoners and among the convicted persons, more than 50 per cent are shot-term convicts. All of them are returning to the society as hardens.

Here, comes the question of human rights of those imprisoned as well as of the law-abiding citizens. Since the conviction rate is low in India, it is evident that majority of the remand prisoners will be acquitted. By this time, they would have remained in prison for several months. This is drastic violation of their Human rights.

In event of those remand prisoners and short-term convicts coming out as hardens and involves in serious and series of crimes, it results in the violation of the human rights of law-abiding members of the society who constitute the majority.

One of the solution, is the wide and intelligent application of Probation Supervision as provided by the existing law. In this regard public awareness and public support is necessary. This books is written with a view to provide deep and concise knowledge to the students, social workers, planners, policy makers, lawyers and to the general public with hope that it would kindle hope to the neglected part of our Criminal Justice System.

P. Prathapan

1

Introduction

Probation is a method of dealing with specially selected offenders and that it consists of the conditional suspension of punishment, while the offender is placed under personal supervision and is given individual guidance and treatment. It applies to a person, who admits the criminal offense, committed by him and reports.But the selection is based on the presentence investigation by the Probation Officer. The Magistrate may or may not exercise this discretion over the case in placing a person under the supervision of Probation Officer. Since it involves individualisation of treatment, probation is said to be the best alternative to short term sentences, which are proved to be harmful to several convicts. Probation involves professional Casework, Job placement, Counseling, Family counseling, Financial assistance, resuming education, supervision.

The Four Basic Elements

1. Probation is a method of dealing with offender

It denotes a gradual transition from the method of punishment of offenders to their social and psychological treatment similar to the treatment of maladjusted individuals. Thus, crime is considered to be the product of a diseased mind.The success of probation depends upon 'the personal relationship of trust and guidance, with the help of community resources'.

2. Probation is a method, which is applied on a selective basis

The probationer is selected on the basis of the scientific study on the family and social background and criminal antecedents of the individual. The persistence enquiry is conducted on the antecedents, family background, age, circumstances and gravity of the offence, and examines the offender's personality and needs, to be subjected to individual treatment. It depends mainly on the reports enacted between the probationer and Probation Officer. Presentence enquiry and the consequent follow up programmes are part of the probation treatment. The final selection is the discretion of the court.

3. Probation involves conditional suspension of punishment

The original offence remains punishable throughout the period of probation and the offender is liable to get the original sentence in event of the violation of the conditions of his probation supervision order or in case of a fresh offence. Hence, Probation is not a 'let off'. The probationer should voluntarily accept the conditions of the bond and co-operative with the Probation Officer. Probation permits a more normal social experience than institutionalisation, hence it is a form of community treatment, and it does not disrupt the offender's relationship with his family, relatives, with his friends, with the opposite sex, with his educationor, with his occupation.

4. Probation involves supervision and treatment

Probationers provided with the systematic assistance and the society accepts his future lawful course of conduct. Unlike police supervision probation supervision involves personal relationship. Since the Probation supervision as a personal relationship between the probationer and Probation Officer has its negative and positive implications. On the negative side, it is essentially the use of legal authority for the protection of the probationer form the "unwise use of personal freedom", and as such, it is an authoritarian restrictive and disciplinary measure. Supervision is having educational, therapeutic and rehabilitative objectives. The positive aspect of the treatment part includes Counseling, professional Casework and skilled profession. The personal relationship created between the probationer and Probation Officer should be with a rehabilitative objective.

Misconceptions about Probation

1. A Misconception exists among the public, offenders, Judicial officers and other officials charged with enforcement of the law, that the probation is a form of leniency or as a 'let-off'. Mainly because the probationers escape the penalty for their offences and the inadequate use of necessary safeguards like the careful section

of probationers and the maintenance of close personal supervision,

2. Probation is to be distinguished from 'pardon' and 'commutation'. Pardon involves the absolution of the offender for punishment and may be granted at any time; communication consists of the substituting of a less severe punishment for that which was originally imposed.
3. Another misconception is that probation is applicable only or mainly to first offenders. But probation can be successfully applied to adult offenders and to offenders with a previous criminal record. Since the essence of probation is that 'each case should be considered on its merits, and the real criterion is the likehood of the offender to respond if a probation order is made'.

Some Related Measures of Probation

1. **Parole:** Convicted persons are released from prisons for shorter period so as to mingle with his family and community;
2. **Pre-delinquent supervision:** Here the use of supervision is similar of the probationary type with respect to pre delinquents and other maladjusted persons;
3. The recognizance and binding over; and,
4. The conditional suspension of the imposition, or of the execution of sentence without probation supervision.

There are many eminent persons in the world who stood for human rights and social rehabilitation of the delinquents. As Mahatma Gandhi wrote in **Young India dated 19-9-1931**, about the India of his dreams:

> "There will be no exploiter or exploited and hence every individual enjoys equal and dignified treatment in the India. I shall work for an India in which the poorest shall feel that it is their country in whose making they have an effective voice, an India in which there shall be no high class or low class of people; an India in which all the communities shall live in perfect harmony. There can be no room in such India for the curse of untouchables or the curse of intoxicating drinks and drugs.

Women will enjoy the same rights as men. Since we shall be at peace with all the rest of the world, neither, exploiting nor being exploited, we should have the smallest army imaginable. All interests not in conflict with the interests of the dumb millions will be scrupulously respected whether foreign or indigenous. Personally, I hate distinction between foreign and indigenous. This is the India of my dreams".[1]

In the introductory remarks of the Report of All India Jail Manual Committee 1957-59 quotes a speech from Dr. S. Radhakrishnan, the then Vice- President of India stated that:

> " There is not a single individual, however criminal he may be who is beyond redemption. All men are the children of immortality, "amrtasyaputrah". The spirit is in every one, as a part of oneself, a part of the substratum of one's being. It may be buried in some like a hidden treasure, beneath the barren debris of brutality and violence, but it is there all the same, operative and alive, ready to come to the surface at the first suitable opportunity".[2]

The famous **'talisman'** proposed by Gandhi can very well be applicable to Probation Officers. In order to achieve the ideals of equality and brotherhood, the mankind must act on the principles of paying the highest attention to the prime needs of the weakest sections of the populations or 'Daridranarayana' as Mahatma had called them, as is well known. Gandhiji had given a remarkable, 'talisman':

> "Whenever you are in doubt, or when the self becomes too much with you, try the following expedient. Recall the face of the poorest and most helpless man whom you may have seen and ask yourself if the step you contemplate is going to be of any use to him"[3].

Eminent persons and several Jail Reforms Committee reports spoke about the advantages of probation and its wide application. One derivation of probation is from the word 'probare' which means to prove. That is to prove the worth. Another etymological origin on the word Probation:

> "Derives from the Latin term 'probatio' that means a period of proving or trial and forgiveness. Thus, offenders who prove themselves during the trial period by complying with the conditions of their probation are forgiven and released from further involvements with the criminal justice system."[4]

Probation was introduced in many provinces in the British India in different ways. But an uniform legislation named Probation of Ofenders Act was passed after independence. The Joint Parliamentary Committee constituted to draft Probation Law in India, in its report states:

> "The Probation of Offenders Bill was introduced in the Lok Sabha on the 11th November, 1957. The motion for consideration of the bill was moved in the House by Shri. B.N. Datar on the 14th November 1957. An amendment to the motion for reference of the Bill to a Joint Committee of the house was moved by Shree Narayan Das, on the 18th November, 1957 and was discussed in the Lok Sabha and adopted on the same day.

The Rajya Sabha discussed the motion on the 25th and 26th November 1957 and concurred in the said motion on the 26th November, 1957. The Committee held several sittings. The Committee considered the report on 17th and 19th February, 1958 and adopted the same on the 19th February, 1958. Recommending the Bill to be passed, Shree Hukam Singh, Chairman of the Joint Committee submitted the Joint Committee report on 21st, February, 1958."[5]

Probation in its rudimentary form was present in ancient India as is evident from the Smritis. The item numbers (6), (8) and (9) noted below from the scriptures are present in the existing Probation of Offenders Act 1958, as section 3 and 4 respectively. The penances of various kinds were exercised with a religious touch but it involves repentance of the offender. The punishments to which the offenders are liable under the provisions of ancient Hindu Law were:

> "(1) Death Sentence under various modes; (2) Arrest and imprisonment; (3) Corporal punishment of various degrees; (4) Banishment or Deportation; (5) Forfeiture of property; (6) Fines; (7) Harsh reproofs; (8) Gentle admonitions; and, (9) Penances of various kinds"[6].

Modern Criminal Justice System aims for the reformation and social rehabilitation of the offender. This is to be done by the scientific study of the offender regarding his family background by the personnel in the criminal justice system and implement the plan of action chalked out.

> "The goal of correctional treatment is to help the criminal understands his own problems and enable him to deal adequately with them. The Probation Officer must use the resources in the community skillfully to enhance his effectiveness in working with the probationers. Correctional treatment of probationers must be done on the basis of mutual trust, cooperation and responsibility between the Probation Officer and the criminal".[7]

Shri. V. Krishna Menon, former Chief Probation Superintendent Madras wrote, with regard to the importance or relevance of probation as found in the Report of the All India Jail Manual Committee, that:-

> "Of all the modern methods of corrective treatment, the one which has achieved the greatest prominence is probation. Probation has now been recognised on all hands as the most dynamic, realistic and the democratic method of dealing with an offender. It is an invaluable method of protecting society by means other than punishment, and provides a real and more satisfactory alternative method of fulfilling those purposes, which the welfare of society needs to be fulfilled by a punishment

consisting of imprisonment. It is now increasingly being realised that there are few more ways of manufacturing criminals than by sending young offenders unnecessarily to prison where they may easily find themselves far more comfortable than they expect to be, where perhaps they may make acquaintance with men and methods likely to bring them to ruin, and where after serving some short sentence of complete futility, they may abandon for ever their repugnance to prison and all that it involves. Years of experience in the field of law enforcement in the advanced countries have forced the conclusion that the safety of society cannot be assured by putting all our trusts in prisons and that we must increasingly place more and more emphasis on preventing our youth from gravitating towards a life of crime and upon the salvaging of a vast proportion of our delinquents through the enlightened system of probation".[8]

The kinds of punishments as per ancient Hindu law were: Death under various modes, arrest and imprisonment, corporal punishment of various degrees, banishment, forfeiture of property, fines harsh reproof, gentle admonitions, and penances of various kinds. The last mentioned methods of punishments are very similar to probation service of modern times.

> "Kautilay Smritis (IV-10) lay down the award of punishment must be regulated by a consideration of the motive and the nature of the offence, the time and place, the strength, age, conduct (or duties) learning and monetary position of the offenders and by the fact whether the offense is repeated."[9]

Probation, Victimology and restorative justice are increasingly be used judicial officers within the previews of the existing legal system. Probation was in existence time immemorial in a rudimentary form in India also. In many countries the judicial officers under the criminal Justice system has developed in such an extend to give compensation to the victims of crime.

> "Sentencing becomes a delicate art of healing and is now increasingly practiced such by enlightened courts".[10]

> "The usual pattern is the suspension of the execution of the sentence and a further action by the court on successful completion by way of quashing the previous sentence"[11]

In these days the role of voluntary organisations and persons in probation supervision is becoming increasingly relevant:

> "In view of the vastly increased dimensions of probation work, it is considered now a days to have a nucleus of professional service with voluntary workers in adequate numbers to assist the organisation. A distinguishing feature of probation is that unlike every other disposition it enlists the willing co-operation of the offender, his family, teachers, workers, neighbors, and other social and professional workers as needed."[12]

Criminology being scientific study of crime as a social phenomenon, in India, it was introduced as a subject in Jail Officers Training School, at Lucknow in the year 1940. Among the conservative, Liberal and Radical criminologists, the Liberal criminologists are more pro-probation. Liberal Criminologists are of the view that:

> "Crime is the result of learning process occurring within criminogenic culture. Criminality is the result of breakdown of personal and social control. Crime is a normal response to a situation of cultural discontinuity between ends and means".[13]

Justice V.R. Krishna Iyer, in one of his articles on the Relevance of Probation in the changing contours of Criminology and Law, states that:

> "The new philosophy and benefits of non- institutional treatment needs to be publicised so that intelligent public opinion and popular good will may be mobilised in support of the theory and practice of probation as an alternative to jail term".[14]

Probation in a primitive form was present in ancient India. Mahesh Kumar wrote quoting ancient scriptures:

> "Administration of justice was then equitable. ' Manu' used the power of discrimination too far. If it is the first crime of the offender he could be "let off" with a warning to behave properly in future. If the same offender commits a second criminal act, he must be 'censured' and let go. 'Fines' will be imposed for a third offense. Even then he continues to commit offense in any manner, nothing but corporal punishment is suitable. But those who does wrong second time and that too knowingly, are liable to punishment as found in the Manusmriti, Chapter VIII, stanzas 128-129)".[15]

The various wings of Criminal Justice System are to act in coordination and cooperation with a 'correctional mind'; so as to prevent persons involved in crimes from becoming hardens criminals.

> "A hardened criminal is not born. It is the system, which throws him outside the pale of society. If the police and the law were guided by the dictates of justice then the term undertrail should have been obsolete.

> The attempt is not to shield the criminal, nor it is to overlook the working constraints of the police. The effort is to clear the choking undergrowth in the jungle law as also simplify the arduous trek from the political lock-up to the final court verdict. Attempts have also to be made to ensure that the police or the law do not misuse the powers entrusted to them. It calls for a sense of commitment to what is right-and just-rather than treatment of the suspect as a prospective 'sentencingguineapig'".[16]

Internationally the United Nations Standard Minimum Rules for Non-custodial Measures (**Tokyo rules**) provide the basic principles in this regard. The member nations shall develop non-custodial measures within their legal systems. A proper balance is to be maintained between the individual offenders, the right of the victim and public safety. At the time of its implementation the political, economic, social and cultural conditions of each country are to be considered. It promotes greater involvement of the community in the treatment of offenders. It was adopted by General Assembly Resolution 451110 of December 1990.The Tokyo Rule (1990) stipulates in its rule 13, the treatment Process as:

> "Within the framework of a given non-custodial measure, in appropriate cases, various schemes, such as casework, group therapy, residential programmes and the specialised treatment of various categories of offenders, should be developed to meet the needs of offenders more effectively;

Professionals who have suitable training and practical experience should conduct treatment:

> When it decided that treatment is necessary, efforts should be made to understand the offender's background, personality, aptitude, intelligence, values and, especially, the circumstances leading to the commission of the offence;

> The competent authority may involve the community and social support systems in the application of non-custodial measures;

> These assignments shall be maintained as far as practicable at a manageable level to ensure the implementation of treatment programmes;

For each offender, a case record shall be maintained by the competent authority".[17]

With regards to Discipline and breach of conditions the Tokyo **rules** states:

> "A breach of the conditions to be observed by the offender may result in a modification or revocation of the non-custodial measure;

The competent authority shall make all modifications or revocation of custodial measure; this shall be done only after a careful examination of the facts adduced by both the supervising officer and the offender.

The failure of non-custodial measure should not automatically lead to the imposition of a custodial measure.

In the event of a modification or revocation of a non-custodial measure, the competent authority shall attempt to establish a suitable alternative non-custodial measure. A sentence of imprisonment may be imposed only in the absence of other suitable alternatives.

The power to arrest and detain the offender under supervision in cases where there is a breach of the conditions shall be prescribed by the law.

> Upon modification or revocation of the non-custodial measure, the offender shall have the right to appeal to the judicial or other competent authority."[18]

The United Nations Guidelines for the Prevention of Juvenile Delinquency (Riyadh Guidelines) passed in the year 1991 states with regards to the General Prevention, the main guidelines stipulated in article 9 are as below:

"Comprehensive prevention plans should be instituted at every level of government and include the following:

(a) In-depth analysis of the problem and inventories of programmes, services, facilities and resources available;
(b) Well defined responsibilities of the qualified agencies, institutions and personnel involved in preventive efforts;
(c) Mechanisms for the appropriate coordination of prevention efforts between governmental and non-governmental agencies;
(d) Policies, programmes and strategies based on prognostic studies to be continuously monitored and carefully evaluated in the course of implementation;
(e) Methods for effectively reducing the opportunity to commit delinquent acts;
(f) Community involvement through a wide range of services and programmes;
(g) Close interdisciplinary co-operation between national, provincial and local governments, with the involvement of the private sector, representative citizens of the community to be served, and labour,

child-care, health education, social, law enforcement and judicial agencies in taking concerted action to prevent juvenile delinquency and youth crime;

(h) Youth participation in delinquency prevention policies and process, recourse to community resources, youth self help, and victim compensation and assistance programmes;

(i) Specialized personnel at all levels."[19]

In the modern times the Restorative Justice system had developed where the victims were restored from the trauma suffered out of the crime by making the relationship with offender and his family. The points considered by the traditional Justice System and Restorative Justice are markedly different as written by Tim Newell:

"The Traditional Justice System focuses upon blame and pain in considering, the relevant points:

- What law has been broken?
- Who has broken it?, and
- How should the offender be punished?

Whereas the Restorative Justice considers, the issues like:

- Who has been harmed?
- What is the nature of the harm?
- Who is responsible for that harm?
- What can be done to repair the harm?
- How can the person responsible put things right for the harmed person now and avoid harming others in future."[20]

The judiciary has to go long way to reach this goal.

A similar version was written by Justice V.R. Krishna Iyerin in his book Social Mission of Law urging the need to educate the Judiciary:

> "There is a great and urgent need to civilise and sophisticate the penal law, educate the criminal judiciary and allied agencies with a new accent on rehabilitation of delinquents to broaden and deepen the probation system and diversify the punitive process, to strengthen and modernise social defense, in order to save the exchequer good money in the bargain, as probation is certainly less expensive and if wisely used, more effective than prison bars in certain areas of crime. These contours need to be understood in the proper perspective by those in charge of the nation's policy making and applied by those charged with the enforcement of relevant laws. More than all, the new philosophy and the benefits of non-

> institutional treatment needs to be publicised so that intelligent public opinion and popular good will may be mobilised in support of the theory and practice.

The Probation Officer who is to play a key role in the implementation of the probation system seems to be handicapped seriously in many ways-like that lack of infrastructure to lack of proper orientation. The society refuses to come or aware of the inherent multifarious potentialities of the probation system. That if a person is prevented from becoming a hardened criminal, the society gains a lot materially and morally in the long run, apart from the happiness and well being bestowed to the person so saved. Thus the spread of juvenile delinquency and the consequent immorality and other hardships could be controlled to a great extent with the strengthening of the probation system, though it relates to the prevailing mass poverty, illiteracy and ignorance ".[21]

The Preamble to the Indian Constitution is the key to the Constitution, which is the mother of all laws:

> "In the Preamble to our Constitution we have resolved to secure to all our citizens 'Justice-Social, economic and political'. In the Directive Principles of the State Policy, the Constitution has enjoined that the "State shall strive to promote the welfare of the people, by securing and protecting social order, in which justice- social, economic and political shall inform all the institutions of national life."

The Directive Principles also entrust the State to direct its policy towards securing that "childhood and youth are protected against exploitation and against moral and material abandonment" Unless we carry out a more enlightened approach in the field of criminal justice and offer the right dessert to they ounger generation, even when found wayward, we shall be failing in our solemn obligation to fulfill the promises given in the Constitution to the nation. Article 37 of the Constitution of India;

> "The state shall strive to promote the welfare of the people by securing and protecting as effectively as it may make a social order in which justice, social, economic and political shall inform all the institutions of the national life."[22]

Similarly there are safeguards against all forms of cruelty, exploitation of the vulnerable groups like young, women and aged.The Constitution of India provided special protection to children.

Article 15(3) states that"nothing shall prevent the State from making any special provision for the welfare of children, even if the provision may be deemed to be discretionary".

Article 24 provides for prohibition of employment of children in factories, stating that 'no child below the age of fourteen years shall be employed to work in any factory or mine or engaged in any other hazardous employment'.

Article 39(f) has been substituted by the Constitution (Forty Second Amendment) Act of 1976 providing that the state shall direct its policy towards securing that, 'children of the tender age are not abused and that children are given opportunities and facilities to develop in a healthy manner and in conditions of freedom and dignity and that childhood and youth are protected against exploitation and against moral and material abandonment'. The Article 39(e) further enjoins the State to ensure that, 'the children of tender age shall not be abused and that they shall be forced by economic necessity to enter avocations unsuited their age or strength.'

Article 45 prescribes that, 'the state shall endeavour to provide within a period of ten years from the commencement of this Constitution, for free and compulsory education for all children until they complete the age of fourteen years" (amended as fundamental right)".[23]

The historical background the Constitution, the laws all are in favour that the offender and the victims have rights. In order to achieve this, the Probation system has to be developed as an alternative to imprisonment.

"Probation at a comparative international level appears to be static, as if time has stood still. New technologies, attempts at evaluation standards, new roles and organisation structures are resisted by the concerned. This situation may lead the probation to become a kind of 'criminal justice island.' The non-custodial measures are."[24]

Similar is the view of the several Committees on Jail reforms constituted on various occasions by the Government of India.

"So if we look from a welfare point of view: Probation should more extensively be used than at present..."[25]

The All India Jails Committee initiated the legal origin of probation system in India in the year 1919-20 headed by Sir Alexander Cardew that recommended the introduction of probation system

> " ...In India where the system of probation officers has not hitherto existed, considerable difficulty may be experienced in finding suitable persons for the post, but we certainly think that an attempt should be made in this direction. We have touched upon this subject in the section of this chapter dealing with the Child Offender and have proposed that the appointment of probation officer should in the first instance be made in large towns."[26]

The All India Committee on Jail Reforms 1980-1983 chaired by Justice A.N. Mulla, Retired Judge of Allahabad High Court and former Member of Parliament had opined that:

> "It has been established all over the World that short term imprisonment is neither deterrent nor coercive. Indeed it might further criminalises short term prisoners who constitute a large percentage of the prison population. The Committee draws attention to the proposed amendment to section 53 of the Indian Penal Code suggested by the Report of the Joint Committee on the Indian Penal Code (Amendment) bill 1972. The amendment suggestsin addition to imprisonment, alternatives such as:

(i) Community Service;

(ii) Disqualification from holding office;

(iii) Order to payment of compensation;

(iv) Forfeiture of property;

(v) Fine; and,

(vi) Public Censure"[27]

Institutional treatment of young persons was classified into Pre committal, Committal and post-Committal stage institutions like:

(a) Pre-Committal stage: Observation Home/Remand Home, Balbhawan, Boys Clubs, SOS Village, Orphanage, Destitute Home

(b) Committal Stage: Bal Sahayog, Children Home, Fit Persons, Fit Institutions, Special/Certified Approved School Reformatory, Juvenile Jail, Borstal School and any other special institution.

(c) Post-Committal Stage: After Care Homes/ Hostels, Day Care Centres and Half-way-Homes."[28]

The problem of street children was eradicated in the former Soviet Union but the method adopted is still not revealed:

> "One remembers those gangs of homeless children who lived outlaw lives in the cities of Russia in the first years of the Revolution. The task of fitting them into the new society that was emerging was accomplished

with brilliant success. Yet the story of exactly, how it was done has still to be made available for other countries.

The world's Dead End kids will soon be counted, not just by companies as they are here, but by divisions and by armies. Some world organisation for the exchange of information and ideas is urgently necessary if we are to give another start in life to all these young people in trouble."[29]

In India the section 562 of the Criminal Procedure Code 1898 envisages the release of certain offenders on probation of good conduct. The Indian jails committee 1919-20 recommended widening and extend its scope so that children or young persons can be released on probation under the supervision of a Probation Officer. No such amendments were made so far even in the amended Criminal Procedure Code 1973. The Committee recommended in its report during 1919-20 that:

> "When the court is possession of all the necessary facts, it will make a final order. We wish to draw attention here to the opinion held by the best authorities both in England and in America that the most satisfactory solution of the problem will be to entrust the child to his relatives, if there is any reasonable prospect of their exercising better care of him in the future than in their past and if the home is at all a decent one. In order that this plan may be adopted it is desirable that the scope of section 562 of the Criminal Procedure Code should be extended, so that in the case of children and young person sat least, a wider discretion may be conferred on the courts to release children under that section, which should, we think, be made as elastic as possible. It should be possible for the court, in addition to releasing the child offender on his own recognizance or on those of a relative or other fit person, to combine such an order with a stipulation regarding payment of fine, damages or costs, or regarding the undergoing of such a period of probation, with or without security for good behaviour; as the court may see fit or both. It is often beneficial to join the parent with the probation officer as surety as bringing home to the former his responsibility regarding his child. The idea of requiring the young offender or his parents or guardians to make some measure of restitution by payment of fine or damages is growing in popularity in the United States, and appears highly desirable. This and other methods of discharge are there freely employed in combination with the system of probation, which we must now notice."[30]

Correctional processes were found to be applicable in the case of dreaded dacoits of Chambal Valley. Violence creates more violence. Gandhiji also stated that by applying the principle of an eye for an eye makes the whole world blind. With regard to the problem of dacoity:

> "The attitude of the Government, of police requires a change to solve this question. Non-violence is the only way to solve the complex problem of dacoity of Chambal ravines. This joint command had 83 encounters in whole in which 74 dacoits are killed, 105 captured, 61 policemen were killed in action."[31]

Ultimate objective of the Criminal Justice System is the rehabilitation of the offender to the very same society he belongs.

Problem of Criminal Justice System in dispensation of Justice to common people" an article written by Anup Kumar Varshney (Sub Editor, Legislative Department, Ministry of Law and Company Affair.) The article is prepared after review of various reports of the Law Commissions like the 4th (1958), 77th (in 1978), and 96th in (1984). It states that:

> "There is generally a lack of understanding that the different limbs of the Criminal Justice System, Viz. the Legislature, the Police, the Prosecution, the court, and the Correctional organisation in order to uphold and make the system effective."[32]

Criminality is a human quality, which was present time immemorial in various forms. Criminal activities were the function of some castes. Gandhi wrote in Young India dated 22-01-1925 (page-25) that Sardar Vallabh Bhai patel was involved in the correction of criminal tribe called Dharalas:

> "Dharalas area fierce military tribe in Gujarat. Their occupation is chiefly farming. But through economic distress they have taken to Thieving. Murder is not an uncommon thing among them. The wave of self purification which pass through India in 1921 could not fail to touch them. The class of workers that have come into being are working in their midst with the sole intention of carrying out internal reform among them. The brilliant Satyagraha movement initiated and led so successfully by Vallabh Bhai during 1923, brought about a great awakening among these people. Their conference at Sojitra was one of the fruits of the reform. They listened to the proceedings in perfect silence. The resolutions carried were about abstaining from intoxicating drinks and drugs, from selling their daughters in marriage and from abduction, a habit which seems rampant among them."[33]

Gandhi wrote in Harijan dated 01-08-1936 under the caption 'a criminal tribe' that:

> "Perhaps there are not many places on this globe where crime is the profession of tribes as it is in India, and it flourishes under the grab of religion. We have therefore a law in this country called the Criminal

Tribes Act. The Aheris of Hissar District are supposed to be one of such tribes."[34]

Gandhi wrote in Harijan dated 13-07-1947 about the way to establish a socialistic society where the criminals also have a place that:

> "Impure means results in an impure end. Hence the prince and the peasant will not be equalised by cutting off the Prince's head, nor can the process of cutting off equalise the employer and the employed. One cannot reach truth by untruthful reason.Therefore only truthful, non violent and pure hearted Socialists will be able to establish a socialistic society in India and the world."[35]

Probation is the result of the evolution in correctional philosophy, starting from the theory of retribution. Various aspects of corrections—

Firstly, the approach of Correctional Officers to clients- based on early criminological thought, physiological approach (physical abnormalities, body type, chromosome abnormalities, biochemical theories, biology and environment).

Secondly, psychological approaches like psychoanalysis, behaviourism, clinical psychology, intelligence and education and sociological approaches like Differential Association, Alienation, Adaptation and Opportunity Theory, Containment Theory and Label ling Theory.

Thus the corporal punishment and capital punishments was to be abandoned, it was necessary to develop an alternation sanction. Then came the eras of reform, and rehabilitation. The corporal punishment and capital punishments was to be abandoned, it was necessary to develop an alternate. Probation is the result of the evolution in correctional philosophy, starting from the theory of retribution. Various aspects of corrections, firstly, the approach of Correctional Officers to clients-based on early criminological thought, physiological approach (physical abnormalities, body type, chromosome abnormalities, biochemical theories, biology and environment). Secondly, psychological approaches like psychoanalysis, behaviourism, clinical psychology, intelligence and education and sociological approaches like Differential Association, Alienation, Adaptation and Opportunity Theory, Containment Theory and Labelling Theory. Thus: "The corporal punishment and capital punishments was to be abandoned, it was necessary to develop an alternation sanction. Then came the eras of reform, and rehabilitation."[36]

In India one of the postulates of the All India Jail Manual Committee (1957-58) was that "probation will be more extensively but selectively used."[37]

And the All India jail Manual Committee had a perspective outlook that,

> "The developments which are likely to take place in our country during the next ten or fifteen years have been taken into consideration. The pattern of delinquent and criminal behaviour which are likely to emerge during the next decade or so."[38]

And the abolition of short-term sentences and the provision of alternative measures was one of the points examined by the All India Jail Manual Committee-1957-59, in Page-4.

By providing public safety, empowering the staff and community, giving attention to human rights and developing good relationships with the stakeholders a humane and just society is envisaged as seen from the Vision Statement of American Probation and Parole Association:

"We see a fair, just and safe society where community partnerships are restoring hope by embracing a balance of prevention, intervention and advocacy. We seek to create a system of Community Justice where:

- **A FULL RANGE OF SANCTIONS AND SERVICES** Provides public safety by insuring humane, effective, and individualised sentences for offenders, and support and protection for victims;
- **PRIMARY PREVENTION INITIATIVES** are cultivated through our leadership and guidance;
- **OUR COMMUNITIES ARE EMPOWERED** to own and participate in solutions;
- **RESULTS** are measured and direct our service delivery;
- **DIGNITY AND RESPECT** describes how each person is treated;
- **STAFF ARE EMPOWERED** and supported in an environment of honesty, inclusion, and respect for differences; and
- **PARTNERSHIP WITH STAKEHOLDERS** lead to shared ownership of our vision."[39]

"Probation is a method of dealing with specially selected offenders, and that it consists of the conditional suspension of punishment while the offender is placed under personal supervision and is given individual guidance or treatment".[40]

Probation is a method, which is applied on a selective basis. This is based upon the principle of individualisation of treatment:

> "The selection of the case is more often circumscribed by statutory restrictions according to the age and the previous record of the offender, the nature and gravity of the offence, etc.The actual selection is based on a careful investigation of the personal traits and social circumstances of offenders prior to the final judicial disposition of the case."[41]

The Liberal Criminology dominated for 50 years from 1940's revolves around the principles laid down by Gibbons and Garebaldian that,

> "(1) Crimes are the result of learning processes occurring within a criminogenic culture; (2) Criminality is the result of breakdown of personal and social control; (3) Crime is a normal response to a situation of cultural discontinuity between ends and means".[42]

Probation is accepted as a method of dealing with offenders. Probation has become the part of the Criminal Justice Act in several countries. Starting with the retribution theory to the restitution theory propounded by several criminologists the position of Probation has become prominent due to the position in the special acts to the major Act in several countries. In India the position still remains the same as the status of Special Law Legislation. The transition of probation form of treatment envisages:

> "With the gradual transition from the punishment of offenders to their social and psychological treatment on a basis similar to the treatment of other maladjusted individuals"[43]

Probation services in India have to perform a number of functions other than usual Probation work like:

"(i) Assisting children before the children's courts

(ii) Making enquires relating to release on parole and of licenses released or about to be released from intuitions;

(iii) Doing welfare and aftercare work in relation to types of discharged offenders;

(iv) Helping women in maintenance and matrimonial cases, as in Tamil Nadu;

(v) Helping 'Nyaya Panchayaths', as in Utter Pradesh

(vi) Making enquiries under section 202 of the Criminal Procedure Code to find out whether it is at all desirable to be preceded with some complaint cases before courts."[44]

As an alternative to corporal punishment the ways of dealing with offenders have been accepted by the United Nations as with various sentencing dispositions. The judicial authority, having at its disposal a range of non-custodial measures, should take into consideration in making his decision the rehabilitative needs of the offender, the protection of society and the interests of the victim, who should be consulted whenever appropriate. Various forms of disposal of cases in the following ways:

"(a) Verbal sanctions, such as admonition, reprimand and warning;
(b) Conditional discharge;
(c) Status Penalties;
(d) Economic sanctions and monetary penalties, such as fines and day-fines;
(e) Confiscation or an expropriation order;
(f) Restitution to the victim or compensation order;
(g) Suspended or deferred sentence;
(h) Probation and judicial supervision
(i) A Community Service order;
(j) Referral to an attendance centre;
(k) House arrest
(l) Any other mode of non-institutional treatment;
(m) Some combination of the measures listed above."[45]

In India these forms of disposals are not present in the Probation of Offenders Act 1958 or in the Indian Penal Code 1860. It only shows that Indian Criminal Justice system has to go a long way to reach in par with the modern forms of treatment of offenders. The Policy makers, Planners, Public and Administrators at Central and State level have to take the lead in the above lines to reach the judicious Criminal Justice System.

Footnotes

1. Davis George(2000), Dynamics of Power: The Gandhiyan Perspective, Frank Bros & Co (Publishers) Ltd, 4675-A, Ansari Road, 21 Daryaganj, New Delhi-110002, p. 209.
2. Report of the All India Jail Manual Committee - 1957-59, Government of India Press, New Delhi, p. 2.
3. Shriman Narayan (1978)- *Towards Gandhiyan Plan*, S. Chand & Company Ltd, Ram Nagar, New Delhi-110055, p. 61.

4. Dean .J. Campion (1990) Probation Parole and Community Corrections, Prentice Hall, Upper Saddile River, New Jersey 07458; p. 32.
5. The Gazetteer of India, (Extraordinary) dated 1958, part II, Sec.2, p. 233.
6. Dr. Mahesh Kumar Sharan (1978), Court Procedure in Ancient India, Abinav Publications, E-37, Hauz Khas, New Delhi-110016, p. 194.
7. V.V. Devasia and Leelamma Devasia (1992) Criminology, Victimology and Corrections, Azhish Publishing House, 8/81 Punjabi bagh, New Delhi-110026, p. 141.
8. All India Jail Manual Committee- 1957-59, Part-I, Annexure- L, Government of India Publication, New Delhi, p. 196.
9. Dr. Mahesh Kumar Sharan (1978), Court Procedure In Ancient India, Abhinav publications, E-37, Hauz Khas, New Delhi-110016, p. 193.
10. Encyclopaedia of Social Work in India, Vol. II, (1987), Govt. of India Publication, New Delhi, p. 330.
11. *Ibid.,* p. 331.
12. Encyclopaedia of social work in India, Vol. II, (1987), Government of India Publication, New Delhi, p. 331.
13. Ram Ahuja (2000), Criminology, Rawat publications, Sathyam Apartments, Sector 3, Jain temple Road, Jawahar Nagar, Jaipur-302004, e-mail: rawatbooks@pinkline.net (page-5)
14. V.R. Krishna Iyer (1976) Social Mission Of Law, Orient Longman Ltd.3/5 Asaf Ali Road, New Delhi-110001, p. 95.
15. Dr. Mahesh Kumar Sharan (1978) Court Procedure In Ancient India, Abhinav publications, E-37, Haus Khas, New Delhi-110016, p. 191.
16. Kum Kum Chedha (1983), The Indian Jail - A Contemporary Document, Vikas Publishing House Pvt. Ltd., 5 Ansari Road, New Delhi-110002, p. 179.
17. The Tokyo Rules (1990)
18. The Tokyo Rules (1990) Article 14
19. U.N. Guidelines for the prevention of Juvenile delinquency (The Riyadh Guidelines) Police Research and Development, (July-September 1991) New Delhi (page- 84)

20. Tim Newell (2000), Forging Justice-Quaker vision for Criminal Justice, Swarthmore Lecture 2000, Quaker Home Service, Friends House, Euston Road, London NWI 2BJ, (page 99)
21. V.R. Krishna Iyer (1976), Social Mission Of Law, Orient Longman Ltd, 3/5 Asaf Ali Road, New Delhi-110001, (page-95)
22. Constitution of India Article 37
23. S.P. Srivastava, (1989) 'Juvenile Justice in India', Ajantha publications (India), Jawahar Nagar, Delhi-110007 (page-14)
24. Jon. F. Klaus (May 1998), Hand Book In Probation Services, Publication No.60/Rome/London, United Nations International Crime and Justice Research Institute 1998 UNCRI- Common Wealth Secretariat, p. 39.
25. Report of the All India Jail Manual Committee 1957-59, Government of India, New Delhi, p. 33.
26. Indian Jails Committee 1919-20, Government Press Simla, Vol. I, para 434, p. 223.
27. Report of the All India Committee on Jail Reforms-1980-83, Vol. I&II, Ministry of Home Affairs, New Delhi, p. 36.
28. S.P. Srivastava (1989), Juvenile Justice in India, Ajantha Publications, New Delhi -07, pp. 78-79.
29. Robert Mayer (1946)] Young People in Trouble, Victor Gallancz Ltd, London, p. 61.
30. Report of the Indian Jails Committee 1919-20, Vol. 1 Government Press, Shimla, Para-374, pp. 198-9.
31. Shrikrishna Datta Bhatta (1962)... And they gave up dacoity, A.B. Sarva Seva Sanghprakasan, Rajghat, Varanasi, p. 299.
32. Anup Kumar Varshney (April 1994) Social Defense, Vol. xxxiv Number 116, National Institute of Social Defense, Ministry of Welfare, Government of India, New Delhi-110066, p. 21.
33. V.B. Kher (1976) Social Service Work and Reform Vol. III, Navajivan Publishing Home Ahmedabad-14, p. 451.
34. V.B. Kher (1976) Social Service, work and Reform, Vol.III, Navajivan Publishing House, Ahmedabad-380014, p. 451.
35. Bharatan Kumarappa, (Ed.) (January 1954) Sarvodaya- M.K. Gandhi, Navajivam Publishing Trust, Ahmedabad-14, p. 154.

36. Vernon. B. Fox & Jeanne B. Stinch Comb (1972), Introduction To Correction, Prentice Hall, Career & Technology, Englewood Cliffs, NJ 07632, p. 113.

37. All India Jail Manual Committee -1957-59, p. 9.

38. *Ibid.,* p. 11.

39. Vision statement of American Probation and Parole Association, www.appa-net.or

40. United Nations (1951) The Origin and Spread of Probation and Related Measure, UN publication, New York, p. 4.

41. *Ibid.*, p. 5.

42. Ram Ahuja (2000) Criminology, Rawat Publications, Sathyam Apartments, Sector-3 Jain temple Road, Jawahar Nagar, Jaipur-302004, p. 3.

43. United Nations (1951) The Origin and Spread of Probation and Related Measures, UN Publication, New York, pp. 4-5.

44. Encyclopaedia of Social Work in India (1987) Vol. II, Government of India, Publication Division, New Delhi-1, p. 334.

45. John F. klaus (May 1998) Hand book on Probation service, UNICRI, New York, (UN Publication sales No. E.98.111N.3), p. 17.

2

Object of Probation

The object of Probation of Offenders Bill, 1958, states, "There has been an increasing emphasis on the reformation and rehabilitation of the offender as useful and self-reliant member of the society without subjecting him to the deleterious effect of jail life It was proposed to have a central law on the subject which should be uniformly applicable to all the States."[1]

By 1985 the set of objective of Criminal Justice System in England has become the following as written by Tim Newell:

> "To prevent and reduce crime; to establish a principled basis for sentencing; to avoid the unnecessary use of imprisonment and stabilize the current prison population; to develop supervision schemes in the community; to reduce re-offending; to give greater consideration to victims; and, to make the system more effective, efficient and accountable."[2]

Ancient Indian scriptures proclaimed the object of punishment:

> "The Kautilya Smritis (IV, 10), lay down the award of punishment must be regulated by a consideration of the motive and the nature of the offense, the time and place, the strength, age, conduct (or duties) learning and monetary position of the offenders and by the fact whether the offense is repeated".[3]

Probation is recognised as a prime measure of correction by extending its activities to encourage public participation, training to relevant personnel and to conduct research and development in the field. It is evident from the goals and objectives of the American Probation and parole Association as below:

- "To encourage public awareness for probation and parole.
- To pursue certification of probation and parole programmes on a national basis.
- To encourage participation of line personnel in the American Probation and Parole Association programmes.
- To develop standards for probation and parole programmes.
- To establish regional training programmes.
- To develop membership internationally in order to become a unified voice for community corrections.
- To sponsor training opportunities for all levels of practitioners giving the membership and others, the opportunity to keep current with practices, issues and innovations as well as continuing to develop professional skills.
- To provide technical assistance through a broad membership network by identifying those individuals and jurisdictions who can provide assistance to others.
- To recognise outstanding contributions in the field for community corrections and administer a national awards programme.
- To provide a public information system.
- To conduct research and develop activities in support of the field of community corrections."[4]

Another version of the Objects of the Probation (Supervision) Order addresses itself simultaneously to four implicit objects of the probation order are as given below:

"1. ***Legal or statutory***, that is, observance of the probation conditions prescribed by the court.

2. ***Therapeutic***, that is, use by the probation officer of his casework skills, group therapy, counseling (including vocational), community organisation methods and rapport with the juvenile's parents, friends, etc.

3. ***Rehabilitative*** that is, extending to the probationer whatever concrete services he may need for his adjustment to employer, co-workers, and family.

4. ***Preventive,*** that is, probation, as social treatment, can justify itself as an alternative to institutionalisation only when the probationer makes good on probation, and the probationer and the probation officer together play a significant role in bringing about the positive eventuation".[5]

The object of Probation is to aid the person placed under supervision to lead a responsible life:

> "F.V. Jarvis quotes Swanson Probation Officers Manual: the aim of probation is a more permanent goal than inhibition under the authoritative restraint of criminal or otherwise anti-social conduct during the limited period of recognisance, that is the permanent assumption of a stable and responsible manner of living."[6]

Bhattacharya as below gives another version of the objectives of Probation work by Probation officer:

> "To conduct presentence inquiry; to reform and rehabilitate the criminal in his own natural surroundings; to help him to stand on his own legs and solve behavioural problems through counseling; and to change his behaviour and also correct his path so as to enable him to become a useful citizen"

The object and reasons of the Probation of offenders Act 1958:

"1. The question of release of offenders on probation of good conduct instead of sentencing them to imprisonment has been under consideration for sometime. In 1931, the Government of India proposed a draft of Probation of offenders Bill and circulated it to then local Governments for their views. However owing to preoccupations with other more important matters the Bill could not be proceeded with. Later, in 1934 the Government of India informed Provincial Governments that there was no prospect of Central legislation being undertaken at the time and there would be no objection to the provinces undertaking such legislations themselves. A few Provinces accordingly enacted their own Probation laws."

2. In several states, however, there are no separate probation laws at all. Even in the states there are probation laws, they are not uniform nor are they adequate to meet the present requirements. In the mean time there has been an increasing emphasis on the reformation and rehabilitation of useful and salient member of the society without subjecting him to the deleterious effect of jail life. In view of the widespread interest in the probation system in the country, this question has been re-examined and it is proposed to have a central law on the subject, which should be uniformly applicable to all the states.

3. It is proposed to empower courts to release an offender after admonition in respect of certain specified offences. It is also

proposed to empower courts to release on probation, in all suitable cases an offender found guilty of having suitable committed on offence not punishable with death or imprisonment for life. In respect of offenders under 21 years of age, special provision has been made putting restrictions on their imprisonment. During the period of probation, offenders will remain under the supervision of probation officers in order that they may be reformed and become useful members of society. The bill seeks to achieve these objects."[7]

The Supreme Court, also upheld that the object of the Act is to prevent the mingling of youthful offenders with the hardened in prisons, that:

> "The object of the Act is to prevent the conversion of youthful offenders with obdurate criminals as a result at their association with hardened criminals of mature age in case the youthful offenders are sentenced to undergo imprisonment in jail and provides for their release on probation or after due admonition"[8]

The object of Probation of offenders Act was reiterated by Justices V.R. Krishna Iyer, P.N. Bhagawathy and S. Murtaza Fazil Ali, of the Supreme Court, that it is a social legislation meant to reform juvenile offenders:

> "As, however the appellant was a boy of 20 years, his case clearly falls within the purview of the probation of offenders Act 1958. The probation of offenders Act is a social legislation which is meant to reform juvenile offenders so as to prevent them from becoming hardened criminals by providing an educational and reformative treatment to them by the government. Unfortunately though the provision of section 6 of the Probation of offenders Act are mandatory the courts do not appear to make wise use of these provisions which is necessary to protect our younger generation from becoming professional criminals and therefore a menace to the society."[9]

Majority of the offenders commits the crime due to the influence of the circumstances or at the spur of moment. Organised crimes are often very generally serious crimes. Serious criminals can also be corrected in conducive atmosphere with experts correctional officers. It is generally believed that that the correctional treatment meted out to the prisoners are not so effective for their reformation and converting them to useful citizens.

This is mainly because the prisoner gets ample chance to interact with the hardens in prisons. Even if it is for a shorter period imprisonment embeds a deep and lifelong negative marking in the mental set up of the person. In Many cases it is an injustice to the person, violates of his human rights and can create harmful results, affecting the human rights of the other members of the society who are leading a law abiding life.

Footnotes

1. Published in Gazette India, Extraordinary, 1957, Part II, Sec 2, p. 842.
2. Tim Newell (2000), Forgiving Justice, Quaker Home Service, Friends House, Euston Road, London NWI, 2BJ, p. 33.
3. Dr. Mahesh Kumar Sharan (1978) Court Procedure in Ancient India, Abhinav Publications, E-35, Haus Khas, New Delhi-110016, p. 39.
4. www.appa-net.org
5. M.S. Sabins (1995), Juvenile Justice and Juvenile Correction, Pride and Prudence, Somaiya Publications, Pvt. Ltd., New Delhi, p. 274.
6. Hilary Walkar, Bill Beaumont (1981) Probation Critical Theory and Socialist Practice, Basil Blackwell Publisher Limited, 108 Cowley Road, Oxford, ox4, IJF, England, p. 27.
7. Gazette of India, (1957 Extra.) Pt. II Sec 2, p. 842.
8. Jugal Kishore Prasad Vs State of Bihar, AIR, (1972), SC, 2522 (2524) 2525.
9. Musa Khan and others Vs State of Maharashtra (AIR (1976) Supreme Court cases 2566.

3

Origin of Probation

Origin and Development of Probation in India

The Dharma and Adharma, sin and sinners were some of the concepts associated with crime and punishment in ancient India. Non-Injury, Truth, Non-Theft, Purity and Control of senses constitute Dharma according to Manu, the ancient Lawgiver. The Code of Manu embodies different Forms of punishments like deterrent Expiatory, Retaliatory, Protection and Poetic. It some way exemplifies in the words Samam, Dhanam, Bhedam, and Dhandam.

It means initially giving a chance to reform and in the case of unavoidable circumstances as a last resort imposes serious punishment.

According to other lawgivers like, Kautilyanand Yagnavalkya, the Personal Qualities, Aptitude, Antecedents' Previous Criminal Records etc., are to be considered before imposing punishments.

At the sametime Vigneswara, the lawgiver, points out that before imposing punishment to an offender, whether the accused person is a first offender or not is to be considered by the judiciary.

Mithramisan, the lawgiver, prescribes that the circumstance in which the crime was committed also is to be taken into consideration.

The story of 'Valmiki', a hardened thief who realised his wrong doings, became penitent over the crimes and does the 'thapas' which turned him in to a noble man, can be cited as an example of the reformation of a criminal in ancient times in India. Many of the principles of correction can be traced in the Upanishads and the epics.

Thiruvallur had stated on the subject: 'Inna siethaare oruthal avar nanne; Nannayam 'Siethy vidal' means the best way of punishing offenders is by doing them good in such a way that it is put them to shame.

These are all the traces of the origin of crime and punishment in India as well as the origin of probation in the rudimentary form.

The section 562 of the Criminal Producers Code 1923 states that the specially selected first offenders who have committed offences punishable with imprisonment for life and all men below 21 years of age were eligible for the benefit of probation with or without sureties. The Criminal Procedure Code amended in 1973 envisages these benefits under section 360. Here the Age, Character, Antecedents, and the Circumstances in which the offence was committed, were taken into consideration before releasing them on probation by the court. Accordingly the Chief Metropolitan magistrate of Bombay has instructed to constitute police courts/metropolitan magistrate court to consider a minor offence under the section 562. The accused were interviewed with the help of a social Service Institution, for finding out sureties, his home surroundings and to impose supervision. The work may not be entrusted to police since it may lead to suppression.

Indian Jail committee Report-1919-20, recommended the first offenders were to be treated liberally and could even be released unconditionally, after admonition. The first offenders were classified under two categories, (i) the male adult offenders over 21 years of age, and (ii) young male offenders under 21 years of age and female offenders of any age.

In 1931, the Jail Reforms Committee found that many persons were sent to jail unjustly and recommended for a common central legislation. This was in view of the successful implementation of section 562 of Criminal Procedure Code 1923; and observing the success of probation system in England and U.S.A., but the bill could not be passed mainly due to the unrest existed throughout India.

After independence leaders who experienced bitter experiences in Jails recommended radical changes in jail administration. Accordingly the government of India convened a conference in Bombay during 1952 on the advice of United Nations Technological experts on correctional services. The world famous Criminologist Dr. Walter C. Reckless from the United Nations Technical Expert group, who addressed the conference and later undertook a survey on the correctional administration in India and submitted a valuable report contained recommendations based upon the philosophy of modern jail administration and rehabilitation of offenders. His observation on probation was that there was good evidence to show that probation supervision, as an alternative to jail sentence is the best, most satisfying and the most economical way of handling the juvenile and adult offenders.

Consequently, the All Indian Jail Manual Committee was formed to review the working of Indian Jail. The Committee in its report on 1957-59 pointed out that "there was no liaison between the government the probation personnel, the police and the prison administrators in the implementation of probation law; and also recommended for a central legislation.

In para 135 of the above report states that "the probation should be more extensively used than at present in respect of delinquent children and adolescent offenders. To facilitate this, each state should organise a wide network of probation services".

During that period each state had its own probation laws like; Madras Probation of Offenders Act 1936; Andhra Pradesh Probation of Offenders Act 1938 for Bombay and U.P., central provinces Probation of Offenders Act 1936 for M.P., Good conduct prisoners probation release Act. 1926, by the state of Punjab; West Bengal offender's release on Admonition and probation Act 1954, and Uttar Pradesh First Offenders Act 1938.

Hence to accomplish the recommendation of the Jail Committee, a Bill on probation was introduced in the Lok Sabha on November 11, 1957. Late Shri B.N. Datta moved in the motion for consideration of the bill into the house on November 14, 1957, and later referred to a Joint Committee of the House headed by Sardar Hakum Singh, who handed over it on February 25, 1958 to the Lok Sabha, which passed it and got the President's assent on May 16, 1958.

Now most of the States had enacted rules to carry out the purpose of this Act. But section 18 of the Act provides that nothing in the act shall affect the provisions of section 31 of the Reformatory schools Act 1897, or sub section (2) of section 5 of the Prevention of Corruption Act 1947, or of any laws in force in any State relating to juvenile offenders or Borstal Schools.

As per the other provisions of the Probation of Offenders Act 1958 an offender can be convicted and released on admonition, or on probation with or without supervision by the court after considering his Character, Antecedents, Home Surroundings, and the Circumstances in which the offence was committed.

A report from the Probation Officer was made mandatory in the case of offenders below the age of 21 years. There is provision as per section 5 of the Act for ordering compensation and costs as the court thinks reasonable for the loss or injury caused to any person by the commission of the offence.

There are provisions on the Borstal School Acts of different States to send the convicted offenders in the age group of 16 to 21 years for their reformation to a corrective institution instead of sending them to jail.

Children Acts were in force in different States. All these Acts were codified and a uniform Act called Juvenile Justice Act was enacted in 1986 followed by Juvenile Justice Rules in the respective States. As per the provisions of the Act Separate Courts were established for delinquent and for neglected Juveniles. Juveniles below the age of 16 years, in the case of males and 18 years in the case of females shall not be kept in police custody or in jails. The age limit for both male and female were made uniform 18 years in the Juvenile Justice (care and protection of children) Act 2000. This Act was amended in 2006 by incorporating stringent punishments to offences against juveniles relating to Cruelty, Giving Intoxicants and using them as Labourers.

Justice S.M. Sikri, the former Chief Justice, Supreme Court of India, in his inaugural address on the eve of the Probation Year during May 1971 observed that, not only probation officers should be convinced of the advantages of probation but the judiciary and the bar must become its votaries". And Mr. Justice V.R. Krishna Iyer, former judge of the Supreme Court expressing his views on probation and other correctional services in the National Correctional Conference on Probation and allied measures held in October 1971 at New Delhi, observed,

> "Twenty five years of freedom have not freed our judiciary form the obsolete British Indian penology, bearing on suppression of crime and it is time our magistracy bends to the winds of social change".

Want on use of the provisions of that may result in making a mockery of the Act It should not be extended to educated and experienced person who deliberately flout the law, since it would create an impression in the minds of the criminals that they could commit crimes with impunity thus defeating the very object of the Act.

In a judgment, justices V.R. Krishna Iyer, P.N. Bhavathy and S. Murtaza Fazil Ali stated the object of the Probation of Offenders Act, in Musa Khan and others Vs. State of Maharastra. It is preventing neither the juvenile from becoming hardened criminals, nor the courts are making wise use of its provisions.

Another version of the object of the Act found in Jugal Kishore Prased Vs. State of Bihar is "to prevent the conversion of youthful offenders into obdurate criminals as a result of their association with hardened criminals of mature age, in case the youthful offenders are sentenced to undergo imprisonment in jail, and provide for their release on probation or after due admonition.

The observation made by the Hon'ble High Court of Kerala in Chandrasenan Vs. State of Kerala, charged under the Abkari Act, in worth mentioning especially at this time of increase in organised crime of youngsters, that, "the area and pattern of crime are fast changing in our country that the courts must also play is own role, in ensuring that the course of public justice is not abandoned".

"The first real Probation Law was enacted in New Zealand in 1886, establishing conditions of probation and providing for salaried officers to investigate cases of first offenders and to recommend probation in appropriate cases. England adopted Probation of First Offenders Act in 1887. A more comprehensive probation law was enacted in England in 1907, which provided for investigation and supervision by salaried officers for special conditions, as they might be considered suitable to be contained in the recognizance.

The origin of probation was not the result of a deliberate creation, legislative or judicial act, but rather the result of a gradual growth, an almost unconscious modification of legal practices.

"In the history of criminal policy, the development of probation and related measures is, thus, to be viewed as a part of the general movement away from the traditional, punitive and repressive approach towards the substitution of humanitarian, humanising and utilitarian considerations for those of deterrence and retribution. The main thrust, which the new approach primarily aimed at, was the recognition of the social rehabilitation of the individual as being the main objective of criminal policy thereby achieving the other equally important objective of bringing about improvement in social conditions and development of basic social services favourable to prevention of crime and to social defense generally".[1]

Probation Law was enacted in the State of Massachussets, United States of America in the year 1878, but there were no paid Probation Officers.

In 1619, the colony of Virginia regularised an agreement for the shipment of orphans and destitute children from England. That same year 'Africans' another group of coerced immigrants, made their first appearance in the Virginia Colony. This importation of African slaves displaced youthful poor from U.K."[2]

"In California, U.S.A, in 1941 the Youth Correction Authority was passed under which, a Youth Correction Authority was set up which coordinates all facilities, educational, medical, and rehabilitation work for juvenile delinquents carried on, in social agencies, children' institutions, training schools, clinics and hospitals. Besides, the rehabilitation programme the youth Correction Authority assists in the development of facilities for sports, recreation and leisure time activities for children and young persons in community level as a preventive measure".[3]

With regard to the Study of delinquents R.K. Merton developed the term 'anomie' in 1938. In his article, 'Social Structure and anomie', published in the American Sociological Review:

> "'Anomie' develops because of a breakdown in the relationship between goals that place great stress on success and to which all groups in our society are indoctrinated without equivalent emphasis on institutional or legitimate channels of access to these goals. In the areas where the discrepancy between goals and means, is greater, a condition of anomie prevails and individuals resort to illegitimate means to achieve the goals".[4]

> "In 1899 the first Juvenile Court was established in Cook County, Illinois, USA and within a generation practically every state had enacted Statutes establishing juvenile courts or their equivalents... the courts are like families, Universities social clubs".[5]

A full-fledged probation law was enacted in New Zealand, in 1886, where paid Probation Officers were appointed; and other provisions very similar to the Acts of today. The united nations report on Probation States.

"New Zealand, in 1886 enacted by far the most significant of the early probation statutes of the countries of the British Commonwealth, and was, in fact, the first country or territory in the world to follow Massachusetts, in making statutory provision for the introduction of a full-fledged probation system. The Governor made provision for the appointment of salaried probation officers, and such officers were required to investigate the cases of first offenders, to report to the court, and to recommend the use of probation in hopeful cases. The Act was limited in its application to first offenders. Similarly excluded from its provisions were offenders found guilty of a number of specified major offences and of offences indicating the existence of an established criminal intention on the part of the offender. The statute authorised the release of offenders on probation, instead of their being sentenced to punishment, for any period not exceeding the longest term of imprisonment to which they might be sentenced. The reinforcement of the release on probation by requiring the offender to enter into a recognizance to be of good behaviour was made optional. Provision was also made for certain mandatory conditions of release on probation (periodic report to Probation Officer, honest means of earning a living; etc.), and the statute permitted the court to impose any additional condition which it might deem fit. As regards the legal effect of successful probation, the statute specified that an offender, who satisfactorily fulfilled all the conditions of his release, should "be deemed to be discharged as if, he had been sentenced and served the same". Where an offender failed to comply with the conditions of his release, the court could, at its discretion, commit the offender to prison for the offence of which he was originally convicted, or again release him on probation".[6]

The Early Criminologist, Magistrate and novelist, Henry Fielding of the late 18th century, categorically stated that the total effort to defend society against the problem of crime and criminals should be organised in three fronts:

First, the traditional methods of preventing crime through the provisions of law, then the legally approved executive methods of the police, life patrolling and surveillance.

Second, the public cooperation methods of preventing crime through programmes involving the utilisation of precautions, equipment, personnel and organisation, in short erecting a defensible space around, calculated to make criminal operations more difficult; and,

Third, the basic removal of causes of crime from the individual and from society, involving all relevant preventive and correctional strategies which are Third, the basic removal of causes of crime from the individual and from society, involving all relevant preventive and correctional strategies which are normally thought of when social defense is mentioned".[7]

During the period 1951-52, probation was in existence only in three states of India. W.C. Reckless suggested the use of various other alternatives to Jail also along with probation and aftercare, since it will be more economical and socially salvaging. He wrote in Jail Administration in India, there was no alternative to Jail except in three states.

"There are only three States in India which have developed probation to a point where it might be considered as a perceptible or imperceptible alternative to a jail sentence. The important thing is that Government, Magistrates, Police, Jail Officers, and the public believe that there should be and can be alternatives to jail sentence for a large proportion of ordinary offenders. Each country must work out what these alternatives are. But probation is already here in India and should be developed to the point of being more important than the jails. Likewise, premature release to the supervision of whole-time after care officers is the best alternative to lengthily jail sentences, if retributive punishment and protective detention are not the main concern. The extent to which day fines (commensurate to wages), judicial reprieve, personal recognizance, sureties, warnings, dismissals, filing (case to be brought out if and when a person gets involved again), in addition to probation, can be used will depend on local circumstances. But all of them will involve a calculated risk, which the Magistrate should be willing to take or should be instructed to take, if he is unable to take responsibility. All of us need to remember that we are doing more harm than good in sending most prisoners to jail. This would even be true if the jails were much better organised than they are today. If a society persists in saying to itself that we just cannot find alternatives to jail sentences, then this society really wants to perpetuate the jail system as the chief instrument of social control. Alternatives to jail sentence will not only be more satisfactory from the standpoint of social salvage but they will also prove to be much more economical in actual social and monetary cost."[8]

Ram Ahuja wrote about origin and development of Probation as below:

> "Credit for the introduction of probation and enacting the first law for placing offenders on probation goes to the state of Massachusetts in the United States of America in 1869. Earlier, an experiment under the leadership of one John Augustus — a shoemaker of Boston– was successfully carried out for suspending the sentence of the offenders and supervising their behaviour and helping them in rehabilitation in society. Augustus had assumed responsibility for assisting about 2,000

persons- 1,152 males and 794 females - between 1841 and 1858-during the period of their suspended sentences (Cf. Sutherland, Principles of Criminology, 1965: 423). He was thus called the first probation officer".[9]

The official origin of probation as a legal system authorising the courts to place offenders on Probation was made in 1887 when Massachusetts (US) passed a law. During the period 1951-52, probation was in existence in three states only. W.C. Reckless suggested the use of various other alternatives to Jail also along with probation and aftercare, since it will be more economical and socially salvaging. He wrote in Jail Administration in India, there was no alternative to Jail except in three states.

The appointment of a paid Probation Officer by 1917 about 21 States in America introduced the probation system in their States. The Federal Court of the United States enacted such law in 1925. By 1953 about 45 States and the Federal Courts in the USA had been provided with some sort of legislation authorising probational release of the offenders.

"In England, the parliament passed the Probation of First Offenders Act in 1887. It restricted probation to first offenders and did not authorise the appointment of probation officers. This limitation was removed in 1907 while the appointment of probation officers in all courts was permitted in 1925. France enacted such a law in 1891."[10]

"In India, the Probation of Offenders Act was enacted in 1958 which was gradually extended to all states except Jammu & Kashmir, Karnataka, Sikkim, Tripura, Arunachal Pradesh and Mizoram. Of these six states, Tripura enacted its own Act in 1960, Jammu & Kashmir and Karnataka in 1966, while Sikkim, Mizoram and Arunachal Pradesh have still to enact Probation Acts in their States."[11]

John Augustus, the Father of Probation, because he invented probation and became the first unofficial Probation Officer. "Probation in the United States was conceived in 1841 by the to this phenomenon may be found in writings as early as 1820's. Of course, some scholars may interpret the actions of Judge Thatcher as probation, since he sentenced convicted offenders to release on their own recognizance in lieu of incarceration. However, John Augustus is most frequently credited with implementing probation on a fairly large scale, even though, no local or State statutes were in effect at the time to condone it. Strongly influenced by the temperance movement of the period. Augustus made a concerted effort to rehabilitate alcoholics and to assist those arrested for intoxication-related offenses. Appearing in a Boston municipal court, one morning to observe offenders charged and sentenced for various crimes. Augustus intervened on behalf of a man charged with being a "common drunkard" (Augustus, 1852). As an alternative to having the convicted offender placed in the Boston House of Corrections. Augustus offered to supervise the man's behaviour for a three-week period and guaranteed his subsequent reappearance in court. Knowing Augustus's reputation for philanthropy and trusting his motives, the judge agreed. When Augustus returned three weeks later with the reformed drunkard, the judge was so impressed that he fined the offender only one cent and court costs (which amounted to less than 4 cents!) and suspended the usual sentence of incarceration (which was sometimes six months or more). Between 1841 and 1859, the year Augustus died, it is estimated that he saved nearly 2000 men and women from incarceration by building them our and supervising them for a fixed probationary period.

During that same period, Augustus attracted several philanthropic volunteers to perform similar probation services. These volunteers worked with juvenile offenders as well as adults. However, since few records were kept about the dispositions of juveniles because of their status, the precise number of those assisted by Augustus's volunteers is unknown. Estimates are that thousands of youths benefited as the result of these voluntary services."[12]

With regard to the origin of probation, the U.N. Report states that in 1841, John Augustus; a cobbler, in front of the Police Court, Boston, Massachusetts, USA, bailed out a drunkard.

Due to the effective and close association between them even though for a shorter period, the drunkard turned into a sober man. The noble and positive outcome positively encouraged him to continue the work till his death, in 1859.

United Nations report, on Probation States that, "Probation is a method of dealing with specially selected offenders, and that it consists of the conditional suspension of punishment while the offender is placed under personal supervision and is given individual guidance or treatment."[13]

Probation is a method of dealing with offenders. Historically it developed as an alternative to imprisonment, applicable in cases where guilt was established but where the administrators of justice were led by other considerations, to refrain from imposing a prison sentences. It had its pre-statutory origin in the realisation of the ineffectiveness and actual harmfulness of short-term prison sentences.

"The first essential constituent of probation is the conditional suspension of punishment. It is clear, however that from the point of view of social expediency the suspension of punishment is only feasible when there is a reasonable basis for expecting that the released offender will not resume a criminal career".[14]

In 1897, the Reformatory Schools Act came into force in India. In 1923 the amended Criminal Procedure Code stipulates different procedures for children as per section 29. B. Section 360 of the Criminal Procedure Code empowers the court to release first offenders that had committed offences, not punishable with imprisonment for more than 7 years or women will be released on probation of good conduct. Then came the introduction of the Probation of Offenders Act in the year 1958.

The earliest introduction of the Probation of Offenders Act was in the provinces of Madras, Madhya Pradesh, Bombay and Uttar Pradesh starting from the year 1936. The United Nations Report on Probation States: "Probationary supervision for juvenile offenders was introduced in the provinces of Madras (1920), Bengal (1922) and Bombay (1922)."

"During the years following the amendment of the Code of Criminal Procedure in 1923, the introduction of probation proper for adult offenders was repeatedly under consideration. At successive annual conferences of the provincial Inspectors-General of Prisons resolutions were passed requesting the Government of India to introduce probation legislation along the lines of the British Probation of Offenders Act, 1907. In 1930, the Government of India announced its intention to introduce probation legislations as an All-India measure, and in 1931 an All-India Probation Bill was actually drafted by the Government and was circulated to the provincial Governments for criticism and opinion. The Bill was never written into the national statute book, however, chiefly as a result of the great political upheavals associated with the Indian independence movement that followed. The government of India, however, gave permission to the provincial governments to introduce legislation along the lines of the All-India draft. Statutory provision for probation on a provincial basis was subsequently made in the Central Provinces (now Madhya Pradesh) and Madras in 1936, and in the United provinces (now Utter Pradesh) and Bombay in 1938. In the remaining provinces the provisions of the Code of Criminal Procedure (as amended) with respect to the conditional release of offenders without supervision, continue to constitute the only relevant legislation with respect to adult offenders".[15]

Part of the above said Provinces are now overlapping with adjoining States that the Madras Provinces, includes northern parts of present Kerala and Southern part of Andhra Pradesh State. And these provinces constitutes more than 50 per cent of the total area present in India. The Criminal Procedure Code 1923 was in force in other parts of India, which empowers courts to release certain persons on probation as per section 562, though there were no Probation Officers.

In judicial reprieve the convicted person is given a chance to go for pardon. The United Nations report on Probation States:

"The judicial reprieve was a temporary suspension by the court of either the imposition or the execution of a sentence. It was used for specific purposes such as to permit a convicted person to apply for a pardon or under circumstances such as where the judge was not satisfied with the verdict or where the evidence was suspicious"[16]

In Australia the initial probation services was in the form of suspension of the execution of sentence:

> "The most important innovation introduced in the early Australian statues under consideration was the substitution, by Queensland (followed by most of the other colonies), of the suspension of the execution of sentences, for the suspension of the imposition of sentence- an innovation which seems to have been introduced quite accidentally."[17]

Among the provinces, in India the Madras province implemented the scheme more widely, as stated in the Report by United Nations: "Indian Provincial probation legislation authorities the official appointment of Probation Officers, special provision being also made in some cases for the official designation, of an officer provided by a suitable voluntary organisation. In the provinces where legislative provision for probation has been made probation services have generally been made available by stage to serve larger and larger areas. As yet, however, Madras is the only province in India where probation services are in operation on a province wide basis. In India the present tendency would appear to be, to look upon probation work as a branch of social work requiring suitable technical training".[18]

Pursuant to chapter 526 Statutes of 1998 (Assembly bill (AB) 2331, CDC is required to develop and report to the Legislature by December 31, 2000, a plan that would ensure that all prisoners and parolees who are substance abusers receive appropriate treatment, including therapy, community and other appropriate therapeutic programmes by January

1."[19]

The prevalence of the use of probation in Sweden as a method of dealing with offenders can be seen from the following statistics from the report of the United Nations:

> "Statistical data concerning the use of probation in Sweden in 1945-46 are presented in table below. It appears that, in cases of probation (i.e., cases of offenders placed under supervision), the suspension of the execution of the sentence is used from 3.5 to 4.2 times, as frequently as the suspension of the imposition of the sentence. In the majority of cases of probation (72 per cent in 1945, and 68 per cent in 1946) no special conditions were attached to the probation order, and where there were such conditions the great majority of probation orders contained only one condition.

Table 1. The Use of the Suspension of Punishment and of Probation in Sweden, 1945- 1946

Year	*Total number of cases of suspension of imposition or execution of sentence*	*Cases put on probation i.e., Placed under supervision*				
		Total	*Execution of sentence suspended.*	*Imposition sentence suspended*	*No special conditions imposed*	*Special conditions imposed*
1945	4483	3247	2642	629	2340	931
1946	4591	3207	2492	715	2178	1029

While it is impossible to deduce any significant trends from figures for two years only, it is of interest to note that in 1946 the suspension of the imposition of sentence was used in a significantly larger proportion of cases than in 1945; there was a similar significant increase in the use of special conditions attached to probation orders."[20]

In the United kingdom several voluntary organisations were established as a forerunner to the present Probation service: "In 1876, a step of major significance in this connection was taken by the Church of England, Temperance Society, and these-called "Police Court Missions," were established. Agents of the Society (so-called police courts Missionaries") for not sending their children to school, the giving were subsequently assigned to the different London Police Courts, particularly with a view to reclaiming those charged with drunkenness or with offences resulting from the abuse of liquor. The police court missionaries were soon assigned to tasks other than helping drunkards to reform; these included the placement of women and girls in suitable homes, assistance in finding employment for men and youths charged with petty offences, home enquiries in cases in which parents were charged of relief to needy cases etc. Police court missionaries were soon assigned to the task of supervising the behaviour of conditionally released offenders. 'Supervision now became, for the first time a practicable method for courts which were fortunate enough to possess the services of a police court missionary, and while the primary object of the first appointment was the reclamation of offenders whose downfall was the result of drink, it was soon found that other offenders could be helped in the same way', Additional police court missionaries were soon appointed in London and elsewhere, and other voluntary organisations also entered the field." [21]

It is worth emulating the procedure of Children's Courts of U.K of the last century by the Child Welfare Committee in India under the Juvenile Justice (care and protection of children) Act 2000 for the care and protection of children in need.

Robert Mayer wrote in 1946:

> "A magistrate considers that the ideal judge is the person who keeps fresh by sitting in court only once a week, keeping up contact with ordinary children during the rest of the week. If this is accepted, the lay magistrate must be superior to the professional for this particular job."[22]

The number of cases dealt on probation in the State of Massachusetts during the year 1917, shows the importance given to the probation service about 90 years ago. In New York 3/4 of the persons placed on probation have previous conviction. The Report of the Indian Jails Committee 1919-20, reveals about the probation in America:

> "The subject of probation has already been noticed in connection with the child-offender and the adolescent, but there are special aspects of the matter, as applied to the adult criminal, which require some attention. In the United States of America This method of dealing with the grown-up offender has achieved a great development of late years. It is generally held there that to be beneficial, the period of probation should not be less than one year. The release of a prisoner on probation was at first intended to be applicable to the first offender only but it is no longer so restricted. In the State of New York, three-fourths of the persons placed on probation have some previous conviction on record against them. In one

city in that State 46 per cent of all person convicted by juries of felonies, from manslaughter in the first degree downwards were placed on probation. In the State of Massachusetts 30,588 persons were placed on probation in the year 1917, this total including 14,201 cases of drunkenness, 3,289 cases of larceny, 1,631 cases of non-support, 1,188 cases of breaking and entering, 1,114 cases of assault and battery, besides smaller numbers of such grave crimes as, forgery, robbery, receiving Stolen property, incest, rape, sodomy, and even in one case, murder. Thus in some of the United States the system of release on probations is now extended to all crimes".[23]

The Indian Jails Committee 1919-20 recommends the introduction of probation service in India, as was present in Great Britain and in America.

"In Great Britain and in America the practice as already noticed has been to appoint special officers to exercise supervision over persons released on probation. All who have paid attention to the subject in those countries attaches great importance to this supervision and we also were impressed with the advantage that the existence of a properly selected force of probation officers confers on the working of any system of release on condition of good behaviour. In India, where the system of probation officers has not hitherto existed, considerable difficulty may be experienced in finding suitable persons for the post, but we certainly think that an attempt should be made in this direction. We have touched upon this subject in the Section of the chapter dealing with Child Offender and have proposed that the appointment of Probation Officer should in the first instance be made in large towns. In other parts of the country, it may be necessary for the present to allow the system of release on probation to be carried out as it now is without any formal agency for supervision, but we would record the opinion that the probability of the successful working of the system would be much enhanced if it were possible to secure a supply of suitable probation officers. We think, further, that there is no reason why in India, other Countries as in where probation is used, there should not be power to recognise the private individuals as voluntary probation workers although for reasons already noticed, this method is subject to certain limitations and disadvantages. In England the Criminal Justice Administration Act, gives power to recognise and subsidies societies for the care of youthful offenders on probation and it is possible that if similar provisions are introduced in India they may have a good effect. It is to the societies engaged in social work that it will probably be necessary at first to look for a supply of persons suitable for employment as probation officers and presumably the local Government will begin by utilising the services of those individuals who have already shown an interest in the subject or a readiness to take up social work. We would here notice the fact that there is a very general opinion among authorities interested in the matter that it is not desirable to employ the police in the capacity of probation officers. It should be clearly understood, also, that when a person has been released on probation by the courts, the police should not exercise surveillance over him, or interfere with him in any way, unless he commits further crime."[24]

The origin of probation service was due to efforts of voluntary persons. Phyllida Parsole wrote in 1967, that:

> "By 1887, such changes were possible due not only to experiment in this country but also to the news of the success of a system of probation in Boston, Massachusetts. This started as a Voluntary scheme by one shoe maker, John Augustus in 1841 and had become official in 1878 when the first Probation Act was passed (USA) the 1887 Probation of first Offenders Act only partly met their wishes in the UK."[25]

Legal Origins of Probation in England, have its roots in the English common law practices like, Benefit of Clergy, Judicial reprieve, the Right of sanitary, and the Recognizance.

The term 'probation' appears to have been derived from one of the Latin words: '*probare*'(to prove), or '*probatio*' meaning 'I prove' (my worth) or test on approval. The legal origins of modern probation and related social treatment measures may historically be traced to the devices used for the mitigation of punishment, in England in the thirteenth century. The origins had their roots in the English Common Law practices namely:

(a) The benefit of clergy, which granted certain privileges to, ordained Clergy and exempted them from the rigors of punishment, (This benefit was, later, extended to all non-clerical offenders who could read the scriptures),

(b) The judicial reprieve which was a temporary suspension by the court of either the imposition or the execution of a sentence, if the presiding judge was not satisfied with the verdict on the evidence and felt that leniency was justified to enable the convicted person to apply for a pardon,

(c) The right of sanctuary which gave a convicted offender (usually a felon) immunity from arrest in a place of worship or sanctuary (this practice was abandoned in England in 1623 for a criminal act and in 1723 for a civil process); and

(d) The recognizance or binding over, which has and is being used even today as a measure of preventive justice both to ensure the presence of an offender before the court at a future date when called upon and as a disposition (or a part thereof) in the case of a convicted offender. The use of the recognizance in connection with probation was abandoned in England with the enactment of the Criminal Justice Act, 1948."[26]

In Canada various alternative methods to imprisonment are adopted, like, Adult Day Reporting Centers (DRC), Adult work release, Drug Court, Electronic Monitoring, and work Furlough, as found in the Website of Government Canada:

> "Adult Day Reporting Center (DRC): Allows inmates to complete their disciplinary sentence while participating in the 90 day DRC programme. Participants are required to report to the DRC daily, wear a GPS Tracking device and participate in individual and group counseling programmes. Individuals participating in the DRC can utilise the on site resource to complete their supervision period, attend counseling programmes and obtain employment. Services are funded through the Indian Gaming Special Distribution Fund, which is supported by the Thunder Valley Casino.

Adult Work Release: Allows inmates with sentences to county jail of 60 days or less to serve their sentence on work crews, supervised by probation department personnel instead of physical custody. This programme helped to build an addition to the placer county Fair managers' facility a Johnson Hall, located on the Placer County Fairgrounds.

Drug Court: Provides for up to one-year of drug or alcohol treatment services, outpatient and or residential, with case management by county Probation and Health and Human Services staff, and regular oversight by the court.

Electronic Monitoring: Enables offenders who have been ordered to serve 15 days or more in Jail to serve their time in their home. Participants are monitored using a GPS tracking device and intensive supervision by a probation officer.

Work Furlough: This programme is for offenders who do not meet electronic monitoring criteria. Participants are allowed to work at outside jobs while staying"[27]

Suspended sentence is a concept developed in Belgium and France during the year 1888 is similar to probation release. The aim is to reduce the overcrowding in Prisons. But there is no supervision by the Probation officer. Mare Ancel, London wrote:

> "The suspended sentence which is essentially a European innovation in modern penology implies the concept of suspension of the imposition of sentence. The concept originally derives from the Franco-Belgian legal system. As incorporated in the Belgian law of 1888 (drafted by Berenger), the concept has, for its aims, avoidance of criminal contagion (due to imprisonment and its brutalities) and prevention of recidivism. The suspended sentence is a conditional sentence, which is a penalty consisting of the threat of execution, or a true sentence comprising a penalty whose execution is suspended."[28]

During the supervision period up to one-year treatment services on drug or alcohol, outpatient and or residential, with case management by county Probation and Health and Human Services staff, and regular oversight by the court are undertaken.

Alternative measures to imprisonment were one of the issues examined by the All India Jail Manual Committee of 1957-59. The Government of India directed that the Committee should also examine and make recommendations among other issues:

> "(ii) Abolition of short term sentences and provision of Alternative measures. (iv) Care of children and women offenders etc.

The Committee consisted of the following members:

1. Shri. R.G. Selvi IAS, Joint Secretary to Government of Bombay, Home Department (Convener)
2. Dr. C.P. Tandon PMSI, Inspector General of Prison Uttar Pradesh.
3. Dr. P.K. Biswas, Special Officer and Ex-officio Dy. Secretary Home (jails) Dept. Government of West Bengal.
4. Shri. B.C. Katoch, Inspector General of Prisons, Punjab.
5. Dr. A.B. Rudra IAS, Inspector General of Prison, State of West Bengal
6. Shri. M.B. Selvi, IAS, Inspector General of Prison, Bombay.
7. Shri. M.A. Sheriff, IAS, Inspector General of Prison, Madras.
8. Shri. C.P.S. Menon, Dy Secretary to Government of India, Ministry of Home Affairs.
9. Shri A.V. John, Inspector General of Prisons, Kerala.

10. Shri. J.J. Panakal, Head, Department of Criminology and Correctional Administration, Tata Institute of Social Sciences, Bombay.
11. Shri. D.J. Jadhav, Principal, Jail Officers Training School, State of Bombay."[29]

In the U.K. the probation of First Offenders Act, 1887 was enacted mainly to prevent children from sending to prisons. Robert Mayer wrote:

> "The growing recognition of the disastrous results of imprisoning children was responsible for the probation system. First mooted about 1827 and thereafter the subject of prolonged agitation, it finally found its way on to the Statute Book in the Jubilee year of 1887 under the title of Probation of First Offenders Act."[30]

'Thuggs' were prevalent in India prior to dacoit's emergence.

"During the reign of Ferozhe Shah Tuglak (1351-88) 1000 thugs were arrested in Delhi, later they were let off. During the reign of Akbar (1556-1605) both Meadow Taylor and Balfour affirm that many Thuggs were then executed and according to Balfour they numbered 500 and belonged to Etawah District"[31]

In 1936, The Madras Probation of Offenders Act, the first one in India came into force, followed by U.P. Probation of 'Offenders' Act and Bengal Probation of Offenders Act.

Article 15(3) of the Constitution of India provides special provisions for women and child as a fundamental right of non-discrimination. Art 39, Art 45 of the Constitution gives directive principles for the welfare of the disadvantaged class like women aged and children. These are in par with the correctional principle and human rights of the persons concerned.

Immediately after the adoption of the Constitution of India, Walter. C. Reckless the United Nations' expert in Criminology visited India during the year 1951-52, as per the request from the then Prime Minister, Pundit Jawaharlal Nehru; and studied the prison system in India. He had recommended the introduction and expansion of probation and other alternatives to imprisonment. He also suggested the enactment of the Probation of Offenders Act by the Central Government. He also prepared a model for drafting a bill on probation. Consequently B.K. Menon, Chief Probation Superintendent of Madras Province drafted the bill, which was passed by the Parliament of India in the year 1958.

The United Nations Report on Probation States:

"In England the origin of probation was not the result of a deliberate creative, legislative or judicial act, but rather the result of a gradual growth an almost unconscious modification of existing legal practices."

"The direct precursors of probation, are the so-called benefit of clergy, the judicial reprieve, the release of an offender on his own recognizance, provisional release on bail, the provisional "filing" of a case, and other legal devices for the suspension of either the imposition or the execution of sentence. With a view to a full understanding of the legal origins of probation, it is necessary to review briefly the nature of these practices".[32]

Offenders are considered for release on probation after finding him guilty and before considering the sentence. Similar is the view of the ancient practice of the Benefit of clergy. On the benefit of clergy the United Nations report States:

"The so-called benefit of clergy was a special plea of dubious origin by virtue of which certain categories of offenders could, after convictions, but before judgment, claim exemption from, or mitigation of, punishment. In practice, it was primarily a device to avoid capital punishment. The importance of this plea in the criminal proceedings of the eighteenth and early nineteenth century is beyond any doubt: 'According to the common practice in England of working out modern improvements through antiquated forms, this exemption was made the means of modifying the severity of the criminal law.' It is, however, extremely doubtful whether this device had any direct influence on the later development of the suspension of sentence or any other immediate precursor of probation."[33]

Section 562 of the Criminal Procedure Code 1898, empowers the courts in India to release certain offenders, who had committed an offence punishable with imprisonment, up to 2 years, after executing a bond of good behaviour. But an amendment to the section in the year 1923 extended purview of the section to first offenders below 21 years of age who had committed an offence punishable with imprisonment up to 7 years or a woman not committed an offence punishable with death or imprisonment for life. At the same time there were no probation officers to conduct enquiry or supervision.

So probation in its preliminary form was present in section 562 of the Code of Criminal Procedure Code 1898, which was in operation in India.

"In India the release of offenders on probation is regulated by section 562 of the Code of Criminal Procedure. This section was first introduced into the Code in 1898 and was based on section 1 of the Probation of First

Offenders Act, 1887, (50 and 51 Act, s. 25), which has been replaced by the Probation of Offenders Act, 1907 (Edw. VII, s.17). Under this section release on probation is limited to offenders under the Indian Penal Code punishable with not more than two years' imprisonment, to which are added theft, theft in a building, dishonest misappropriation and cheating; it cannot be resorted to if a previous conviction is proved against the offender; in using it regard is to be had, 'to the youth, character and antecedents of the offender, to the trivial nature of the offence, and to any extenuating circumstances in which the offence is committed;' finally, the power to proceed under the section can only be used by courts not of lower grade than magistrates of the first class or by second class magistrates, if specially empowered in this behalf."[34]

The origin of probation dates back in the ancient scriptures in India and the Christian religious backing like do good to others; and no one is born criminal, in the western world. Later certain socially spirited persons took the mantle and worked on their own in collaboration with the courts. It paved the way for legislations in several States.

Then the United Nations came to the picture and compiled the laws and procedures on Probation prevailed in different Nations and gave guidance for the wide use of Probation. Consequently most of the Nations enacted legislations on Probation as an alternative to imprisonment.

Footnotes

1. M.S. Sabins (1995), Juvenile Justice and Juvenile Corrections, Somaiya publications Pvt. Ltd., Bombay, pp. 253-54.
2. Barry Krisberg, James. F. Austin (1993) Reinventing Juvenile Justice, Sage Publications, New Delhi, p. 13.
3. B.N. Mishra (1991) Juvenile Delinquency and Justice System, Ashish Publishing House, 8/81 Punjabi Bagh, New Delhi 110026, p. 34.
4. B.N. Mishra (1991) Juvenile Delinquency and Justice System, Ashish Publishing House, 8/81 Punjabi Bagh, New Delhi-110026, p. 122.
5. Robert. K. Merton and Robert. A. Nisbet (1966) Contemporary Social Problems- Harcourt Brace and World Inc. pp. 84-86
6. United Nations (1951) Probation and related measures U.N. Publication Division, New York, p. 52.

7. N.K. Chakrabarti (1999) Social Defence - In the Administration of criminal Justice, Deep and Deep Publications Pvt. Ltd., F-159, Rajouri Gardens, New Delhi- 110027, pp. 28-29.
8. W.C. Reckless (1951-52), Jail Administration in India, Government of India Publication, New Delhi, p. 13.
9. Ram Ahuja (2000) Criminology, Rawat Publications Satyam Apartments, sector-3, Jain Temple Road, Jawahar Nagar, Jaipur-302004, p. 336.
10. Ram Ahuja (2000) Criminology, Rawat Publications, Satyam Apartments, Sector 3, Jain Temple Road, Jawahar Nagar Jaipur – 302004, p. 336.
11. Social Defense, (January 1990; 59) National Institute of Social Defense, New Delhi, p. 59.
12. Dean. J. Campion (1990), Probation Parole And Community Corrections, Prentice Hall, Upper Saddle river, New Jersey 07458, p. 35.
13. United Nations, (1951), Probation and Related measures, Department of Social Affairs, New York, p. 47.
14. *Ibid.,* p. 3.
15. United Nations, (1951), Probation and Related measures, Department of Social Affairs, New York, p. 88.
16. *Ibid.,* p. 17.
17. *Ibid.,* p. 53.
18. *Ibid.,* p. 89.
19. California Department of Corrections, Overview of Substance Abuse Programmes (December 1999), California Dept. of Corrections, Office of the substance Abuse Programmes, P.O. Box. 942883, Sieramento, CA 94283- 0001 (916) 3273707 Calnet 467-3707, p. 4.
20. United Nations (1951), Probation and Related Measures, Department of Social Affairs, New York, p. 61.
21. United Nations (1951), Probation and Related Measures, New York, p. 46.
22. Robert Mayer (1946), Young People in trouble, Victor Gallanc Ltd., London, p. 27.
23. Report of the Indian Jails Committee 1919 20, Vol. I, Government Central Press, Shimla, Para – 420, p. 216.
24. Report of the Indian Jails Committee 1919 20, Vol. I, Government Central Press Simla, Para – 422, p. 23.

25. Phyllida Parole, B.A., (1967), The Work of The Probation And After Care Officer, Routledge and Kegan Paul Ltd., Broadway House, 68-74, Carter Lane, London, EC4, p. 3.
26. M.S. Sabins (1995) Juvenile Justice and Juvenile Correction Pride and prudence, Samia publications Pvt. Ltd., Bombay, pp. 251-52.
27. http:/www.placer. ca. gov/probation/Alternative downloaded on 12-12-2006.
28. M.S. Sabins (1995), Juvenile Justice and Juvenile Correction, Pride and Prudence, Somaiya Publications Pvt. Ltd., Bombay, p. 280.
29. Report of the All India Jail Manual Committee-1957-59, para-8, p. 7.
30. Robert Mayer (1946), Young People in trouble, Victor Gollancz Ltd., London, p. 12.
31. Shrikrishna Datta Bhatta (1962). And They Gave Up Dacoity, A.B. Sarva Seva Sangh Prakasan, Rajghat, Varanasi, p. 24.
32. United Nations (1951), Probation and Related Measures, New York, p. 17.
33. United Nations (1951), Probation and Related Measures, New York, p. 17.
34. Report of the Indian Jails Committee- 1919-20, Vol. I Government Central Press, Shimla, Para-431, p. 221.

4

Success of Probation

The success of the Probation supervision depends on the Probation officer as well as the cooperation and coordination among other wings of the Criminal Justice System. The Report of the Indian Jails Committee 1919-20 states that the success of probation depends on the proper selection of person to be released on probation supervision.

"It is, of course, necessary that the courts should exercise their discretion wisely in the selection of cases to be placed on probation and we think it might help them if a pamphlet were drawn up pointing out the rationale of the system and indicating in general outline the classes of cases which are, and which are not, suitable for this method. In particular it should be pointed out that it is useless to place on probation persons of defective intellect. The feeble minded who have drifted into crime through sheer inability to earn a living will, it seems clear, be liable to take the same course again unless some management can be made with friends or relatives for their protection. Otherwise, the proper remedy is the provision of suitable institutions for persons of this class and at present no such institutions are known to exist in this country. The disposal of these cases will, therefore, continue for some time to present very considerable difficulties."[1]

Proper diagnosis of the case during the enquiry and systematic supervision amounts to the success of probation.

"The success and effectiveness of probation depends upon three things: (i) an adequate pre-sentence investigation, (ii) a careful decision by the court that there is a reasonable probability of the offender's making good on probation, and (iii) a systematic supervision of the probationer by a qualified person who is not burdened with excessive caseloads and who takes a real interest in the probationer's rehabilitation out of his commitment and dedication to duty."[2]

The rate of recidivism is an index to find out the rate of success or failure. Robert Mayer wrote: "It is almost impossible to evaluate the degree to which the schools are successful. Recidivism, or the return to crime, is probably the best index. The basis of computation that has been adopted is the percentage of those who have been guilty of new offences within three years of being placed out from a school. In pre-war years this amounted to about 20 per cent for boys and a rather smaller figure for girls."[3]

Success of Probation depends upon the stability of the environment, which the probationer belongs. The United Nations report states:

> "The significance of the association of the outcome of release on probation with age, and with material and family status, was considerably smaller, but tended to indicate (a) that young offenders are more likely to violate probation than older offenders; and (b) that single persons are more likely to violate probation than married persons.

The results of the study under consideration seem to, point to the general conclusion that relatively stable social and employment connection, and the absence of criminal antecedents, tend to be conducive to a favourable outcome of release on probation."[4]

The Success of Probation primarily depends on the nature and quality of the relationship between the probationer and Probation Officer. The cooperative relationship is to gain confidence of the probationer, as found in the UN Report on Probation.

> "Probation treatment is of a varied nature, ranging from religious counseling or the unskilled assistance of volunteer probation officers on one hand, to professional social case work sometimes supplemented by Psychiatric treatment on the other. The work of the probation officer is being increasingly recognised as a skilled profession requiring specific technical training"[5]

The success of probation relates to the proper enquiry correct diagnosis and effective supervision. The main factors associated with success and failures are as found in the Report of United Nations:

> "In discussing the factors associated with success and failure on probation, it is necessary to begin by emphasising that there can be no simple, categorical guide to the determination of the suitability of a particular offender for release on probation. Individuals present such a

> wide variety of combinations of separate psychological and social traits that no single trait can be taken to constitute an adequate indication of suitability or unsuitability. The final decision can only be made on the basis of an understanding of the total personality in his environment. It should be remembered, moreover, that not only the personality and circumstances of the offender, but also the nature and adequacy of the available supervisory personnel, are decisive in determining success or failure in probationary treatment. With these reservations, however, it is possible to enumerate specific factors, which are most generally associated with a favourable or unfavourable outcome of probationary treatment.

In the case of younger offenders, home circumstances seem to be of primary importance. Probation practice has repeatedly shown that unfavourable home surroundings reduce very considerably the chances of probation being successful, particularly if the offender is left in his previous environment; if no suitable arrangements are feasible for the removal of the offender from his unfavourable home environment, appropriate institutional training or treatment may be much more suitable and effective.

It is probably generally accepted that the best results can be obtained by using probation at the earliest possible stage in an offender".[6]

The period of supervision of persons released from Borstal schools were usually one year but often it extends up to 5 years if the person under supervision wishes to receive such assistance. And the success rate up to the period ending 1914 was 66.8 per cent, as is found in the Report of the Indian Jails Committee-1919-20:

> "The representatives or associates of the Borstal Association are drawn from all classes. Paid workers are remunerated sometimes, by fixed salary sometimes, by fees per case. In London some agents are ex-police inspectors who receive £ 3. 10s a week. When the remuneration is by fees, three shillings are allowed for the first visit and one guinea a year afterwards, but the association endeavours to avoid a fixed rate of the fee as tending too much towards a routine performance of duty. In other parts of the country they include officials of other societies for the aid of discharged prisoners, police courts missionaries, clergymen volunteers engaged in social work and, in fact, any one ready to befriend and look after a youth or girls entrusted to his one her care. About half the workers are unpaid. The supervision exercised by the Borstal society's agents extends, properly speaking, only up to the end of the period of detention ordered by the court, and to one year further, but in practice they often continue their service and assistance much longer if the boy wishes it

> and the Association generally endeavours to keep in touch with boys for five years after their release. No definite statistics are available to show the results in the case of boys whose period of detention and probation has expired, but the figures for the five-year period ending with 1914 are claimed to show 66.8 per cent of successes. Since the commencement of the war it has been difficult to trace the further career of boys discharged from Borstal institutions as large numbers entered the Army".[7]

Linkages with relevant agencies and activities are to be adopted for the success of supervision:

> "Suitable mechanisms should be evolved at various levels to facilitate the establishment of linkages between services responsible for non-custodial measures, other branches of the criminal justice system such as developmental and welfare agencies, both governmental and non-governmental, in such fields as health, housing, education and labour, and the Mass Media."[8]

Probably the most profound axiomatic observation that could be made about the nature of correctional supervision is that it is, or should be, a teaching position. Staff development directors, training officers and personnel-orientation supervisors can at best prepare staff for trainings; the real training occurs on the job for the most part of the first line supervisor.

"The individual is released if he so desires and is offered 'high support counseling, job development, job training and other services with the dual aim of stabilising his behaviour so that he will avoid further criminal activity and obtain a dismissal of his charges. At the end of his probationary continuance he returns to court where: (1) the charges may be dropped; (2) another trial continence under programme supervision may be imposed; or (3) trial may be set. It is reported in the National District Attorneys Association, Alternatives to the criminal warrant process: The Prosecutors Discretionary Decision to Charge. Screening of Criminal Cases: Chicago."[9]

With respect to the role of Judiciary in the implementation of probation and advocating the use of probation, Justice V.R. Krishna Iyer commented that,

> "This twentieth century approach to crime and punishment is, for us of Gandhian vintage, it runs counter to the traditional theory of harsh deterrence writ large in the Indian Penal Code and Criminal Procedure Code. The ghosts of Macaulay and men of his ilk haunt our Criminal

Courts still, so much so, Probation fares ill in the courts... And it is time our magistracy bends to the winds blowing for a long time now. Orthodoxy and ignorance die hard-even among judicial personnel."[10]

Thus the success depends upon the Probation officer, his enquiry, selection of offenders and the circumstances of the offender in which he ordinarily lives. Supervision by the judiciary is also plays a cardinal role.

Footnotes

1. Report of Indian Jails Committee - 1919-20, Vol. I, Government Central Press, Simla, Para 436, p. 224.
2. Ram Ahuja (2000), Criminology Rawat Publication, Jaipur – 302004, p. 347.
3. Robert Mayer (1946) Young People in Trouble, Victor Gallancy Ltd, London, p. 38.
4. United Nations - (1951), Probation and Related Measures, New York, p. 240.
5. United Nations (1951) Probation and Related Measures Department of Social Affairs, p. 7.
6. United Nations (1951), Probation and Related Measures, New York, p. 238.
7. Report of the Indian Jails Committee 1919-20, Vol. I, Appendix IX, Government Central Press, Simla, p. 494.
8. The Tokyo Rules (1990).
9. Allan Coffey, Santa Clara County (1975), Correctional Administration, The Management of probation institutions and parole, Prentice-Hall, Inc, Engle wood Cliff, New Jersey, p. 102.
10. V.R. Krishna Iyer (1976) Social Mission of Law, Orient Longman Ltd., 3/5 Asaf Ali Road, New Delhi-110001; p. 97.

5

Needs of Probationers

Probation officer, who conducts the social investigation report, is to supervise the offender upon his release on probation. Accordingly the Probation work falls into three divisions, each interlinked with one another, forming a continuum of social investigation, diagnosis, adjudication, deposition, adjustment, social treatment (probation supervision) and social rehabilitation of the offender:

"1. Social investigation (diagnosis) and presentation by the probation officer of his report to the competent authority.
2. The Juvenile Court (or Juvenile Welfare Board) work (hearing, adjudication and disposition).
3. Probation supervision and follow-up (social treatment and rehabilitation)." [1]

The Probation Officer as the case worker in the correctional setting, has to observe the following four main tasks:

1. Firstly Investigation and surveillance for the purpose of securing information about the client's failure or success in meeting the obligations of his legal status.
2. The use of controls to modify client behaviour.
3. Acting as a legal authority in the client's life with responsibility for value change.
4. Correctional decision-making" [2]

Supervision is one of the important duties of a Probation Officer. The Tokyo rule 10 stipulates:

> "The purpose of supervision is to reduce re-offending and to assist the offender's integration into society a way which minimise the likelihood of

a return to crime. If a non-custodial measure entails supervision the latter shall be carried out by a competent authority under the specific conditions prescribed by law.

Within the framework of a given non-custodial measure, the most suitable form of supervision and treatment should be determined for each individual case, aimed at assisting the offender to work on his or her offending. Supervision and treatment should be periodically reviewed and adjusted as necessary. Offenders should, when needed, be provided with psychological, social and material assistance and will opportunities to strengthen links with the community and facilitate their reintegration into society."[3]

Marital discords of those under the Supervision of Probation officers are settled by:

> "Each worker sees one member of the marriage and deals with the problems as they are expressed in the marriage. References for instance, by the wife, to her husband's behaviour are discussed in terms of the needs and expectations of the wife and not as symptoms of the husbands, disturbances.... this method was found useful."[4]

It is generally believed that the probation office where the probationers assemble periodically would become a venue for their intermingling and plan for further offences; and hence several Probation Officers discourage it. But considering the purpose of probation supervision the clients can be seen in groups also.

"The traditional method in probation has been individual meetings between officer and offender, but experiments are taking place in the use of the groups... groups are being formed either of probationers unknown to each other, or of those jointly charged or living together in a hostel. Others have provided various kinds of group experiences such as summer camps, weekend outings or play groups".[5]

Family, education and employment are social institutions where the Probation Officer has to concentrate with a view to uplift the offender under supervision. The better way is to give focus on the rehabilitation of the whole family in which the offender belongs. It helps the reconciliation process in a better way:

> "There are two major approaches which mould the methods of family therapy. The first is the application of the family as a center of correctional treatment on behalf of one or more of its members. The second approach visualises the whole family as the target for correctional treatment. This

is the essentially reiterative type of family therapy. Its objectives are the rehabilitation of the entire family as a healthy functioning unit in the community.

Among social institutions, education is second only to the family in its impact in socialisation. The general problems of education for youth have great relevance to corrections.

The type and nature of job, an individual holds determines, to a large extent, the kind of life he leads, because employment is a major variable in a person's social status according to others and indeed of himself. Work is, therefore, significantly related to the goals of correctional treatment in probation".[6]

Through the intervention of the Probation Officer, right notion and conduct are to be inducted into the Probationer who is under supervision; and to help him/her to develop and express the hidden abilities in him. In other words, the Probation officers are to induct right notions and good conduct in the probationer and to help him to express the latent potentialities in him. This process involves three phases:

" (i) Social inquiry into the total situation of the probationer.

(ii) Social diagnosis, that is inquiry in to the relationships and attitudes of the criminal and

(iii) Correction or reformation of the criminal's behaviour and personality."[7]

Supervision of delinquent juvenile requires the Probation Officer to be more re-educative and capable of instilling confidence in the wards. Walter C. Reckless stated that the probation officers are to:

> "develop a constructive relationship with the probationer and working out with him a plan that will lead to a more satisfactory and acceptable level of adjustment, the probation officers are to be a friendly counselor and guide, who encourages, interprets and implants suggestions, and who is a leader, executive and a social therapist."[8]

In reality many Probation officers are ill equipped and overburdened. " The probation service is crammed full of dedicated officers who have an accumulation of complex though partial an half digested psychoanalytic theories and insights into human behaviour well meaning they blunder their way through their case loads hoping it all makes some kind of sense." [9]

"Probation service is said to be a casework in authoritarian setting. Probation Officer is viewed, as an agent officer of the court/prison by the probationers under supervision and it is a hindrance in creating a counseling relationship based on warmth of acceptance and absence of coercion.

"A quotation from Carl Rogers... Therapy and authority cannot be co-existent in the same relationship. There cannot be an atmosphere of complete permissiveness when the relationship is authoritative. If the delinquent accepts a counseling relationship with the probation officer and tells him of further delinquencies, the worker must at once decide if he is a therapist or officer,"[10]

Upon the successful completion of the period under supervision, the Probation Officer submits a completion report to the Court. At this juncture the Court orders, that:

" 1. The charges may be dropped.
2. Another trial continuance under programme supervision may be imposed; or
3. Trial may be set."[11]

"During Supervision a Probation Officer is to make all earnest efforts to maintain a disciplined behaviour of the probationer and at the same time giving the probationer a moral strength and support in his economic and social adjustment to life in the free community. The therapeutic aids, materials, social and emotional should be used to help in the process of rehabilitation."[12]

Norway a Scandinavian country had introduced a Council to consider the cases of juveniles and take care of them up to the age of twenty one years. The council was more comprehensive than the existing Juvenile Justice Boards in India. The Juvenile Justice Board has a Principal Magistrate and two Social Workers as members.

"Before the war Norway had no Juvenile Courts. Every municipality had Child Welfare Council consisting of judge, clergyman, doctor and four members elected by members of the local council of whom two at least two were women.

The Council inspected homes and schools; and when decisions were taken, parents and guardians had the right to attend.

Under the law concerning the treatment of neglected children which was first introduced in 1896 and gradually extended, the council was responsible for the care of:

(a) Children under fourteen who had committed punishable offences;

(b) Children between fourteen and eighteen who had committed offences, but against whom the jury considered a charge should not be made;

(c) children up to the age of eighteen, if their conduct, caused by bad home conditions or by personal defective character, made it necessary to take preventive precautions other than a serious warning.

Once committed, young people can be kept under the care of the council up to the age of twenty-one years.

Two special types of schools were available:

(a) Corrective Schools, which existed in every large town and in which, by order of the Council or School Board, the child could be kept for one year. They also served as observation centers for the Council. After a year, the child could be placed with a family if the Headmaster though fit.

(b) School Homes, or reform schools for those requiring treatment after corrective school."[13]

Probation Officer and the Probationer shall develop, a mutual trust and faith between them, which may lead to useful cooperation. This can be achieved through, helping the offender to understand himself and not by controlling him through correction. In order to achieve this, the following principles were stipulated in the Manual published by American Correctional Association. They are:

"1. Change comes from within the person; therefore a probationer must be a participant in any correctional treatment programme designed to help him.

2. The needs, problems, capacities and limitations of the individual criminal must be considered in planning a treatment programme with him."

3. Legally binding conditions of probation are essential and in the best interests of the criminal and the community.

4. The goal of correctional treatment is to help the criminal understand his own problems and enable him to deal adequately with them."[14]

The Probation Officer is to be aware of the needs of the probationer and act accordingly. Similar to the way a Caseworker responds to his client. The interview between the Probation Officer and Probationer, helps to generate mutual understanding, as well as making the Probationer independent and to carryout socially acceptable behaviour. The needs of the client and principles behind it are:

"The need of the client	*The principle*
1. To be treated as an individual	1. Individualisation
2. To express feelings.	2. Purposeful expression of feelings
3. To get empathetic responses to Problems involvement.	3. Controlled emotional
4. To be recognised as a person	4. Acceptance of worth.
5. Not to be judged	5. Non-judgmental attitude
6. To make his own choice and decisions.	6. Client self-determination.
7. To keep secret about the self.	7. Confidentiality"[15]

The quality time spent between Probation officer and Probationer shall influence the quality of supervisions. A Consumer Survey by Nottingham Probation Officers on the impact of Probation supervision described probation Service is worth mentioning.

"A five minute talk which was unrelated to the rest of their activities and which, because it happened infrequently (although definitions of frequency varied, e.g., only once a month to only once a week) could not therefore have any impact."[16]

Complete rehabilitation of offenders in the very same society requires the development of friendship between the offender and the victim of the crime. In that sense restorative justice becomes an extension involved from Probation service. Quakers or Society of friends mainly in United Kingdom developed this concept. Tim Newell Writes:

> "Friends have experienced prison from both sides of the bar. This gives us unique insights into an important social institution. We are aware that criminal justice is an area of social activity which reflects the values of a society most clearly and which has the strongest impact on the most vulnerable groups."[17]

A report of group discussion on the duties of Probation Officers,

"**Group A** report contains:

1. Preliminary Enquiry in respect of the accused-both adult juvenile
2. Constitutional Enquiries
3. Supervision of Probationers, ex-convicts and ex-inmates.
4. Rehabilitation of probationers, ex-convicts, ex-inmates and ex-pupils, who are placed under supervision.

Group B report contains:

1. Presentence enquiry
2. To reform and rehabilitate the criminal in his own natural surroundings.
3. To help him to stand on his legs and solve behavioural problems through counseling; and
4. To change his behaviour and also to correct his path so as to enable him to become a useful citizen.

Group C report contains:

1. Rehabilitation of probationers
2. Counseling and supervision
3. To help him to stand on his own legs and solve behavioural problems through counseling; and
4. Court duty and contact with judiciary
5. Office interview, administration record keeping"[18]

The workload of the Probation Officer is a determinative factor on the quality of supervision. Hence the number of supervision cases is limited to maximum 60 at a time, as opined by the Indian Jails Committee 1919-20:

> "Another criticism was that the probation officers, even if properly selected, often had an excessive number of cases interest to Probation Officer, for more than they could reasonably manage. The witnesses differed as to the number of cases that a Probation officer could supervise effectively, but on the whole, sixty seemed to be the maximum limit most generally accepted. In Glasgow and in London, cases were mentioned of a Probation Officer with no less than 200 cases. It seems evident that a Probation Officer thus burdened cannot devote to individual cases, the amount of time and attention necessary to produce a satisfactory result. A hasty visit paid by an official, unacquainted with the previous history of the boy and his family and ignorant of the causes, which have brought the child into trouble, can hardly be expected to accomplish much, and it is essential that no Probation Officer should be given too many cases to look after at one and the same time."[19]

It is apt time and necessary to develop a Code of Ethics to Probation survive for its smooth and uniform functioning. Because it emphasis that the personal qualities of a Probation officer is having a decisive role in the effectiveness of Probation service. The Code of Ethics developed by American Probation and Parole Association reproduced below.

1. I will render professional service to the justice system and the community at large in effecting the social adjustment of the offender.
2. I will uphold the law with dignity, displaying an awareness of my responsibility to offenders while recognising the right of the public to be safeguarded from criminal activity.
3. I will strive to be objective in the performance of my duties, recognising the inalienable right of all persons, appreciating the inherent worth of the individual, and respecting those confidences which can be reposed in me.
4. I will conduct my personal life with decorum, neither accepting nor granting favours in connection with my office.
5. I will cooperate with my co-workers and related agencies and will continually strive to improve my professional competence through the seeking and sharing of knowledge and understanding.
6. I will distinguish clearly, in public, between my statements and action as an individual and as a representative of my profession.
7. I will encourage policy, procedures and personnel practices, which will enable others to conduct themselves in accordance with the values, goals and objectives of the American Probation and Parole Association.
8. I recognise my office as a symbol of public faith and I accept as a public trust to be held as long as I am true to the ethics of the American Probation and Parole Association.
9. I will constantly strive to achieve these objectives ideals dedicating myself to my chosen Profession."[20]

Probation without proper selection of the offender and effective supervision may result in the failure of supervision. This situation developed the following arguments against Probation services are as below:

"1. Probation is not a form of correction but it is a form of leniency which pampers an offender.

2. Probation enables an offender to avoid punishment, which is necessary not only as a deterrent to crime and delinquency but also for maintaining law and order.

3. After release on Probation, the offender returns to the same family and community environment that contributed to his crime. He is therefore exposed to the same influences all over again.

4. Probation does not protect the community since the offender lives in the community and may repeat his crimes or delinquencies.
5. Since social investigation has not been made compulsory, the judge finds it difficult to decide whether or not the offender should be released on probation.
6. There is no provision for compulsory supervision, i.e., offenders are released under suspended sentences but without supervision. This needs to be criticised and looked into.
7. The probation officers do not supervise the probationer properly due to heavy caseloads. The number of trained personnel is also insufficient. The supervision thus remains both inadequate and questionable."[21]

But the probation helps the offender in reshaping his life, is the Community setting:

> "Probation is a method of correctional process for the guidance and treatment of the criminal and his family, the discovery and correction of the criminals personality and character and criminogenic environment, with the help of the resources of the community. (Home Officer, 1960; 8)."[22]

Probation involves conditional suspension of punishment:

> It means that probation is not a let off and the probationer is liable to be punished in case of violation of the conditions of the bond. "The success of supervision is therefore the determination of the" probationer to reform from unlawful activity, and to cooperate with the probation officer charged with his supervision, rather than the conditions imposed by the court. The conditional suspension of punishment, however, does provide an 'authoritarian setting' for the supervision and treatment carried out by the probation officer."[23]

Probation is a form of "community treatment" of offenders, Probation permits a more normal social experience than institutionalisation, it does not disrupt the offenders' relationships with his family, with his friends with the opposite sex, or with his occupation. While involving the conditional suspension of punishment, probation is directed at the social rehabilitation of the offender as a self-supporting and law abiding member of the community.

Kautilya smriti in chapter IV para 10 lays down that:

> "the award of punishment must be regulated by the consideration of the motive and nature of the offence, the time and place, the strength, age,

conduct (or duties) learning, and monetary position of the offenders and by the fact whether the offence is repeated."[24]

Proper family background enquiry, selection of the offender and supervision order by the Court is a continuous process in the probation service. Conducting a presentence investigation is the basis for the proper selection of persons to be released on probation. Such a person considered for probation is thus placed under the supervision of a Probation Officer. Cooperation and understanding between the Probation Officer and Probationer is necessary for the success of supervision. The Probation Officer and Probationer had to discuss and together assess the needs of the probationer, prepare on action plan and implement the same meticulously so that the probationer gets adjusted with the community. The quality and integrity of the Probation Officer counts much in the success of understanding the needs of the probationer.

Footnotes

1. M.S. Sabins (1995) Juvenile Justice and Juvenile Corrections, Pride and Prudence, Somaiya Publications Pvt. Ltd., New Delhi, p. 255.
2. Boehm, Werner W. (1959) Objectives of Social Curriculam of the Future Social Work Curriculum Study, New York: Council of Social Work Education, New York, p. 124.
3. United Nations Standard Minimum Rule for Non-custodial Measures (The Tokyo Rules) (Rule-10).
4. Phyllida Parsloe B.A. (1967) The work of Probation and After Care Officer, Rutledge and Kegan Paul Ltd., Broad way House 68-74, Carter Lane, London EC4; p. 39.
5. Phyllida Parsloe B.A. (1967), The work of a Probation and Aftercare officer, Rutledge and Kegan Paul Ltd., Broad way House 68-74, Carter Lane, London EC4; pp. 44-45.
6. V.V. Devasia and Leelamma (1992), Criminology Victimology and Corrections, Ashish Publishing House 8/88 Punjabi Bagh, New Delhi-110026, p. 143.
7. *Ibid.,* p. 144.
8. Walter. C. Reckless (1950), The Crime Problem, Appleton Century Crafts Inc. New York, p. 382.
9. Geoffrey Parkinson I gave them money, New Society, p. 34.

10. Hilary Walker, Bill Beaumont (1981) Probation critical theory and socialist practice, Basil Blackwell Publisher Limited, 108 Cowley Road, Oxford OX4, England, p. 33.
11. Allen Coffey, Santa Clara (1975) Correctional Administration- The management of Probation Institutions and Parole, Prentice Hill Inc, Engle wood Cliff, New Jersey, p. 102.
12. Jyotsna H. Shah. Ph.D DSSA (1973), Studies in Criminology, Probation Services in India, N.M. Tripathi, Pvt. Ltd., 164, Samaldas Gandhi Marg, Bombay-400002, pp. 31-32.
13. Robert Mayer (1946) Young People in Trouble, Victor Gallancz Ltd, London, pp. 58-59.
14. Manual of Correctional Standards (1966) American Correctional Association, New York, p. 107.
15. Biestek, Felix P. (1957), The Casework Relationship: Loyola University Press, Chicago, p. 90.
16. Hillary Walker and Bill Beaumont (1981) Probation work Critical Theory and Socialist Practice, Basil Blackwell Publisher Limited, 108, Cowley Road, Oxford OX4 1JF, England, p. 30.
17. Time Newell (2000)], Forgiving Justice-Quaker Vision For Criminal Justice, Swarthmore Lecture, 2000, Quaker Home Service, Friends House, Euston Road, London NWI, 2BJ, U.K., p. 19.
18. Dr. Sunil Kanta Bhattacharya (1986), Probation System In India-An Appraisal, Manas Publications, 18-D, Kamala Nagar, Delhi-110007, pp. 151-52.
19. Report of the Indian Jails Committee- 1919-20, Vol. I, Appendix, Government Central Press, Simla, p. 482.
20. www.appa-net.org/down loaded on 25-11-2006.
21. Ram Ahuja (2000) Criminology, Rawat Publications, Satyam Apartments, Sector-3, Jain temple Road Jawahar Nagar, Jaipur-302004, p. 348.
22. V.V. Devasia and Leelamma Devasia (1992), Criminology Victimology and Corrections, Ashish Publishing House, 8/88 Punjabi Bagh Delhi-110026, p. 137.
23. United Nations (1951) Probation And Related Measures, United Nations Publications New York, p. 6.
24. Dr. Mahesh Kumar Sharan (1978) Court Procedure In Ancient India, Abinav Publications E-37, Hauz khas, New Delhi-110016, p. 193.

6

Personal Qualities of Probation Officers

In earlier days in England and United States of America, the Probation personnel were influenced by religious considerations. But in these days Probation Officers with technical knowledge and skill combined with positive favourable personal qualities are the ideal model. He is to instill confidence in the wards placed under his/her supervision. And probation officer is the pivot of probation supervision. With regards to the personal qualities by a Probation Officer, the United Nations Report States:

> "The vital importance of the personal qualities of the Probation Officer for the success of the system is very widely recognised, and such qualities tend to be of great importance in the selection of supervisory officers, both voluntary and paid. The requisite personality traits are not always very well defined, but there seems to exist wide-spread agreement as to the desirability of adequate intellectual endowment and maturity ; emotional stability; a high degree of personal integrity; dependability and sincerity; respect for the human personality, genuine interest in and concern for people, humor, tolerance, objectivity and the capacity for understanding and accepting other people for what they are and without moral condemnation; the ability to work with others and to win confidence, and tact; a strong sense of reality, a practical disposition, resourcefulness, adaptability and patience; firmness and strength of character. In addition, the qualities of health and physical endurance are frequently considered to be of paramount importance".[1]

Probation Officer is a quasi-judicial officer and hence the qualifications prescribed for a judicial officer can be attributed to him also:

"Yajnavalkala, Visnu, Katyayana, Narada, and Sukra requires the following qualifications of a judge:

1. They should be endowed with the study of the 'Vedas'
2. Should know dharmasastra
3. Should speak the truth
4. Should be steady
5. Should be devoted to their work
6. Intelligent
7. Hereditary
8. Proficient in 'Arthasastra'"[2]

The Probation Officer as correctional officers should have a positive attitude towards human beings, because,

"The success of correctional administration mainly depends on the faith, philosophy and efficiency of the correctional personnel. A correctional officer is expected to socially re-educate the offender. He is supposed to have an operational theory of behaviour in tune with the basic principles of correctional work. He must have a balanced personality and faith in the improvability of human beings."[3]

On the contrary, "Best rules and regulations and the most progressive measures of prison reform may be nullified by unsuitable personnel."[4]

The Indian Jails Committee 1919-20 opines, that the Probation Officer is to report to the Magistrate about the failure, if any, to observe the conditions bond. Further probation is to be combined with fine to make it more effective:

> "The Probation Officer ought usually to be, a full time officer receiving a fixed salary and not paid by fees. In some cases where the probation officer is the agent of a philanthropic society, duly attached to the court for probation duty. It is the practice to pay him a fee, for every case, sends under his care and whether, he gets these fees himself or hands them over to the society to which he is an agent, there is a temptation to him, to retain a case on probation which he really ought to report to the magistrate as a failure. There was a general consensus of opinion, also that as a measure of central control and supervision over probation officers is necessary. Another important point is that any failure to carry out the conditions of probation should be immediately brought to the notice of the magistrate, as neglect to enforce, the terms of probation orders is to bring the system into contempt. Under the existing English law, a youthful offender who is convicted and sentenced to fine or other punishment cannot simultaneously be placed under probation. Power to combine probation with fine or an order for restitution is very desirable".[5]

The appointment of Probation Officers, introduction of an all India Probation of Offenders Act, and premature release of prisoners were introduced on an all in India basis attributed to the solution No. 26 of the Reckless Committee, which state that:

"(a) It was resolved that a Probation of offenders Act, should be introduced in all States and the provisions of the Act should be made applicable to all prisoners regardless of age.

(b) It was resolved that an Act, on the lines of the Uttar Pradesh Release of prisoners on Probation Act (Act VIII of 1938) should also be aimed by all the States.

(c) It was also resolved that a system of releases as now obtaining in Uttar Pradesh under the ticket of leave rules should be introduced in all leave States.

(d) It was resolved that probation officers should be appointed in every state. It was generally agreed that the appointment of probation officers would result in a considerable saving to the state governments in as much as the release of prisoners under probation would avoid expenditure on the maintenance of prisoners in jails."[6]

Brise, considers that no less than from thirty to forty per cent of the population of local prisons have been under probation.

"It is, how hardly just to condemn the probation system on the ground that a number of the children have been through it find their way subsequently to those institutions, without the collection of statistics which are not available, as to the number of children placed under probation and most of those thereby reclaimed, as well as of those who later on, get into further trouble. Even the most accurate statistics could hardly be other than misleading, because so much depends, upon the class of case which individual magistrates might think suitable for probation. If only the worst cases were selected, the proportion of those who fell again would obviously be higher, while if almost every case, however trivial, were placed on probation to the pro of success would be greater."[7]

The Indian Jails Committee in the year 1919-20, recommends the personal qualities required for a Probation Officer, and suggests that the salary per mensem be rupees 250/-. In the 2014 the equivalent of the amount would approximately be Rs. 125000/-. So the Probation Officers are not receiving adequate remuneration even in these days.

With regard to the selection of probation officers the committee recommends persons with higher degree of character, judgment, discretion and if possible, enthusiasm is required. Securing the right type of person in India is a challenge. There needs to be Code of Conduct for Probation Officers since the Probation Officer is considered as to be the friend, philosopher and guide. Caldwell has also pointed out a few generally accepted principles to which the probation officer can look for guidance. The qualities required are:

"1. He must be a leader, i.e., he must always be in command of the situation and that he, and not the probationer, should be the one to decide what techniques are needed and how and when they should be used.

2. The Probation Officer should set a model of behaviour for the probationer by his own conduct. He should not be inconsistent with the values he expects the probationer to accept.

3. The Probation Officer should focus on both the environment and the personality traits of the probationer; keeping in mind the fact that criminality is the product of interaction of pressures of both.

4. He should try to seek help from all the available resources in the community-an interested employer, a loyal friend, a helpful neighbor, understanding parents, cooperating relative, a skillful psychiatrist, a recreation Centre, if any-for changing the attitudes of the probationer.

5. He should avoid threatening, ordering, and preaching but should seek the participation of the probationer in the solution of his own problems."[8]

The Code of Ethics published by the Government of Canada States: "We recognise the profound responsibilities in a profession dedicated to the protection of the community. Following are our guiding precepts both on and off duty:

> We will serve with humility, uphold the law with dignity, honesty and integrity, and act without prejudice.
>
> We will respect the inalienable rights of others, respect the privacy of clients, and be objective in the performance of our duties.
>
> We will treat each other with co-operation, respect, and fairness regardless of position or assignment.
>
> We will remain aware of our responsibilities to the community, the department and the individual.
>
> We will improve professional standards through continuously seeking knowledge, education, and training."[9]

The qualifications Donald. T. Shanahan wrote about for Probation Officers; other personnel, that:

"(a) The educational and occupational requirements of probation Officers should be possession of a Bachelors Degree supplemented by:

(i) a year of graduate study in social work, corrections, counseling, law, criminology, psychology, penology or related fields; or working experience along with a recognised social, community, correctional or juvenile agency dealing with offenders or disadvantaged persons or its equivalent as determined by the hiring agency.

(b) A significant number of probation officers in a department should have graduates degree in one of the subjects enumerated in this section.

(c) While the core of any probation department should be professionally educated and trained personnel, it is desirable that the staff include individuals who may lack such professional qualifications but have backgrounds similar to those of the probationers themselves. In addition, in appropriate cases citizen volunteers should be used to assist probation officers." [10]

Section 4 of the Probation of Offenders Act 1907 of Great Britain states the duties of a probation officer which is wider than the present probation of offenders Act 1958 in India; as below:

The duties of a probation officer are laid down in section 4 of the Probation of Offenders Act 1907, as follows: -

"(a) To visit or receive reports from the person under supervision at such suitable intervals as may be specified in the probation order or, subject thereto, as the probation officer may think fit;

(b) To see that he observes the conditions of his recognizance;

(c) To report to the court as to his behaviour;

(d) To advise, assist and befriend him, and when necessary, to endeavour, to find him suitable employment."

It is generally agreed by those best related to form an opinion that mere surveillance is not probation and there needs to be an earnest personal relation between the Probation Officer and the child. While there was an almost unanimous approval of probation in theory, there is much criticism of its practical working, more frequently by superintendents of reformatory and industrial schools, which necessarily often get failures of the probation system as stated by Sir Evelyn Ruggles.

"No definite Professional qualifications are essential but in practice men of good education and of the stamp found among the masters of the upper classes in secondary schools or colleges will be suitable. The pay must be sufficient to attract the right type of man. We would suggest a scale rising from Rs.100 to Rs. 250 per mensem, and it may be necessary to offer even a higher salary for a Chief Probation Officer. We saw in Calcutta two probation officers there employed but the pay (Rs. 50 per mensem) was insufficient to attract really suitable men nor had the requisite powers been conferred by law to enable these probation officers to do justice to their position. Probation officers should always be remunerated by a fixed salary and not, as in some parts of England, by per capita grants based on the number of probation cases entrusted to them."[11]

Probation Officers are to be a person with strength of character and sound mind in order to exert positive influence over the offender's future conduct and behaviour. And the Committee recommends that the released children be placed under the supervision of Probation Officer to receive assistance to get a job, counseling, and to dissuade them from associating with unsuitable friends. "The idea of the probation system is to provide a method by which an offender, instead of being whipped or sent for a prolonged period to a reformatory or other school can be placed under the direct personal supervision of some person chosen if possible for strength of character and sound personal influence, who will watch over the offender's future conduct, give him assistance in procuring work, advise him on occasions of difficulty, dissuade him from associating with unsuitable friends and generally direct and influence his conduct for good. The person to be thus entrusted with supervision over a young offender may be paid official, generally termed a Probation Officer working under the orders of the court, or he may be a private individual interested in philanthropic or social work, in this country possibly a missionary connected with some recognised mission. The court when discharging a child offender would place him under the supervision of such a probation officer or probation worker for a fixed period imposing such further conditions or penalties as it saw fit."[12]

Shri R.S. Rastogi, Principal, Jail Training School, Lucknow writes that:

> "A correctional officer should be able to register positive impact on the offender. He can only do so when he has the right personality and possess knowledge of influencing other."[13]

He also suggested that a Correctional Manual is required. "Mere training will not be sufficient in converting the older staff and changing their attitude. It is necessary that, the whole correctional policy should be carefully planned. A correctional manual containing, detailed instructions about correctional work should be framed. This work should no longer be left to individuals but should be supervised and guided by capable and well-trained officers at the head quarters. Care should however be taken not to discourage individual initiative."[14]

Probation Officers should have strong base in knowledge and positive attitude towards reformation and rehabilitation of the offender in the same society. At the same time they may find it difficult to include a boarder perspective in their presentence of enquiry reports to the courts. The reason behind it is :

"In the courts the focus is on the individual defendant, the individual criminal act, the defendant's guilt, criminal responsibility, criminal record and background history. Criminal acts are viewed purely as a particular aspect often individuals behaviour and not a more widespread social phenomenon with social, economic and political causes."[15]

Other qualities required to a Probation Officer are as per the recommendation of the Indian Jail Committee-1919-20 are:

> "Persons of high character judgment, discretion, and it possible enthusiasm are required."[16]

Further States about Refresher Course- All correctional workers should undergo, a refresher course on attaining promotion. Every member of the staff should be given a refresher course once in five years. Training should remain a continuous process. Correctional workers should always be up-to-date in their knowledge of correctional practices through these courses and visits to advanced countries.

The duties of Probation Officer are to advise, assist and befriend the offender under supervision for a permanent change and it requires frequent meetings by visiting the probationer's houses and asking them to report periodically to probation office. Hilary Walker and Bill Beaumont wrote in this regard:

> "The Probation Officer is expected, to encourage a person on probation to make use of any statutory or voluntary agency which might contribute to his welfare, and to take advantage of any available social recreational or educational facilities suited to his age, ability, and temperament."[17]

Probation Officers have to be men of character, and strong will in order to discharge their duties. The Indian Jails Committee recommended with regard to the role of probation Officer that "an offender can be placed under the direct personal supervision of some person chosen, if possible for strength of character and sound personal influence, who will watch over the offender's future conduct, give him assistance in procuring work, advise him on occasions of difficulty, dissuade him from associating with unsuitable, friends, and generally direct and influence his conduct for good, (termed probation officer) working under the orders of the court."

[Report of the Indian Jails Committee-1919-20 Vol-I, Government Press, Simla, Para 375, (page-199)]

Unfortunately some Probation Officers mistakenly undertake the work in a prejudiced way. "Few Probation Officers will have, envisaged the job as tailoring clients to meet the needs of society and few attempts to do this."[18]

Survey Reports in England shows: "Most Probation Officers, if asked to describe what they do, would explain that they give, "general support" to their clients and find it hard to be any more specific. Despite a trend towards exploring, different methods of social work to be practiced under probation orders, there is little evidence of any wholesale adoption and most work is still carried out on a one-to-one basis."[19]

The persons under supervision of Probation Officers often are unaware about the role of Probation Officer in their life and this results in several misunderstandings and unexpected developments in between the probationer and probation officers. So it becomes relevant. to keep the relationship official and objectives as written by Phyllida:

> "One very important part of the job of a Probation Officer is to give to his probationer the experience of being under the authority of someone, who takes pains to understand his point of view, is concerned about him as a person and yet set limits and ultimately take action."[20]

The total number of probation officers in India is estimated to be about 615, of whom 17 per cent are females a 83 per cent are males. The Probation Officers are to be the pivot of probation service as stated by B. Krishna Menon, former Chief Probation Superintendent of Tamilnadu:

> "Probation provides a method by which an offender instead of being sent to a correctional institution or a jail can be placed under the direct

> personal supervision of the Probation Officer chosen for strength of character, sound personal influence and high social instinct, who will watch the offender's future conduct, give him assistance in procuring work, advise him on occasions of difficulty, dissuade him from associating with unsuitable friends, direct and influence his conduct for good, and thus in all possible ways, control and enhance his life."[21]

The qualities required for an effective Probation Officer with regard to knowledge, skill and attitude are similar to the one required Aftercare officer. The job satisfaction and stress of Probation officers vary from person to person and place to place.

"The work is rarely dull, need never become repetitive or routine and constantly gives them the opportunity to develop and make use of their own personality. Using yourself as the tool of your work is both satisfying and exhausting.

The probation officer should expect that his job will give him opportunities to come to terms with some of his own conflicts and that it will satisfy some of his own needs."[22]

The ratio between the Probation Officer and Population in India is 1:15,00,000 and the number of male Probation Officers are for higher than female Probation Officers.

The qualities required for a professional worker to be effective while dealing with delinquents and criminals are:

> "Knowledge of Delinquent and criminal behaviour as one form of deviance; The Psychological and social strains which in various constellations press individuals towards such behaviour; The body of techniques, which is learned by the offender, in order to commit offences and to protect himself in dealing with community authorities; The diagnostic approaches now in use and problems inherent in applying them to the correctional caseload.

Skills in: Identifying the social as well as psychological strains effective in the causation of offending behaviour; Modifying the offender's environment so that strains towards conformity are substituted for those which press toward criminal deviance.

Attitudes of: Acceptance of delinquent and criminal deviants without condoning anti-social behaviour; scientific interest in the contributions of social structure to causation and treatment as well as in psychological determinants:

Readiness to work experimentally and without undue discouragement in a field where present knowledge is limited, prognosis is uncertain, and failures frequent."[23]

"The efficacy of the probation system is to large extend depended on the quality of the Probation Officers, who play vital role not in determining the quality of supervision services but also in the programme of rehabilitating the first and young offenders back in the society. They mechanise the whole philosophy of the institution of probation, obviously in a given societal circumstances. Carney has rightly observed that, 'the key to effective probation lies in the quality of the professional staff that implements the probation service'. The job of a Probation Officer is both technical as well as voluntary. It is technical in the sense, that it concerns remoulding or reshaping the personality of the offenders. It is technical and sensitive because concerned with the care and treatment of Juvenile and adult offenders. Professional interchange of ideas is very necessary for the growth of new ideas and the dissemination of these ideas."[24]

Concerted attempt in this regard is to be done in this area.

In United Kingdom Probation officers are appointed under government and they are receiving assistance from voluntary persons, as stated in the report of the United Nations. While each probationer must be placed under the supervision of a Probation Officer this does not exclude the use of voluntary assistance.

"Voluntary help is sometimes of value, though it must not be regarded as in any way a substitute for the services of a salaried probation officer. While every case should be placed under the supervision of a probation officer, voluntary helpers of the right type may be used. It is voluntary, because it grows as a professional service and not as a simple government assignment, it is voluntary service because it entails the various personal interests, areas and it covers a very wide range of individualised relations between the system - delivery source and the recipients of the system. Naturally Probation Officers are deemed to be an expert, a technologist and service minded professional being. Such a highly technical expertise professional attitude can be made available in a person, provided:

"(a) he has a suitable academic background;

(b) an aptitude for taking a challenging profession; and

(c) a very thorough and motivating training course."[25]

Probation Officers are scattered throughout India and they are frequently travelling very nook and corner and interacting with probationers and related persons. Their deep and wide experience related to social problems are not shared with Probation Officers from other parts of the country due to lack of opportunity. W.C. Reckless recommends after his study on Jail Administration in India:

"The Central Government should encourage the development of a professional conference among the superior staff members. It concerns the handling of human mind in its various impulses and emotions in the set up of physical circumstances, the job is highly technical in the sense that it concerns high psychological, sociological, environmental and many other socio-economic and cultural inputs and be able to give useful assistance to him especially in scattered areas where he is stationed a long way from a person placed under his care."[26]

Provision is made in the Probation Rules, 1949 for the appointment, by probation committees subject to the consent of the Home Secretary, of Senior and principal Probation Officers.

"The duties to be performed by these officers include the supervision of and advice upon the work of Probation Officers, the organisation of office work, the distribution of work between Probation Officers, and the supervision and guidance of Probation Officers with respect to the keeping of records; in addition, Principal Officers are to advise probation committees on technical matters relating to the probation service."[27]

With regard to the service conditions of Correctional personnel the All India Jail Manual Committee- 1957-59 recommended:

> "The correctional personnel should feel that they are members of an important social service demanding, ability and good team work. Correctional personnel are continuously exposed to conditions of service that are complex, exacting and arduous; Correctional Administration should therefore afford necessary safe guards and protection to correctional personnel."[28]

Probation is a purposeful activity, which aims a permanent exchange in the offender. But a survey held at Nottingham United kingdom in 1981 showed the work of a Probation Officer is:

> "Boring and routine" "go down there for a chat and come. Home again... It is a waste of time" "a process of aimless talks".[29]

The quality of probation service basically depends on the quality of the Probation Officer and the rules relating to probation is comparatively unimportant.

The Departmental Committee on Probation of Offenders Act 1907 in United Kingdom stated during 1909:

> "The probation officer must be a picked man or woman, endowed not only with intelligence and zeal, but, in a high degree, with sympathy and tact and firmness. On his or her individuality the success or failure of the system depends Probation is what the officer makes it."[30]

The personality traits required for Probation Officers listed out by National Probation and Parole Association of America are:

> "good health, physical endurance, intellectual maturity, emotional stability, integrity, tact, dependability, adaptability, resourcefulness, sincerity, humor, ability to work with others, tolerance, patience, objectivity, capacity to win confidence, respect for human personality, and genuine affection for people."[31]

In the United Kingdom the Probation Officers were initially voluntary persons and after enactments of various legislations, Government appointed Probation officers. The United Nations report on Probation states:

> "The probation service in the United Kingdom has made a gradual transition from a system relying on the use of voluntary personnel and a system providing for the official employment of agents of voluntary societies, to a complete public service. Decided preference is given to full-time trained officers."[32]

The duties of the Probation Officers are prescribed in section14 of the Probation of offenders Act 1958, and in section of the Juvenile Justice (care and Protection of children) Act 2000. It is very similar to criminal Justice Act 1948 of United Kingdom. The words 'inquire' and 'supervision' are not defined in the Act. So it gives ample freedom and opportunity to Probation Officer to utilise his personal skills as a correctional officer.

The Criminal Justice Act, 1948, of United Kingdom defines the duties of Probation Officers in its section 30:

"(a) To supervise the probationers and other persons placed under their supervision and to advise, assist and befriend them;

(b) To inquire in accordance with any directions of the court, into the circumstances or home surroundings of any persons with a view to assisting the court in determining the most suitable method of dealing with his case;

(c) To advise, assist and befriend, in such cases and in such manner as may be prescribed, persons who have been released from custody; and

(d) To perform such other duties as may be prescribed or may be imposed by any enactment."[33]

It is interesting to note that the section 30 of the Criminal Justice Act 1948 of England, which defines the duties of Probation Officers is copied as almost verbatim into the section 14 of the Probation of Offenders Act, 1958, in India. One indication is that the Probation Service everywhere, is similar in nature.

Footnotes

1. United Nations (1951), Probation and Related Measures, U.N. Publication, p. 262.
2. Dr. Mahesh Kumar Sharan (1978) Court Procedure in Ancient India, Abhinav Publications, E-37, Hauzkhas, New Delhi-110016, p. 39.
3. Report of the All India Jail Manual Committee 1957-59, para 48, p. 28.
4. *Ibid.,* para. 50, p. 29.
5. Report of the Indian Jail Committee 1919-20, Vol. I, Appendix IX Government Central Press, Simla, p. 494.
6. W.C. Reckless (1952), Jail Administration In India, Government of India Publication, New Delhi, p. 45.
7. Report of the Indian Jails Committee 1919-20, Vol. I, Appendix-IX, p. 481.
8. Ram Ahuja (2000) Criminology, Rawat Publications, Satyam Apartments, Sector-3, Jain Temple Road, Jawahar Nagar, Jaipur-302004, pp. 340-41.
9. www.placer.ca.gov/probation/Alternative
10. Donald. T. Shanahan, (1977) The Administration of Justice System, an Introduction, University of Louisville Holbrook Press Inc 470 Atlantic Avenue Boston, p. 57.
11. Report of the Indian Jails Committee- 1919-20, Vol. I, Para 376, p. 200.
12. Report of the Indian Jails Committee-1919-20, Vol. 1, para 375; p. 199.
13. All India Jail Manual Committee-1957-59, Part-I, Annexure-K, p. 190.

14. *Ibid.,* p. 194.
15. Hilary Walker, Bill Beaumont (1981) Probation Critical Theory and Socialist Practice, Basil Blackwell Publisher Limited, 108 Cowley Road, Oxford OX4, IJF, England, p. 21.
16. All India Jail Manual Committee-1957-59, Part-I, Annexure-K, p. 194.
17. Hilary Walker, Bill Beaumont (1981) Probation Critical Theory and Socialist Practice, Basil Blackwell Publisher Limited, 108 Cowley, p. 199.
18. *Ibid.,* p. 35.
19. Hillary Walker, Bill Beamont (1981) Probation Work Critical Theory And Socialist Practice, Basil Blackwell Publisher Limited, 108 Cowley Road, Oxford, OX4, IJF, England, p. 34.
20. Phyllida Parsloe (1967), The Work of Probation and Aftercare Officer, Routledge and Kegan Paul, Ltd., Broad way House, 68-74 Carter Lane, London Ec 4, p. 81.
21. B. Krishna Menon, (1959) All India Jail manual Committee Reports, 1957-59 Part-I, Annexure-4, Government of India Publication, New Delhi, pp. 196-97.
22. Phyllida Parsloe (1967), The Work of Probation and Aftercare Officer, Routledge and Kegan Paul, Ltd., Broad way House, 68-74 Carter Lane, London Ec 4, p. 81.
23. Boehm, Werner, W. (1959) Objectives of Social Curriculum of the Future, Council of Social Work Education, New York, p. 125.
24. W.C. Reckless (1950) Jail Administration in India, Government of India Press Publication, New Delhi, p. 360.
25. Nirmal Kanti Chakraborti (October 1989) Social Defense (Vol. XXVIII, No. 98, National Institute of Social Defense, New Delhi, p. 46.
26. W.C. Reckless (1950) Jail Administration in India, Govt. of India Press Publication, New Delhi, p. 360.
27. United Nations — (1951), Probation and Related Measures, U.N. Publication, New York, p. 124.
28. Report of the All India Jail Manual Committee - 1957-59, Government of India, New Delhi, Para 60 pp. 35-36.

29. Hillary Walker, Bill Beaumont (1981), Probation, Critical theory and Socialist Practice,' Basil Blackwell Publisher Limited, 108 Cowley Road, Oxford, OX4 IJF, England, p. 34.
30. United Kingdom, Home Department, Departmental Committee on the Probation of Offenders Act, 1907(1909), Report (Cd.5001), Para. 28.
31. Standards for Selection of Probation and Parole Officers, (1945), National Probation and Parole Association, United States of America, New York, p. 5.
32. United Nations: (1951) Probation and Related Measures, New York, p. 123.
33. *Ibid.*, p. 124.

7

Pre-sentence Investigation

The Pre-sentence Investigation or Preliminary Enquiry report by the Probation Officer helps the Judicial Officer in determining the appropriate sentence. As per section 14 (a) of the Probation of Offenders Act 1958, it is the duty of the Probation Officers to "Inquire in accordance with any directions of the Court, into the circumstances or home surroundings of an person accused of an offence and found guilty with a view to assist the Court in determining the most suitable method of dealing with the offender and submit report to the court".

The report shall contain facts regarding the home surroundings, criminal record and social history of the offender and the circumstances under which the offence was committed and the gravity of the offence.

Section 7, of the Probation Offenders Act 1958, states that the Probation Officers shall not divulge any information concerning their enquiries or probation work to any person other than, the authorities to whom they are required to report, except in so far as, it is necessary to do so in the interest of any probationer. United States Supreme Court judge Black states:

> "Probation Officers reports have been given high value by the conscientious judge who want to sentence persons on the best available information rather than a fuss work and inadequate information".

In the case of institutionalisation, the inquiry report may be submitted in duplicate for one copy can be sent to the institution concerned.

Contents of the presentence investigation report

Generally it contains the personal details and information about his surroundings. The personal situation depends on his position among his friends, companions and his family; also in relation to his popularity, emotional conditions like jealousy, indifferent repressed with or without outlets. The external surroundings include economic and social status, home and neighborhood, employment and the use of spare time. The main source of information is his own story and his reactions to the Probation Officers approach.

The Probation Officer has to visit the home or place of residence and talk with the members of his family, and meet his relatives, friends, associate, and companions, for eliciting the necessary information. A report is to be created with the offender and his neighbors and employers, if any, be approached with caution so that it may not adversely affect his reputation or employment proper, the Probation Officer, is to collect information from police station, Jails, if any, his school etc., and interviewing the offender. An interpretative analysis to, ascertain of the facts during the investigation will be helpful to the Judge and also important for later treatment. It should be written legibly and concisely in the prescribed Form.

Areas for investigation are:

1. ***Identifying Information:*** It includes the name aliases, address date and place of birth, Religion, Education, Caste, Sex and Nationality.
2. ***Personal History:*** Pre-natal and childhood events, adolescents events, his attitude and conduct towards family, relatives and associates.
3. ***Family:*** The age, education, employment and place of parents, brothers, sisters, wife or husband, children and interested relatives.
4. ***Home and neighborhood:*** Includes a short description of the home, type of the area, status of ownership like own or rental, and neighborhood influences.
5. ***Religion:*** Affiliation, belief and attitude towards religion.
6. ***Health:*** Present and past conditions, diseases, injuries, handicaps, behaviour and habits relating to smoking, alcohol, drug and sexual.
7. ***Mental and emotional:*** Present and past situations personality recurrences, history of mental or emotional instability.
8. ***Education:*** The class up-to which studied; whether dropout, if so, reasons; course passed or, completed, aptitude towards teachers and school; desire for higher studies and on any learning problems.

9. ***Interest and activities:*** Leisure time activities; special abilities' group affiliations; social adjustment; and achievements.
10. ***Employment and resources:*** Employment present work, wages; change of work. Skills; cum, investment; pension; financial liabilities etc., written in the chronological order.
11. ***Offence:*** Includes a brief inscription of the charge, duration of detention; name and address of sureties; opinions of the officers, co-accomplices; witnesses and the offender's own opinion and attitude and reaction towards the crime. Whether he is penitent or not.
12. ***Previous Convictions:*** Name of the Courts, place, date and nature of disposal regarding previous conviction and Finger Print result.
13. ***Agencies and individuals interested:*** Name and address of individuals, agencies and two sureties, if available.
14. ***Victim compensation:*** Opinion about the victims and victims' relations; and the possibility of recovering compensation.
15. ***Summary and Diagnosis:*** includes the analysis of the offenders' social situation; history, problems, and causes of past and present offences; his motives and attitudes; with a view to his proper reformation and rehabilitation.
16. ***Summary and recommendation:*** Summarise from the body of the Probation, report the assets and liabilities of the offender and give a fitting recommend quoting the relevant section and the Statute.

Conducting presentence investigation is one of the primary duties of Probation Officers. The contents of the report include the family back ground, personal history, criminal antecedents, personality traits, the nature of the offence, the circumstances of the crime, the gravity of the offence whether he is penitent or having repentances, opinion of the offender towards the crime, and attitude towards the victim as well as the possibility of reformation if he is released on probation supervision.

The views expressed by the National Association of Probation Officers in the United Kingdom:

> "The subject of pre-sentence investigation is dealt with in a complementary statute, adopted at the same time as the new Probation statute (1939) and also coming into force on 1 January 1944. This Act, as amended in 1945, provided for mandatory pre-sentence investigations, in certain cases, including all cases where the defendant is under 21 years

> of age and in custody. A pre-sentence investigation is also a pre requisite to a conditional sentence, to conditional suspension of the imposition of sentence and to various other specified court dispositions. In addition, the court is also authorised to order a pre-sentence investigation in all criminal cases, where it appears to be necessary for gaining knowledge concerning the defendant's personal situation and concerning the measures, which would appear most suitable to reform him.

The court is authorised to designate 'a suitable and willing person' to conduct the pre-sentence investigation in each individual case. Investigators are paid fees, which are fixed by the court, after examination, in each case. The persons appointed for the purpose are, in many cases, young law school graduates attached to the court but it is common to find social workers, staff members of Prisoners aid Associations, policewomen, or child welfare workers, teachers, ministers or physicians accepting appointment.

The nature and scope of the investigation are regulated by royal decree. The investigator is required to makes as complete enquiry as possible into the character, circumstances of life, and personal situation of the defendant; to furnish the court with advice, on the suitability of any form of punishment or measure of treatment under consideration; and, where a conditional sentence is being considered, to make recommendations with respect to the special conditions to be attached, to take preliminary steps for the application of such conditions, and to propose a suitable Volunteer Probation Officer. The investigator is further instructed to make, personal contact with the defendant, to make home visits to secure information from his family and relatives, and to evaluate the defendant's environmental situation on the basis of personal observation. He is to verify and his family are not unnecessarily harmed by the enquiry.

While the case records thus compiled vary considerably in quality, they contain a wide range of information about the defendant. The greater majority of persons brought before the courts are at present being subjected to such investigation."[1]

Preliminary Enquiry or Presenting Enquiry by the Probation officer is decisive document over the suitability of the case to be considered, for probation and for the success of supervision. Thus the objective of preliminary enquiry stated in the Report on Probation by United Nations is:

> "From the point of view of probation practice, the preliminary enquiry has a twofold function, namely the determination of suitability for release

on probation, and the establishment of a basis for subsequent probationary treatment.

The *first* function is one of selection as well as one of elimination. It involves a comprehensive investigation into both, the personal history and characteristics and the environmental circumstances of the offender. It includes the investigation of such factors as the criminal record of the offender, the motivations for and the circumstances of the offence, but its approach is not legalistic, and its purpose is not being determination of guilt or criminal responsibility. Similarly the preliminary enquiry is not intended to seek for mitigating factors warranting, the release of the offender on probation. The primary consideration is the assessment of the offenders susceptibility, to reformative treatment, taking into account the total social and psychological situation.

The *second* function of the pre-sentence investigation, is to establish a sound basis for subsequent treatment on probation, i.e., if the offender is placed on probation. The investigation and subsequent treatment on probation constitute a continuous process and the "diagnosis" of the personality and situation of the offender gives direction to, subsequent planning for his rehabilitation.

Pre-sentence social investigations cannot be self-contained, and no investigation can be adequate, if the investigator fails to make full use of the information relating to the offender, which is already available in the files and records of, various organisations, and agencies in the community. Educational records, records of contacts with welfare organisations, Police and Court records, etc. should be utilised and brought into relationship with the results of the direct enquiries of the investigator. This task is facilitated where a centralised exchange of social service information is in operation, but the systematic follow-up of leads obtained in the course of, direct enquiries is essential. Ideally, the agency responsible for presentence investigations may organise, its own system of personal files and records, with the necessary co-operative and exchange relationships with other centralised and community agencies (schools, etc.), and with due regard to the confidential nature of the information involved. In the United States of America, the State Commission on Probation in Massachusetts has pioneered, in developing such an independent system of personal files and records.

In making an adequate diagnosis of the personality and situation of an offender, it is necessary to bring together several specialised skills. In the absence of the medical, psychological and psychiatric examination of each offender brought before court, it will be the task of the person performing the pre-sentence investigation to determine which offenders particularly need such examinations".[2]

Presentence Enquiry and supervision by Probation officer are the two important components of Probation. But there are some measures similar to probation for dealing with offenders. According to the United Nations report on probation:

> "Probation, in the strict sense of the term, should be distinguished from certain closely related measures which correspond to probation in some respects but lack one or more of the essential elements listed above. Among the most significant measures in this category are to be found; (a) parole; (b) the use of supervision of the probationary type with respect to pre-delinquents and other maladjusted persons; (c) the recognizance and binding-over and (d) the conditional suspension of the imposition, or of the execution of sentence, without probationary supervision."[3]

Presentence Enquiry, Correct diagnosis and meticulous plan of action with regard to the rehabilitation and its prompt implementation is required for the effective probation supervision. Otherwise it will create public apathy towards it.

"The careful selection of probationers is important from the point of view of the outcome of the cases involved. To place persons on probation where the circumstances do not justify, it imposes an unfair burden on the probation officer, and brings discredit on the system. Failure in unsuitable cases may even deter Courts from using probation in cases, which are suitable. Public interest also demands that it shall not be used indiscriminately without due regard to all the circumstances of the case, including the character of the offence".[4]

The Presentence investigation report is presented to the court, after the criminal has been convicted but before awarding a sentence in order to help the court in the sentencing procedure. It includes an evaluation of the criminals:

(i) Family background
(ii) Social relationship
(iii) Occupational strengths
(iv) Educational backgrounds
(v) Criminal background and all other factors pertinent to the problem."[5]

Presentence of data collection consultation with specialists are to be considered by the Judiciary to deliver judgments from a reformatory angle:

> "New therapeutic measures and new institutions must be created. It is here that criminal law, psychiatric medicine and correctional supervision at homes and outside meets at the sentencing level. Here does the judge play a lesser role or rather, leans heavily on Psychiatric or other experts, social workers and Probation officers. It is a pity that the Indian Criminal System does not, extend in a few special statutes provide for the post-conviction, presentencing collection of data and consultation with specialists so as to prescribe personalised judicial directions potent from a reformatory angle."[6]

> "The pre-sentence investigation is performed by the Probation Officer to learn the family and social background of the offender and to assess his strengths and weaknesses with a view toward working out a treatment programme."[7]

> "The Probation Officer should jointly arrive at a common understanding of the goal as the result of Intimate heart to heart discussions... but over kindness in very often be mistaken for weakness."[8]

Ingredients of Social Investigation

Social investigation is designed to fulfill three main functions:

(a) Making an objective appraisal of the offenders mental and emotional make-up in relation to the commission of offence,

(b) Arriving at a diagnosis of his behaviour (and if possible, prognosis) and

(c) Facilitating the judicial process.

That means the investigation report must first correctly analyse and interpret certain basic identifying data about the offender's personality antecedents and character. The report may take the following format:

1. ***A Review of Legal Facts :*** the nature of offence, precipitating factors (if any), time and place of commission of offence, the complainant's attitude, mitigating and aggravating circumstances of the offence, previous record (if any) and previous commitment to institution.
2. ***Analysis of Personality:*** Intelligence, temperament, attitudes, character, bearing and conduct, abnormal or peculiar mental traits.

3. ***Analysis of Environment:*** Development history, early life, school history, education level, home and family environment, neighborhood influences habits and interests, associates, employment and operation history.
4. Diagnosis and interpretation.
5. Tentative plan for treatment and rehabilitation for the competent authority's consideration.
6. Prognosis
7. Synopsis."[9]

The report of the Probation Officer is to be considered before releasing a person on probation.

"It embodies modern humanitarian approach of reformation with freedom rather than punishing the offender. Question of releasing an accused on probation is left to discretion of court come to its own conclusion on consideration of all the factors, including the report of the Probation Officer".[10]

The social enquiry report by Probation Officer is a comprehensive professional document to aid the court to come to judicious decisions. Professionalism includes correct diagnosis of the case and appropriate treatment plan. Reports to the court should be:

"1. Readable
2. Comprehensive and
3. Objective;

   In order to assist the court in deciding upon the appropriate sentence they should be,
4. Relevant to the courts sentencing function
5. Match the offenders with the correct form of treatment.
6. Enable the needs of both society and offender to be met."[11]

American courts and the probation system

Report of the Probation Officer is called for by the court after the guilt is established and for receiving the report the court adjourns the case for one week, as was the practice in America during the year 1907. Various forms of legislation have been resorted to in the United States of American courts to legalise the probation system. Thus in the State of Indiana a law of 1907 gives the courts power to suspend sentence or to withhold judgment in the case of persons charged with any crime except murder, treason, arson, rape, burglary and kidnapping. The law varies from State to State. Sometimes it applies only to minor offences, sometimes only to a first offender, and sometimes only to a first conviction for felony. In a case where the law is applied it is usual for the court, after the guilt of the accused has been established, to grant an adjournment from three to seven days, before sentence is pronounced. This period is employed by the Probation Officer in making inquiries into the prisoner's previous history, the circumstances leading up to the commission of their crime of which he has now have convicted, his family circumstances, physical and mental condition and the like. A report on the result of this enquiry is drawn up and is placed before the judge, who then has the prisoner before him and before disposing of the case, questions him as to any extenuating or aggravating circumstances appearing in the report. Under the American practice no copy of the Probation Officer's report appears to be furnished either to the prosecution or the accused, but counsel on both sides are usually present when the judge questions the accused and can take exception to any statement which the judge may read out from the Probation Officer's report. A special Committee of the State Commission of the Prisons, New York in a report submitted in 1918, held that any reports of preliminary investigation submitted by a Probation Officer to the judge should be treated as confidential and considered that it would be open to serious objection to put into the witness- box an officer who might subsequently be entrusted with the supervision of the offender."[12]

The judge has to consider the Social Investigation report for selecting the offender for community treatment. Hence the probation revolves round:

> "(i) The judge; (ii) The Probation Officer, and (iii) The criminal himself. Although infect the criminal has to achieve his own reformation under the guidance of the probation officer, the major responsibility lies with the court."[13]

> "Presentence investigation report is a valuable help to the Probation Officer himself in his efforts during the period of probation supervision for rehabilitation of probationers ... and scientific research."[14]

It is the duty of the magistrate to examine the following points before pronouncing the judgment because probation is meant for those persons who are willing to abide by the conditions stipulated in the bond at the time of release.

"(i) Has been arrived at by procedures that were valid and free of prejudice;

(ii) Is consistent with the facts known about the criminal;

(iii) Make the most productive use of the criminal's abilities;

(iv) Embodies a realistic correctional programme for the criminal which can achieve its purpose;

(v) Protects the community".[15]

The presentence investigation report by the probation officer is to be considered only after finding the accused guilty or pleaded guilty.

Presentence Investigation Stages

"The probation service of the court shall make a presentence investigation and report to the court before the imposition of sentence or the granting of probation unless the court otherwise directs. The reports shall not be submitted to the court or its contents disclosed to anyone unless the defendant has pleaded guilty or has been found guilty. The Report of the presentence investigation shall contain any prior criminal record of the defendant and such information about his characteristics, his financial condition and the circumstances affecting his behaviour as may be helpful in imposing sentences or in granting probation or in the correctional treatment of the defendant, and such other information as may be required by the Court."[16]

Federal Rules of Criminal Procedure

James. B. Pearsons (March 1964) stated: "Presentence Investigation report must preserved as a Confidential Document."[17]

The reports of the Probation Officer are to be "diagnostic in nature and readable, comprehensive and objective in order to assist the court in deciding upon the most appropriate sentence they should be relevant to the courts sentencing function, match the offenders with the correct form of treatment and thus enable the needs of both society and offender to be met." The Probation Officer has to reach a judgment quickly, often starting completely from scratch. The offender is usually preoccupied with unresolved issues about arrest, conviction or problems unrelated to the courts appearance. In practice social enquiry reports are often hasty judgments made under considerable pressure on the basis of inadequate information. Since the Probation Officer completes many reports choosing recommendations from a small range of possibilities, it is not surprising that reports emerge in a highly routinised (though sometimes idiosyncratic) conceptual form."[18]

The main functions of the presentence investigation report are:

"The pre-sentence investigation report serves five functions:

1. To help the judge in deciding the appropriate sentence.
2. To assist the prison authorities in planning the classification and correctional activities in the institution.
3. To furnish the probation department with information related to the criminal's release on probation.
4. To aid the probation officer in rehabilitative efforts during probation supervision, and
5. To serve as a source of information for systematic research."[19]

The presentence investigation report submitted before a judicial officer shall contain satisfactory answers to the following questions, like:

"1. Is the defiant dangerous?
2. Will imprisonment help or harm this person?
3. Is probation an acceptable constructive substitute for this particular person?
4. Is he mentally and emotionally of such make-up as to be careful of profiting from community corrections?
5. Is his attitude towards community and probation such as to justify the use of probation instead of imprisonment?
6. Will community benefit if the defendant is placed on probation?
7. Will granting probation at this point and under the given circumstances be considered as leniency?
8. Does the defiant have a suitable home and a job to give him a start if he is turned back into the community at this time? Moreover, what plans does the defiant himself have for his future? This latter question may have considerable diagnostic significance."[20]

Time Factor in Social Investigation

Two viewpoints prevail, each having its merit and demerits:

(A) The view points that favours the time-limit emphasises the following points:
  1. Time-limit stress the urgency of investigation.
  2. It sooner relieves the offender of the tension attending a prolonged waiting he expects.

3. It reduces his apprehensions and resistance to law.
4. It expedites justice. In the prevailing work culture, the time-limit guarantees that the process is accelerated, and justice to the offender is not delayed.
5. It obviates subjective factors getting unnecessarily complicated by the offender's fresh detention experiences.
6. It reassures the offender who knows where he will soon stand, and who, accordingly, becomes psychologically prepared to make adjustment now.
7. The existing detention facilities do not provide him with a climate conductive to his mobilising inner resources and capacity to face any eventuality.

(B) The viewpoint that does not favour the time limit stresses the following points:

1. No detailed, searching investigation can be envisaged with the Damocles Sword of time-limit hanging over-head.
2. Time-limit subjects the investigation to avoidable stress, and it cracks the investigation officer's morale.
3. It generates stereotyped approach, and a tendency to categorise cases.
4. It vitiates the relationship between the probation officer and the client (the offender), the relationship being always a matter of gradual growth.
5. The interview technique which the probation officer developing is, basically, a casework technique. It aims at developing appropriate objective relationship between the offender and the Probation Officer in which the latter will be a good listener. He will not be the nuances of the hearing and the influenced on what the offender says; allowing him a reasonable degree of freedom and emotional comfort to express himself. The time factor cramps the Probation Officer's style and necessitates a compromise with the tenets of casework.[21]

Since the Probation Officer is a quasi-judicial Officer the preliminary inquiry report by him also bears the status of quasi-judicial work, as it is decisive document for the judicial officer in deciding a case.

Footnotes

1. United Nations (1951), *Probation and Related Measures,* Para 23 to 26; pp. 160-61.

2. United Nations (1951), *Probation and Related Measures,* Para 21 to 23, p. 233.
3. United Nation (1951), *Probation and Related Measures,* New York, p. 9.
4. United Nations- 1951, also United Kingdom, Home Departmental Committee on the Social Service in Courts of Summary Jurisdiction, Report (1936) (Cmd. 5122), (Para. 64).
5. V.V. Devassia and Leelamma Devassia (1992) Criminology Victimology and Corrections, Ashish Publishing House, 8/81 Punjab Bagh New Delhi-110026, p. 140.
6. V.R. Krishna Iyer (1976), *Social Mission of Law,* Orient, Longman Ltd, 3/5 Asaf Ali Road, New Delhi-110001, p. 99.
7. Fox Vernon (1972), Introduction to Corrections, Engle wood: Prentice Hall, p. 105.
8. Dr. J. Visuvathas (1987) *Deviant Children,* Sri Iyengar Industries, Madras, p. 117.
9. M.S. Sabins (1995), *Juvenile Justice and Juvenile Corrections,* pp. 260- 61.
10. (1969) 71 Punjab L.R (D) 158 (161).
11. Hilary Walker, Bill Beaumont (1981), *Probation Critical Theory and Socialist Practice,* Basil Blackwell Publisher Limited, 108 Cowley Road, Oxford OX4, IJF, England, pp. 15-16.
12. Report of the Indian Jail Committee-1919 - 20, Vol. I, para - 428, p. 219.
13. V.V. Devasia and Leelamma Devasia (1992), *Criminology and Corrections,* Ashish publishing House, 8/81, Punjabi Bagh, Delhi-110026, p. 137.
14. Jyotsna H. show Ph.D. DSSA (1973) Studies in Criminology, Probation services in India, NM Tripathi Pvt. Ltd., 164 Samaldas Gandhi Marg, Bombay- 400002, p. 23.
15. V.V. Devasia and Lelamma (1992), *Criminology,* Ashishs Publication House, Delhi 110026, pp. 139-40.
16. V.V. Devasia and Lelamma (1992), *Criminology,* Ashishs Publication House, Delhi 110026, pp. 139-40.

17. *Federal Probation,* Vol. XVIII, Number 1Administrative Office of the United States Courts in Cooperation with the Bureau of Prisons of the Department of Justice, Washington D.C. p. 10.
18. Hillary Walker, Bill Beaumont (1981) *Probation Work,* Basil Blackwell Publisher Limited, 108 Cowley Road, Oxford OX4 IJF England, p. 16.
19. V.V. Devasia and Leelamma Devasia (1992), *Criminology, Victimology and Corrections,* p. 139.
20. V.V. Devasia and Leelamma (1992), pp. 140-141.
21. M.S. Sabins (1995) Juvenile Justice and Juvenile Corrections, pp. 264-65.

8

Aftercare Supervision

In India, the Aftercare of persons prematurely released from Prisons, Borstal Schools and Juvenile Justice institutions are entrusted with Probation Officers. During the year 1952 Walter. C. Reckless an expert appointed by the Technical Assistance Administration of the United Nations, reported that Probation in India is not well developed and suggested that its improvement can be made with appointment of sufficient staff and by involving the services of Voluntary agencies.

"Aftercare Undeveloped: There is very little after-care work actually done, although there are many great societies which are valiantly trying to help discharged prisoners. After-care service must be on a whole-time basis, staffed to take care of the load of cases discharged from prisons, Borstals, Reformatory Schools, and Certified Schools. Private organisations can help but they can never operate the Service to cover the load of cases requiring after-care help."[1]

A system is to be developed so that the aftercare supervision of inmates released from Borstal school/Prison/childrensHome/Special School are organised well and planned, in advance prior to the release from their respective Institutions. The report of the Indian Jails Committee 1919-20, discusses the methods of aiding inmates upon their release from Institutions.

"Under the provisions of the Prevention of Crime Act, 1908, the Prison Commissioners may, by license, release an adolescent from a Borstal institution, at any time after the expiry of six months, or in the case of female, three months, from the commencement of the period of detention, on condition that, he (or she) is placed under the supervision or authority of any society or person willing to take charge of the case. Three months before the date proposed for release the boy or girl is visited at the Borstal institutions by a representatives of the Borstal Association who sees him alone, discuss his plans with him, and obtains the opinion of the institution officials as to his progress and prospects and as to his suitability for the work he wishes to take up. Information is at the same time obtained about the adolescent's home, and arrangements are then made for his reception at the home, or at lodging; if the home conditions are found to be unsatisfactory or if there is danger from old companions, work is found in a new district. No boy or girl is allowed to be discharged from a Borstal institution, until a situation or work has been found. On the morning of release, he is provided with a complete outfit and is brought by an officer of the Association to the Association's office, where he is interviewed, advised and encouraged, and dispatched to his destination. He is there met by the local representative of the Association who has already arranged lodging for him and who supplies working clothes, money for current expenses and for purchase of tools, and gives any other necessary assistance.

This representative is then expected to maintain, a fairly close supervision over the released adolescent, seeing that he is regular at work and of good conduct generally and, if possible, getting him admitted to a boys club' or otherwise providing him with means of healthy amusement. Periodical reports have to be submitted to the Borstal Association's office, and if a boy is found to be going wrong, it is open to the Commissioners to cancel the license and remand the adolescent to the Borstal institution or to Canterbury."[2]

Aftercare is the supervision by Probation officers or by Aftercare Associations on the persons after their release from Prisons and juvenile institutions. It is a continuation of institutional treatment and very critical in the re-induction of the offender into the society. Voluntary Agencies with financial Assistance from Government are also working in this relief work.

"The core of aftercare and rehabilitation is based on the idea that it is unfair to maintain the loss of civil rights for a person, who served his term in a correctional institution and thus ought to be regarded as a corrected or reformed member of society. Once his punishment has been completed, the mark of crime should be wiped out. Legal rehabilitation, however, may restore only the legal civil right."[3]

The All India Jail Manual Committee -1957-59, included a separate chapter on Aftercare in the draft Manual. Aftercare Association is State,

District and Taluk levels are to be constituted. Other recommendations:

"Planning for aftercare begin soon after an inmate's admission in the institution. Aftercare problems of an individual should be treated in their totally and not in isolation. Not only the individual but also his whole social situation must be tackled.

Special attention should be given to the protection and post-release care and help for children, adolescents, women and sick, old, infirm and handicapped persons. Particular attention should be devoted to the aftercare of the released habitual offenders.

After release from the institution, the case of a released person should be followed up for periods ranging from one to five years, depending on the requirements of each case. Follow-up reports should be sent to correctional institutions and to the Central Indexing.

Bureau in the Head Quarters office. These reports should be useful in the evaluation and future planning of correctional programmes. They will also serve as good material for research projects." [4]

Aftercare service is to provide help, service guidance, counseling, support and protection because institutional training, treatment and post release assistance is a continuous process. The aftercare service is looked after by Probation Officers in India, now some of the recommendations of the All India Jail Manual Committee:

"The State Aftercare Organisation should be financed through grants from the State Government and the Central Social Welfare Board and public donations. The State Organisation should allocate grants to the District, Taluka and City branches. The branch organisations should expend the grants, in accordance with the general policy as laid down by the State Aftercare Organisation.

Aftercare service should become an integral part of Correctional Administration. The Director of Probation, Juvenile Delinquency and Aftercare Services in the Head Quarters Office should attend to all matters pertaining to aftercare. Aftercare work should broadly be phased as shown below:

(a) While the individual is under institutional care and treatment,
(b) Immediately after release from the institution.
(c) During post-release period." [5]

Prior to the release of inmates from juvenile justice institutions the Probation Officer has to visit the home of the inmate and endeavour to find someone to look after him/her, as was the practice in U.K. The After-care at Polmont in United Kingdom was narrated in the Report of the Indian Jails Committee:

"In Scotland, there is no society answering to the Borstal Association, and the aftercare of adolescent prisoners discharged from the Borstal institution at Polmontis arranged for, by the authorities of the institution in conjunction with the Superintendent of Youthful Offenders, who is a paid official working directly under the Scottish Prison Commissioners. When a boy is recommended for release from Polmont, the Superintendent of Youthful offenders visits and his home endeavours to final someone willing to look after the boy. The person to whose care a released adolescent is thus confided is turned his guarding. No paid agents are employed and no fee or remuneration of any kind is at present granted to guardians, but the opinion now expressed that power, to grand a small recompense to deserving guardians would be useful. If there is anyone interested in the family or the boy, he is asked to undertake the post of guardians. Of the fifteen boys on license at the time of our visit, two were Belgians, who had been sent back to their country, five were employed in shipyards, three were farming, one was a carpenter and one was an engineer, while the remaining three were employed in a coal-mine, a jute mill and a machine factory, respectively. All these boys were believed to be doing well. It will be observed that none had taken up tailoring or shoemaking. The trade unions objects to a boy's entering a trade unless he has been through a regular course of apprenticeship, and it is often difficult for a boy to maintain himself during this period. Farming was considered to be one of the best openings for boys, but experience, both in Scotland and England shows that town boys will not keep to the land, even if they at first take up that occupations. When a boy goes to sea, it was considered better that he should be placed in an ocean going ship rather than in the coasting trade. The majority of boys released from the Scottish institution had done well but owing to the war there had been a difficulty in tracing boys, and as the institution was only opened in 1911 There were no pre-war figures such as exist, in regard to the operations of the English Borstal Association."[6]

Quakers initiated the Aftercare Programme of released prisoners, in England in the year 1808.

"Aftercare is an extension of services already rendered in an institution. It is an effort to facilitate readjustment and re-assimilation of an ex-inmate of an institution with the community. Initially, John Howard (1728-1790) started aftercare work of the offender in England, for ameliorating the conditions of prisoners both within and outside of the penal institutions.

After the death of Howard, the Quakers continued his work and took increasing interest on crime causation in England. They set up a society in 1808, for providing aids to released prisoners. This was the beginning of efforts for organised aftercare in Europe and America."[7]

Pardon and Commutation are, also release of offenders but there is no enquiry or supervision by Probation officers.

"Probation should also be clearly distinguished from both pardon and commutation. Both of these measures are usually acts of executive clemency, although courts sometimes exercise the latter. Probation is a conditional suspension of punishment, and is granted before the latter has taken effect; pardon involves the absolution of the offender from punishment."[8]

Another misconception noted down by United Nations in 1951, still persists even among personnel of Criminal Justice System in India:

"A final misconception of the nature of probation relates to the idea that probation is a method of treatment applicable only or mainly to young, or to first, offenders. In practice the tendency, to apply probation more readily to young and to first offenders, than to other categories still persists, but experience has shown beyond any reasonable doubt, that probation can be successfully applied both to adult offenders and to offenders with a previous criminal record." [9]

About hundred years ago, probation was widely used as is evident from the following statistics, noted down by the Indian Jails Committee of 1919-20:

"In the State of Massachusetts 30588 persons were, placed on probation in the year 1917; this total includes:

14201 cases of drunkenness

3289 cases of larceny

1631 cases of non-support

1188 cases of breaking and entering

1114 cases of assault and battery besides smaller number of such grave crimes as forgery, robbery, receiving stolen property, incest rape, sodomy, and even in one case, murder. Thus in some of the United State the system of release on probation is now extended to all crimes."[10]

According to Prison Statistics 2013, published by the National Crime records Bureau, New Delhi the prison population in India is higher, than the authorised accommodation in most of the Prisons.

More than fifty percent of the prison population in India are under trials and of them majority are short term prisoners, who idly spend their time in prisons. So special measures are required to reduce prison population as observed by the Reckless Committee in 1951-52:

"***Overburdened with under trials:*** The Jails of India are overburdened with under trial prisoners, who represent a group which is very difficult to handle properly under present laws and regulations. The accumulations of under trials in the jails, on long successive remand stems from the way the police operates and the courts operates, both of which are not set up to expedite, a case within the confines of a few days, a week, two weeks, a month, or at most three months for sessions cases, according to legal gravity. The concept is very widespread in India, that nothing can be done or should be done for the under trial, except to let him languish in idleness. Emphasis needs to be placed on jail advantageously. This should include opportunity to participate voluntarily in a worthwhile work programme. Special counselors and activity project leaders should be provided in the under trial yards and barracks, to render helpful service to under trials and to enable them, to use their time in jail constructively. This would definitely require additional staff and a specialised programme especially designed for under trials and would cost Government money"[11].

A Scandinavian Solution

Child Welfare Council caring for children in:

	Boys	*Girls*
	Per cent	*Per cent*
Families	40.1	46.7
Service	8.3	6.9
Children's Homes	26.0	33.3
Asylums	1.1	0.5
School Homes	21.5	11.9
Coercive Schools	3.0	0.7
Total	**100**	**100**

The Child Welfare Council procedure was also adopted by Sweden, Denmark and Finland.

"Norway has a particularly favourable position in criminal statistics, including juvenile offences, for, various reasons. The population is principally rural, and there are few large cities. There exist very few really rich and really poor people. Class distinction is practically non-existent, and Norwegian people are homogeneous in origin and language."[12]

Statistics for 1940, disclose the following picture:

Decisions:	*Boys*	*Girls*
	Per cent	*Per cent*
Coercive Schools	4.8	2.8
School Homes	10.3	17.6
Children's Homes	6.9	22.2
Families	7.4	17.0
Work	0.6	3.0
Suggested Punishment	6.7	2.7
Serious Warning to Child	56.0	18.3
Serious Warning to Parent	7.3	16.4
Total	**100**	**100**

Thus, it is evident that Aftercare supervision by the Probation Officer or Aftercare Aid Society started even prior to the advent of Probation supervision.

Since, there are discharged prisoners who needs help and assistance for their living in the hostile antagonistic community into which they were exposed to, the effective aftercare is a solution to their problems. Aftercare Aid Society can be formed by like-minded socially committed, professionally lenient and service minded persons. The members of the Aftercare Aid society is to conduct a study on the prisoner, prior to his release by meeting the other members of his family and interviewing the prisoner.

Based on the findings various forms of assistance can be provided to him in the form of Non Formal Education, Life Skill Education, Vocational Training Employment, Legal Assistance, Medical Assistance, Financial Help to start a Trade or Agriculture, Counseling, Family Counseling, Group Counseling, Psychotherapy, forming Self Help Groups or Group work.

These are the areas, where a discharged prisoner needs help from the society. It is said that the most pathetic moment in the life, a person ordered for imprisonment is not at the time, when he enters the prison gates but the moment when he comes out of the prison gates. He wonders how he would be received by the family and community and the problem would be aggravated, if he belongs to the educationally and economically backward strata. Unfortunately the majority of the prison population in India belongs to this category and the activities of the Aftercare associations are nominal or nearly extinct. This one of the grave areas where the social workers, are to look into, for the social rehabilitation of a person who had actually undergone the period of his sentence consequently, finding it difficult to continue a normal family and social life. It violates of his human rights to live a happy and dignified life in the society.

Footnotes

1. Dr. Walter. C. Reckless, (1952) *Jail Administration in India* Prepared for the Government of India New Delhi, p. 13.
2. *Report of the Indian Jails Committee 1919-20,* Vol. I, Appendix IX, p. 494.
3. Srivastava. S.P. (1987) *The Probation System- Evaluative study,* Print House, Lucknow, p. 72.
4. Report of the All India Jail Manual Committee (1957-59), Government of India Publication, New Delhi, pp. 71-72.
5. *Ibid.,* p. 71.
6. Report of the Indian Jail Committee - 1919-20, Vol. I, Appendix - IX, pp. 494-95.
7. Dr. Sunil. K. Bhattacharya (2000) *Juvenile Justice-An Indian Scenario,* Regency Publications, 20/36-G, Old Market, West Patel Nagar, New Delhi-110008, p. 14.
8. United Nations (1951), *Probation and Related measures,* United Nations Publication, New York, p. 8.
9. United Nations (1951), *Probation and Related measures,* United Nations Publication, New York, p. 9.
10. The Report of the Indian Jails Committee-1919-20, Government Press, Simla, Vol. I, para-420, p. 216.
11. W.C. Reckless, (1951-52), Jail Administration in India, p. 14.
12. Robert Mayer (1946): pp. 60-61.

9

The Advantages of Probation

The success rate of probation in the state of Massachusetts was 77 per cent. And the previous conviction was not considered as a bar for invoking for probation again. The Indian Jails Committee 1919-20 observed:

"The value of probation as a substitute for imprisonment is strongly insisted on by those who favour these methods, notably the authorities of the Probation Department, who naturally believe in the beneficent effects of their own activities. They claim that to have control for a considerable period of time and under thorough supervision, of an offender who is living otherwise his moral life is a much likelier means of producing reformation than commitment to a penal institution. Accordingly it is claimed that a large percentage of success is obtained in dealing with persons placed on probation. Statistics are published indicating that in the State of Massachusetts 77 per cent of the persons so treated pass successfully through their probationary period without coming again before the courts. Nor is a second conviction by itself regarded as necessarily a bar to the use of probation. A single lapse or even several lapse, do not prove, it is urged, that the individual is not striving to become a good citizen or is one who deserves punishment. Public option in America seems to be more inclined to regard such relapses with tolerance than in other parts of the world. It is a part of the general optimism of the country".[1]

When compared with imprisonment the probation service provide community rehabilitation to offenders, through necessary assistance and guidance. It is a non-institutional form of treatment. The advantages as:

1. The probationer leads a normal life in the community and continues

to perform the social responsibilities expected of him by society.

2. The probationer is not a liability on the State like a prisoner but supports himself as well as has family members economically.
3. Probation mitigates the adverse consequences of imprisonment. The probationer is not exposed to prison environment and experiences that may leave stigmatised, embittered and may even make him a serious criminal in association with other prisoners.
4. He is not alone in his efforts to reform himself but is assisted by a Probation Officer who guides and advises him from time to time. The Probation Officer also attempts to keep him away from the environment that produces crime and delinquency.
5. It costs the State less to keep an offender on probation than to confine him in a prison.
6. The Prison population is rapidly increasing with increase in crime and in the number of offenders imprisoned every year. As a result, jails officials face serious problems in maintaining internal order and discipline. With a lower population in jails, it would be easier to pay individual attention to offenders".[2]

"Max Grunhut wrote in 1948, that, the rise of probation is the most remarkable feature of the recent history of criminal law; within the lifetime of the present generation; it has profoundly changed the prevailing penal policy".[3]

During the year 1951, the United Nations urged that "all Governments to consider the adaptation and development of probation".[4]

The Government of India asked the All Indian Jail Manual Committee should examine and make recommendations on the following issues:

(i) "Classification of Prisoners

(ii) Abolition short-term sentences and provision of alternative measures

(iii) Care of children and women offenders

(iv) Use of handcuffs and fetters.

(v) Balanced diet for Prisoners".[5]

During 1957-58, the Chief Minister of Bombay State while addressing the All India Jail Manual Committee said, that:

"Crime is not an isolated factor. It is an outcome of various backgrounds. It is said that crime is a bio-psychological and socio-economic problem. My beliefs that this problem cannot be solved only in prisons and that we *must seek remedial measures also beyond the prison walls.* As the adage goes 'Prevention is much better than Cure'. It is necessary to view this question from various angles i.e., prevention, control, investigation, adequate punishments, treatment and finally aftercare of the released prisoners. When all these phases are properly inter-linked then only we can rightly say that our approach to this problem is systematic and methodical".[6]

Gautham Chatterjee Wrote:

"The Juvenile delinquency is essentially a moral issue rather than being merely a matter for State concern. The British introduced the British Juvenile Justice System which has increased the alienation of Juvenile delinquents."[7]

Organised crime was prevalent from the days of Rigveda, which mentions 'dasyus'; Mugal period came 'Pindaris' then came the 'thhugs', and then appeared the 'dacoits'. In 1960 Acharya Vinoba undertook a 'Padayatra' with a view to convert the *dacoits',* which made several, dreaded dacoits to surrender before him. The love force shown through words and deeds by Vinoba Bhave was the main driving force for the mass surrender. Later during the year 1972 another mass surrenders of occurred at Chambal.

"Supported by active social workers, politician, former dacoits and understanding policeman, some 500 outlaws with sizeable quantities of arms and ammunition, surrendered in the presence of either Sarvodaya leader Shri. Jayaprakash Narayan, or the Chief Minister of Madhya Pradesh or the District officials. By any standard, the mass-surrender was phenomenal"[8].

Section 562 of the Criminal Produce Code 1898, which empowers the courts to release certain offenders who committed offences as mentioned in the Indian Penal Code-1860, be release in probation. The Indian Jails Committee 1919-20 recommends that its purview be extended to offenders under other laws also, that:

"It is evident that the restrictions imposed by the terms of this section greatly limit resort to this method of disposing of offences. As it stands section 562 of the Criminal Procedure Code 1898 is applicable only to offences under the Indian penal Code and this prevents its use in many of those classes of case for which it is particularly suited, for example, the numerous petty offences such as committing nuisances, begging, gambling and the like which have been created under the various Police Acts, or the Acts regulating local and municipal administration in the

Provinces of India. Again, the restriction to trivial offences has prevented the section from being applied to more than few crimes under the Indian Penal Code. Certain local Governments especially those of Burma and Madras, have in their reviews of the reports on criminal justice in recent years urged the desirability of more extended use of the section, but it may well be doubted whether, it at present stands is very great extension of the method of release on probation impossible".[9]

The counter arguments against the criticisms put forth on probation service, like:

1. Probation is neither leniency nor pampering the offender. He is selected for this kind of treatment only after the court decides that there is a reasonable probability that he will adjust successfully in the community and that his living in the society will not be a threat to its security.
2. Imposition of conditions and curbing the freedom of the offender is in itself a punishment for him. Besides, if he does not abide by the conditions of the court, he can be committed to an institution. Probation thus does not eliminate all pain. The condition of reporting to the Probation Officer from time to time also inconvenience, embarrassment and disgrace.
3. It is not correct to say that since the offender lives in the community, he continues to be threat to it and the society remains unprotected. Here it is overlooked that only selected offenders are released on probation and in a good number of cases, there is investigation of his background as well as supervision over his conduct during probation, both of which operate to prevent the exposure of the community to further law violations on the part of the offender.
4. Though there is some logic to the argument that on being released on probation, the offender returns to the same environment in which he committed crime yet in a large number of cases, there is supervision by a Probation Officer over him, who guides and advises him and thus seeks to modify the situation. If there is no supervision, the answer is to be found in improvement of the probation system and not in its elimination. It may also be pointed out that the imprisoned offender also returns to his family and community after he is discharged from prison and there is no one there to guide or assist.

5. The courts order social investigation wherever it is considered necessary. The number of cases dealt with by the courts every year is so large (about 16 lakh in our country) that social investigation in all cases would not be feasible.
6. Supervision is made compulsory in all such cases wherever it is considered essential. If supervision is ordered and the Probation Officer is not able to supervise all cases under him because of excessive workload, supervision will be only a mockery. Besides, since the alternative to probation is not permanent imprisonment, but in all probability, a short term of confinement from which there is often release without supervision, probation even without supervision may actually institute a successful alternative to imprisonment.
7. The insufficient numbers of Probation Officers and/or their heavy workload are deficiencies in the implementation of the programme and not the failure of the probation system itself. In view of the great advantages of probation, the solution is not the abandonment of probation but the elimination of the conditions which make its use difficult. [10]

Howard Abadinski writes about on the treatment theory like psychoanalytical theory, casework, behavioural modification, reality theory and conflict theory. Conflict theory primary based upon Max Weber and Karl Mark, which are concerned with differences in power relationships. He also states that Probation is more economical to the State when compared with other forms of correction as is evident form the following, statistics, regarding

Per-day Cost Comparison in Georgia, U.S.A.[11]

Basic probation	$ 1.01
Intensive probation	$ 4.07
Diversion centers	$ 35.54
Detention centers	$ 35.41
Probation boot camps	$ 35.41
Prison	$ 45.33

Probation is more economical than imprisonment as observed by the Indian Jails. Committee in 1919-20:

"In Massachusetts in 1918 the annual cost of a prisoner in jail is placed at 385 dollars, while that of a case on probation is placed at 19 dollars". [12]

The optimum number of caseload and the useful interaction with the probationers results in the success of probation service, Ram Ahuja Wrote:

1. Contract of a probation officer with the probationer in his office, no doubt is necessary, for the purpose of privacy that cannot be secured in the home of the probationer, but frequent contacts in the probationer's home, school, and work-place are likely to be more useful and expedient.
2. Calling a probationer to office (by the probation officer) and just asking him two or three formal questions after keeping him waiting for hours together makes probationer lose confidence in the probationer officer. Unless the probation officer spends an hour or two with the probationer talking to him like a friend, he cannot create in the probationer a sense of participation in the correctional process.
3. The supervision of probationer cannot be conducted satisfactorily without the maintenance of *case records* and the preparation of *regular and adequate repots*. The results of pre-sentence investigations have to be carefully maintained and used in the process of controlling the probationer's environment and personality traits.
4. Excessive caseloads seriously interfere with supervision, maintaining records, and planning the future strategies. If more, full-time probation officers cannot be appointed, part-time probation officers may be appointed to have their help in supervision and community contracts. Voluntary workers cannot strengthen probation work".[13]

Studies conducted in England on Job satisfaction of probation officers are high and often it help to solve his/her own problems because:

"Their work is rarely dull, never become repetitive or routine and constantly gives them the opportunity to develop and make, use of their own personality. Using yourself as the tool of your work is both satisfying and exhausting. The probation officer should expect that his job will give opportunities to come to terms with some of his own conflicts, and that it will satisfy some of his own needs".[14]

"Low rate of recidivism is an advantage of Probation."[15]

"Almost a quarter of those who failed during probation did so within three months and almost half within six months from the time when the probation order was made. The General rate of success was higher for girls than for boys, and for both sexes it increased from the lower to the higher age groups.

"Almost a quarter of those who failed during probation did so within three months, and almost half within six months from the time when the probation order was made."[16]

Recidivism is lower with regard to probation when compared with imprisonment failure of probation service is only 10 per cent, which shows higher rate of success especially with regard to young offenders. The report of the Indian Jails Committee 1919-20 states:

"The foregoing account of the probation system in the United States illustrated the great extension, it has received there. As a corrective to the tendency to clap into prison every offender against the criminal law, it deserve careful consideration. In cases in which a pecuniary penalty furnishes an adequate punishment for crime, the probation method has many advantages. But it is a question whether this policy has not been carried too far in America. One experienced magistrate with whom we had an interview denounced the system in strong terms. It schemed to the thought, he said, that every man is entitled to one crime as he is to one wife; he declared; the system, he thought, works well with the young but with that there is more crime in his State than ever before and that not 10 per cent of it is detected; though it works well with the young but with the adult it is a failure. The weakest point in the reports of the American Probation Departments is the fact that while giving most encouraging information as to the results of probation, i.e., as to the conduct of persons while on probation, and showing that only 10 per cent commit default, they give no information on the crucial question whether crime considered in relation to population and other relevant factors, is increasing or decreasing.

We endeavoured to obtain statistics on this point but without success, and in their absence there are not sufficient data to form an opinion as to the success or failure of American practice in this respect, though it certainly seems to afford a basis for a considerable measure of advance in India, where such a great proportion of total crime is committed by first offenders. Report of a Committee on 1918 appointed in New York State, the importance of Individual treatment by a Probation Officer was emphasised and it was laid down that a single officer should be required to deal with an average of more than fifty cases, it being added that the number should be less if the officer has to perform other duties, such as the conduct of preliminary investigation, attendance at court and clerical work. In practice this standard has not always been attained. The Committee above referred to found that in many courts Probation Officers were attempting to supervise from one hundred to four hundred probationers in addition to special work. Again in the city and country of San Francisco with one Chief and six assistant or deputy Probation Officers, there were 968 adult probationers on the 31st December 1918. Demands for an increased staff of Probation Officers are frequent features of American reports and in consequence of the inadequate number of officers provided, the working of the system has in some area fallen into disrepute." [17]

As per the Crime in India – 2005, out of the total cognizable crimes of 50, 26,337 the crimes in India charged under Indian Penal code are 18, 22,602 and other Special and Local law crimes are 32, 03, 735. It shows a decline of 16.6 per cent over 2004 (60, 28,781) Conviction rate for IPC crimes remained almost static at 42.5 and 42.4 in 2004 and 2005 respectively.

Tamil Nadu (2777) and Karnataka (1241) together reported 68 per cent of cases under Immoral Traffic Act (4018 out of 5908), incest Rape cases increased by 48.5 per cent in 2005) over 2004 (from 505 in 2004 to 750 in 2005. Maharashtra (141) Jharkhand (120) and Chhattisgarh (110) reported 49.5 per cent of total incest rapes case (371 out of 750). Madhya Pradesh reported 24.8 per cent (3721 out of 14975 of total crimes committed against children in the country. The highest crime rate (6.5) was reported in Delhi as compared to the National average (1.4)."[18]

Thus it can be inferred that every year the number of several offenders who are eligible to be considered for the treatment under the supervision of Probation Officer are not getting the opportunity since the total number of cases where the report of Probation Officer was called for, are less.

Footnotes

1. Report of the Indian Jails Committee-1919 – 20, Vol. I, para-421, p. 216.
2. Ram Ahuja (2000) *Criminology* – Rawat Publications, Satyam Apartments, Sector 3, Jain Temple Road, Jawahar Nagar, Jaipur-302004, pp. 347-8.
3. Max Grunhut (1948) 'Penal Reform', Oxford University Press, London, p. 297.

4. *Encyclopedia of Social Work in India (1987)* Vol. III Government of India Publication Division, New Delhi, p. 332.
5. Report of the *All India Jail Manual Committee -1957-59,* Government of India, New Delhi, p. 4.
6. *Ibid.,* Part I, Annexure A, pp. 125-6.
7. Gutam Chatterje (1995) *Child Criminals and the Raj,* Akshaya Publications, 128, DDA flats, Hauz Khas, New Delhi-110016, p. 40.
8. D.P. Jatar and M.S. Khan (1980). *The Problem of Dacoits in Bundelkhand and the Chambal Valley,* S. Chand and Company Ltd. Ram Nagar, New Delhi – 110055, p. 8.
9. Report of the All Indian Jail Manual Committee – 1919 – 20, Vol. I, para-432, p. 221.
10. Ram Ahuja (2000) *Criminology* – Rawat Publications, Satyam Apartments, sector 3, Jain Temple Road, Jawahar Nagar, Jaipur-302004, pp. 384-50.
11. Howard a Abadinski (1997), *Probation and parole theory and practice,* Prentice Hall, Career and Technology, Englewood Cliff, N.J. 07632, p. 416.
12. Indian Jails Committee – 1919-20, Vol. I, para – 432, p. 217.
13. Ram Ahuja (2000) *Criminology*, Rawat Publications, Jaipur- 302004, p. 341.
14. Phyllida Parsole, B.A. (1967), *The work of the probation and Aftercare Officer,* Routledge and Kegan Pual Ltd., Broadway House, 68-74, Carter Lane, London, ECH, p. 81.
15. The Results Of Probation – A Report of the Department of Criminal Science (1958) Macmillan D&Co Ltd., London, p. 58.
16. *Ibid.,* p. 56.
17. *Report of The Indian Jail Committee* – 1919-20, Vol. I, para-427, pp. 218-19.
18. *Crime in India- 2005,* National Crime Records Bureau, GOI, New Delhi Snapshots, p. 5.

10

Problems of Probation Work

Devoted and trained experts are to be entrusted with the care of criminals to make the system successful. The first United Nations Congress on the Prevention of Crime and Treatment of Offenders' states, that, "before entering on duty, staff should be given a course of training in their general duties with a view particularly to social problems and in their specific duties and be required to pass theoretical and practical examinations".[1]

United Nations General Assembly during 1989 passed the Child Rights Convention meant for persons below 18 years of age. India ratified the convention in the year 1992. Child rights broadly includes:

1. Survival Rights
2. Protective Rights
2. Developmental rights
3. Rights to participate

Consequently Government of India enacted the Juvenile Justice (care and Protection of Children) Act 2000. The Act and the consequent rules envisage the appointment of probation officers. Government of India had chalked out a Integrated Child Protection Scheme, a comprehensive scheme for children. These Legislations and Scheme envisages the appointment of Probation Officers for young persons involved in Crime. Funds are available under the scheme but their appointment and training are still in the processes.

The Recommendation of the All India Jail Manual Committee with regard to habitual offenders stated in Para 146 of the report states:

"(ii) There should be statutory provision for presentence social investigation of the cases habitual offenders

(iv) There should be co-ordination between Police, Courts, Probation Service, Correctional Administration matters pertaining to Service Correctional Administration and Aftercare service regarding all matters pertaining to habitual offenders."[2]

The statutory provision was included in Section 6 of the Probation of Offenders Act 1958 and Borstal Schools Act 1961 stating that the home or family inquiry regarding the offender before sending him for incarceration is mandatory. Statistics shows that the number of such inquiries is inadequate.

With regard to volunteers who supervise the probationers, The United Nation's convention on non-custodial measures states its rule 19, that:

"Volunteers shall be carefully screened and recruited on the basis of their aptitude for and interest in the work involved. They shall be properly trained for the specific responsibilities to be discharged by them and shall have access to support and counseling from, and the opportunity to consult with the competent authority.

Volunteers should encourage offenders and their families to develop meaningful ties with the community and a broader sphere of contact by providing counseling and other appropriate forms of assistance according to their capacity and the offenders' needs.

Volunteers shall be insured against accident, injury and public liability when carrying out their duties. They shall be reimbursed for authorised expenditure incurred in the course of their work. Public recognition should be extended to them for the services they render for the well-being of the community."[3]

Mainly because of the geographical distance present between the office of the Probation Officer and the ward is located; and due to the official relationship, there exists problems in meaningful relationships.

Correction manual is yet to be framed with regard to Probation enquiry and Supervision, though a related recommendation can be found in the annexure of All India Jail Manual Committee 1957-59 which states the need of a correctional manual.

It is necessary that the whole correctional policy should be carefully planned. A correctional manual containing detailed instructions about correctional work should be framed. "This should no longer be left to individuals but should be supervised and guided by capable and well trained officers of the Head Quarters. Care should however be taken not to discourage individual initiatives."[4]

An integrated department of correctional Administration is to be set up immediately, leading to the formation of welfare departments, with a Director and Deputy Directors, who should give rehabilitation of offenders, as recommended to Government of India by W.C. Reckless in 1952:

"An Integrated Department of Correctional Administration. The expert feels quite keenly that India needs to have one department of government in which juvenile courts, remand home, certifies schools, Probation, Borstals, Jails, and After-care can join hands and attack the problems of the handling and treatment of Juvenile delinquents and adult offenders in an integrated way, where each segment is approaching the matter form the same point of view of social rehabilitation. Establishing a Department of Correctional Administration under one Minister should do this. Such a Department should have a Director, who is a trained man that can give leadership to all phases of correctional services. The Department can have a Juvenile Branch, with a Deputy In-Charge of the development and oversight of remand homes and certified schools and any other facilities and services for the social treatment of the delinquent child. The Department can have a Probation and After-Care Branch, dealing with the supervision of juvenile and adult offenders in their own homes, villages, and the neighborhoods when released by courts or released by certified schools, Borstals, and jails. The Department should have a Jail Branch, dealing with the prison to which adult offenders are committed. (Note that the Borstal should be placed in the Juvenile Branch or the Jail Branch). The Department should have a Revising Board Branch, with sufficient staff to cover all institutions for Juvenile and adult offenders once a month. The Department should have lockup Inspection Branch, to inspect periodically all lockup and to make constructive suggestion to police in handling this problem.

Such a department will need to have trained personnel and a career service, with appropriate posting of personnel, according to the principle of the best use of personnel. A trained Probation Officer could become superintendent of a remand home or certified school or of a jail or Borstal. A trained Welfare Officer of an adult jail could be transferred to the probation and after-care branch, and so on. The central or district jail should in its way be just as good as a Borstal or certified school in its way.

In view of the fact that the proper handling of the juvenile delinquents and adults offenders cannot wait until India gets a welfare ministry or finally accepts the feasibility of a Ministry of Social Welfare, the expert feels that the suggestion for the establishment of an integrated department of correctional Administration under one Minister, is the most practical at this time.

Each branch of an integrated Department of Correctional Administration should have a deputy in charge. Some branches might need Assistant Deputy Directors In-Charge of special phases of the programmes. The Director and his deputies should give positive, constructive leadership to all aspects of the social rehabilitation of offenders."[5]

Separate annexures are to be provided for women prisoners and to appoint women staff to deal with them. Further the Committee recommended in para 131 that:

" The Possibility of selective release of certain categories of women offenders on probation or of conditional release under supervision should be considered on a more extensive scale than at present. Cases of women offenders who come to prisons because of offences like infanticide, etc. and which are committed owing to cultural and social pressures should be submitted to Government for immediate review. Such women should be kept in institutions like State Homes or Mahilashrams, under the care and protection of the Aftercare service.

Special attention should be given to the aftercare of women offenders and Financial considerations should not in any way handicap programmes of care, welfare, training and treatment of women offenders."[6]

The Recommendations with respect to statistics and Research, the Committee is of opinion that "the Research should be linked up with census, health and criminal statistics".[7]

When the numbers of probations under supervision are large, the services of voluntary Probation officers are to be sought to make it intensive but the number under supervision be limited to fifty or sixty, as recommended by the Indian Jails Committee-1919-20:

"In many districts the number of children on probation is so large that a sufficient number of paid Probation Officers cannot be provided. To meet this difficulty, resource has been had to the employment of unpaid or voluntary probation workers who undertake to look after a limited number of children. Various opinions were expressed regarding this method. Several witnesses criticised the work of voluntary or honorary probations officers severely. It was said that the voluntary worker, besides often lacking experience, may have many other interests which prevent his giving sufficient time to the work, he has undertaken. He perhaps wants an annual holiday and does not realise the necessity of finding someone to replace him in his probation work during his absence. His zeal is apt to evaporate as time goes on. The court has little hold over a volunteer.

On the other hand, a voluntary worker of the right sort may be of great value. It seems probable that if Voluntary Probation Officers are utilised as supplementary to paid officers, they fill a most useful role, and that the best system is to place the youthful offender, under a whole time Probation Officer, with the understanding that he should, as far as possible, for every young person requiring special attention secure the services of a volunteer who is willing to interest himself in the case. By this method more intensive work can be done than by an unaided Probation Officer, however enthusiastic and however conscientious, whose time and attention have to be distributed among fifty to sixty children. In Scotland, Probation Officers are often merely police officers working under another name. This plan is generally held to be undesirable. We were informed that the advantages of the probation system are not yet fully appreciated by the magistracy in Scotland."[8]

V.V. Giri former President of India in his Inaugural address at the National Conference on 'Probation and Allied Measures' held at New Delhi on 25th October 1971, suggested the following ways:

"The society, at large, cannot escape its due share in the task of prevention of crime and treatment of offenders. A successful social defense-policy includes an enlightened public opinion. Such a public opinion should find expression in better laws, more effective Court procedures and judicial disposition, a positive vote in favour of probation and parole and similar non-institutional modes of correcting offenders. The Acts provide for popular participation in the process as volunteer probation officers who undertake as good citizens to supervise an ex-offender as a Voluntary Probation Officer and rehabilitate him, without any monetary compensation. The popular attitude should be educated through discussion form all mass media about the hard facts of crime problems, an enlightened approach in treatment at individual level and correct the blind popular fury, which wants to stigmatise and alienate the ex-offender for a whole life time. Unless these attitudes are corrected, the economic and social rehabilitation of probationers or ex-prisoners cannot be guaranteed. There is need for Forums like these to bring all partners of the programme to come on common platform to review the progress and draw up fresh policies and programmes.

The Probation Year 1971 may mark the turning point in our overall Criminal Justice System and Social Defense policies and may herald a new era with policies based on facts, reason and research, better co-ordination and integration of efforts, aiming at a just order-social, economic and political order as enshrined in our Constitution."[9]

The Indian Jails Committee states about the criticisms about probation, as below:

"It is of more advantage of turn to more practical criticisms. The first one is that Probation Officers are not properly selected. The ideal Probation Officer should be a man specially in his work, sympathetic and tactful, with a high standard of character and a marked person. This ideal is seldom realised. Many Probation Officers are too old. It being important or should be of an age to sympathies with boys and girls and take an active interest in movements. Some witness thought that they should be of a social standing superior to the with whom they have to deal, while others thought that social standing was less important than the securing of young men possessing sympathy with boys and the power to influence for good. Another criticism, which emanates rather from the Probation Officers themselves that magistrates did not sufficiently avail themselves of the power given to them by to attach conditions to the probation order governing the children's conduct. Similarly, complained that in many cases it is not the practice of the magistrates to consult the Probation Officers as to the best method of treating individual cases, with the result that unsuitable cases sometimes placed on probation. It was generally held that if a boy has a very bad home, there is little use to place him on probation, but that it is better to remove him from demoralising circumstances and give him a fresh start under new conditions, by sending him at once to an institution or Reformatory Schools. Another very frequent criticism was directed against the practice, sending a young offender on probation several times but that in spite of his having relapsed in to crime. This is partly due, no doubt to the reluctance of magistrates to send young persons if their reclamation can possible be secured at home for, it is often held that institutionalising tends to discourage initiatives and individuality in those who undergo it. It is due to a desire on the part of the magistracy, to avoid imposing expense on the local and the second offence is a trivial one, it may be unobjectionable to give a second term to him but if a youthful offender, who has been placed on probation once, gets into serious crime he should ordinarily be committed to an Industrial School or Reformatory. This view expressed by two very experienced workers, one of whom admitted that in his earlier days, when he was acting as a Probation Officer he had frequently moved a Magistrate, when reporting a probation order, to give the boy another chance but was quite convinced that he had not."[10]

With the prevailing conditions in prisons no education, vocational or correctional activity could be planned or executed for short term offenders as W.C. Reckless in 1952.

"***Short Sentence Problem:*** Attention has already been called to the necessity for developing substitutes for the jail sentence and this particularly to the short sentence. Jail sentence should seldom be used for prisoners, who are short sentence cases. And the jails are not equipped by programme, work projects, activity projects, or any other kind of helpful service to handle these short term cases. What work can be started? How can the short termer get something out of the present jail progrmme? The answer is that he can get very little, because the programme is not geared for his short stay. It is possible to develop a programme for a one-day, a two-weeks, a three-months prisoner but in first place, it takes a limited objective. Administrators must be admitting that they cannot do for a prisoner in three months, what they can do for him in fifteen months. They can built him up physically in a short stay, they can fit him into work projects and educational and activity projects, which do not require any point of entrance and go forward without discussion and interviews, how to stay out of trouble on the outside. But the jail programme cannot be expected to have a maximum constructive impact on his affecting, his attitude and approaches to life. But so much so good."[11]

Probation officers are constrained with the various above problems which makes it sufficient to make the probation system ineffective:

"The Probation Officers were the backbone but generally not professionally qualified and frustrated due to salary inadequacy, step motherly treatment, inadequate secretarial assistance, frequent transfers, work load (6380 units per month in Delhi though monthly average should be 125 units)."[12]

Selection of personnel and their appointment as correctional officers, the number of vacancies of Probation Officers, professional training to correctional staff, the budgetary allocation for rehabilitation of offenders, inadequate salary for correctional persons and public apathy towards correction and rehabilitation of offenders are the main problems.

Footnotes

1. *Report of the All India Jail Manual Committee, 1957-59,* Government Of India Publication, New Delhi, Para 54, p. 31.
2. *Report of the All India Jail Manual Committee-1957-59,* Government of India Publication, New Delhi, para-146, p. 86.
3. *The Tokyo rules* (1990), p. 3.
4. *Report of the All India Jail Manual Committee, 1957-59,* Government of India Publication, New Delhi, Annexure, k, p. 194.
5. W.C. Reckless (1952) *Jail Administration in India,* Government of India, New Delhi, pp. 30-31.
6. *Report of the All India Jail Manual Committee - (1957-59), Government of India*, p. 77.
7. *Ibid.,* p. 26.
8. *Report of the All India Jails Committee- 1919-20,* Vol. I, Appendix IX, p. 482.
9. Social Defence (1971), Vol. X, Published by Central Bureau of Correctional Administration, New Delhi, p. 7.
10. *Report of the Indian Jail Committee - 1919-20.* Vol. I, Appendix, IX, p. 481.
11. W.C. Reckless (1951-52), Jail Administration in India, Government of India, p. 14.
12. Sneh Lata Tandon (1989), *Probation - A new Perspective,* Reliance Publishing House, New Delhi, p. 32.

11

Techniques of Supervision

Probation Supervision involves treatment and Rehabilitation. The offender is not only getting 'another chance' but also provides with assistance for his social reintegration. Probation supervision implies a personal relationship between the probationer and the Probation Officer, who exercise supervision. The United Nations report on Probation states:

"Whatever the effectives of the techniques used, probationary supervision is characterised by educational, therapeutic and rehabilitative objectives. Indeed, the authoritarian or disciplinary aspects of probationary supervision are hardly separable from the more positive and constructive measures, which may be grouped together under the term "treatment". In the language of social Casework probation is Casework in an authoritarian setting.

Probationary "treatment" is of a varied nature, ranging from religious counseling or the unskilled assistance of volunteer probation officers, on the one hand, to professional social case work, sometimes supplemented by psychiatric treatment, on the other. The work of the probation officer is being increasingly recognised as a skilled profession requiring specific technical training."[1]

The Buddhist story of *'Ungulimala'* is a typical example in which a hardened criminal can be turned into a monk by providing favourable circumstances and through intelligent guidance. But the society may not accept as is evident from Ungulimalas tragic end. But his reformation was complete as is clear from the last words of Ungulimala just before his death, "My mind is calm. I feel happy in spite of the assaults meted out to my body. I have no feeling of ill will or malice towards those who caused injury to my body".[2]

'Here Lord Buddha's role can be equated with the Superintendent of a correctional institution (here, monastery) for adolescents and as a Probation Officer by helping and guiding a criminal to become a sober man.

The Therapeutic techniques used in the monastery are the study of divine literature, Bhajans, Physical works like agriculture and social works for the community.

Supervision by a Probation Officer is a process of treatment of offenders based on sociological and psychological theories undertaken in the field as a professional activity. It is a personal relationship based on trust. The United Nations report on Probationary Supervision in 1951 states:

"1. The essence of the probation system lies in the fact that the offender is not merely given "another chance", but that society provides him with constructive assistance in his struggle for social rehabilitation. It is this "element of constructive treatment in probation supervision which places probation beyond either leniency or punishment". For this constructive assistance, primarily provided through the intermediary of the Probation Officer, the conventional term supervision has come to be "nothing but an expedient abbreviation". The term, in fact, is a misleading one in so far, as it emphasises only the disciplinary aspect of release on probation - the element of authoritative control over the behaviour of the probationer, with the sanctions of the law and the treat of the application of suspended punishment behind it. There term probationary supervision betrays the historical origins of the practice, which it designates, its present day connotation is certainly much wider in scope than is implicit in the term. In its simplest form, it involves the designation of special officers (either paid or volunteer workers) to 'advise, assist and befriend' the probationer. In its most complex and advanced forms, it is a process of treatment, founded on the psychological and social sciences, and consciously undertaken as a field of professional activity. In either case, it depends for its success on 'a personal relationship of trust and guidance' and involves the systematic mobilisation of community resources to facilitate and advance the social rehabilitation of the probationer.

2. While supervision is the essence of the probation system, the effectiveness of the probation services of any given country is equally dependent upon the systematic and wise selection of

offenders for release on probation. It is too difficult to discern the complementary nature of the two".[3]

Probation is a one to one relationship directed to the reformation of the offender. Hence the consent of the probationer is vital for the success of probation. It is stated that asking for consent itself amounts to the beginning of empowerment. With regard to the consent of the probationer with regard to his release on Probation, the United Nations report states that:

"One of the distinguishing features of the probation system in England is that its use depends on the consent of the offender. This feature of probation is an outgrowth of the recognizance, which presumably involves an obligation voluntarily undertaken as an alternative to imprisonment or other punishment. This feature virtually given a contractual character to release on probation in England. Although the recognizance as the legal basis of probation has been abolished by the criminal justice act, 1948, specific provision has been made for the retention of the element of consent.

The element of consent has often been mentioned as of particular value in view of the fact that it may be utilised as a first step in the strengthening of the offender's own will to reform, which is usually accepted to be a prerequisite to self-activity and participation on the part of the probationer in the planning for his own rehabilitation.

Although the consent of the probationer constitutes a legal prerequisite to release on probation only in a few jurisdictions, which have followed British precedents, the subject is of much wider relevance. Even where, as matter of law, a defendant cannot refuse probation, it is doubtful whether release on probation without the probationer's "consent" can be of any value. Actually, the unqualified refusal to accept probation will probably occur very rarely, but the full understanding and acceptance by the probationer of the conditions of his release seems to be a necessary first step in treatment on probation. This is true not only from the point of view of the probationer's susceptibility to social and psychological treatment, but also in view of the fact that the courts cannot "enforce" probation, and have only revocation at their disposal as a sanction in case of the probationer's refusal to co-operate. If this fact is clearly recognised, the voluntary nature of submission to probationary treatment may be constructively utilised, as is done in England, by probation officers."[4]

The correctional *treatment techniques* of David Dressler are:

(I) "*Manipulative techniques* (Job finding, Accommodation finding, Betterment of community conditions)

(II) *Executive technique* such as job training, Education of children, medical care, public grants, Housing loans, institutional Placement, nursery care for children, Legal aid, Educational and vocational guidance, Recreation, social agency help etc.

(III) *Guidance, Counseling and leadership service* imply certain things like psychological, biological and sociological knowledge of human behaviour, Casework, help to make his own decisions".[5]

Techniques for correction (Supervision) stipulated by David Dressler (1969) a caseworker had categorised the techniques of correction into three groups which is suited to probation officers also, like:

(i) Manipulative techniques: to modify both the situation and the personality traits of the probationer.

(ii) Executive techniques: to discover and use other resources - medical, legal, educational, social service-in the community to supplement his own efforts.

(iii) Guidance, counseling and leadership techniques: to reduce probationer's conflicts and modify his behaviour patterns".[6]

Probation can be considered for those under trials:

"A hardened criminal is not born. It is the system, which throws him outside the pale of society. If the police and the law were guided by dictates of justice then the term under trail should have been obsolete."[7]

The objectives of Criminal Justice System changed drastically by around 1985 in United Kingdom which includes the following, as written by Tim Newell, a former Prison Governor and Quaker:

"To prevent an reduce crime; To establish a principal basis for sentencing; To avoid the unnecessary use of imprisonment and stabilise the current prison population; To develop supervision schemes in the community, to reduce reoffending; To give greater consideration to victims, and to make the system more effective, efficient and accountable".[8]

The conditions in Indians prisons during the year 1930-31 are evident from the following narrative, by Gene Sharp:

"Sunday, August 10th was set for 'Political Prisoners Day' for an All-India demonstration of sympathy with the suffering of political prisoners.

All volunteers, workers and the people at large were urged to fast, and conduct processions and public meetings to condemn the ill treatment of political prisoners. Nearly everywhere extremely harsh treatment in prisons was reported, including being confined entirely to one room at all seasons, unwholesome food, and being denied the minimum amenities of life.

An extreme case was reported from Vilasapur Jail, 27 miles from Ahmed Nagar city, Maharashtra. There only 3 of the 12 barracks were fit for human beings, the others being more for fit cattle. The barracks had places where cold, damp blasts of air entered at night and each person was given only one blanket to serve both as a bed and as a cover. In one barrack, 128 by 15 with 10sq.ft. occupied by a larine, 110 prisoners were housed. The floor was made of earth and stones. Prisoners could not go to the latrine without the permission of the warder who was the prisoner – cum-night –watchman. There was widespread dysentery and diarrhea. The jail compound (there was a wire fence around each barrack and another around all 12) was infested with snakes, scorpions and centipedes. The toilet facilities were horrible. There was drinking Can which was also used inside the latrine. Two minutes were allowed for washing in cold water out of doors at a public tank, some distance from the barrack. There was neither soap nor change of clothes. The food contained grit, dirt, and dead insects and was ill-cooked. It was ordinarily uneatable, and was then too highly spiced: there was very little of it and no variety. There was an unbelievable lack of medical facilities. Prisoners were assaulted and beaten, and given no time for prayers.

It was such treatment and even more severe elsewhere which caused the working committee to inaugurate a political Prisoners Day."[9]

Crime is a disease and will be treated as any other disease in free India, as Gandhi wrote in Harijan 5-5-1946.

"In independent India of the non-violent type, there will be crime but no criminals. They will not be punished. Crime is a disease like any other malady and is a product of the prevalent social system. Therefore, all crime including murder will be treated as a disease. Whether such an Indian will ever come into being is another questions."[10]

Gandhi wrote that, foundation of Satyagraha as of a Nation building is undoubtedly self-purification, self-dedication and selflessness. Let each one ask oneself: How then can I purity myself in term of the nation? Rectitude of private character is surely the beginning of the structure. If my private character is foul, I am like a sounding brass and tinkling 'cymbal'. If, then I am not right inside. I must this very instant purge myself and be a fit vessel for dedication. Government cannot help me or interfere with me here. I must be the soul author of my making or unmaking."[11]

Speaking after the evening prayer at Uruli, Gandhi said about crimes and criminals and it was published in Harijan 11-8-1946 that instead of bearing ill will towards a thief or a criminal and trying to get him punished they should try to get him under his skin, understand the cause that had led him into crime and try to remedy it. They should, for instance, *teach him a vocation* and provide him with the means to make an honest living and thereby transform his life. They could realise that a thief or a criminal was not a different being from themselves. Indeed, if they turned the search – light inward and closely looked into their own souls, they would find that the difference between them was only one of degree"[12]

Prayer is having influence on character formation: Gandhi wrote in Harijan, 29-8-1947.

"Just as body cannot exist without blood, so the soul needs the matchless and pure strength of faith. This strength can renovate the weakness of all man's physical organs. That is why, it is said that when Ramanama is enshrined in the heart, it means *the rebirth of man*. This law applied to the young, the old, man and women like. This belief is to be found in the west too. Christian Sciences give a glimpse of it. But India needs no outside support for belief which has been handed down to her people from time immemorial."[13]

Reformation in other words, self purification of the ward placed under supervision is the duty of the Probation Officer. Here the eleven 'vratas' of Gandhi become relevant in the Indian context. It becomes the basis of resocialisation. Self purification is necessity, for personal, family and social development. Gandhi developed the eleven vrates for *satyagrahis*. But it can be applied to every person under supervision also because it is conducive for the transformation of each individual.

The *Elevan Vratas* are:

(1) Ahimsa (non-violence): (2) Satya (truth): (3) Asteya (non-stealing): (4) Brahmachrya (celibacy): (5) Asangraha (non-accumulation) or Aparigraga (non-possession): (6) Sharirshrama (bread-labour): (7) Aswad (control of the palate): (8) Abhaya (fearlessness): (9) Sarvadharma

Sambhava (equal respect for all religions): (10) Swadeshi (love for one's own country): (11) Sparshabhavana (abjuring untouchability): and of these, only five vratas were mentioned in the ancient Indian religious texts, and they were prescribed for attaining *chitta-shuddhi (purification of mind)*, spiritual progress, and the emancipation or liberation of the self or soul. Gandhi added the next six vratas after taking into account the demands of modern and democratic values and the *contemporary conditions in India.* He had made the recitation of eleven vratas compulsory during the daily morning and evening prayers in his ashrams. He regarded the observance of these vratas as necessary not only for the ashramites but also for everyone in the ordinary business of life: he saw in them the only means for the liberation of both the individual self and the social self." [14]

Probationers require positive reinforcements in personal values in order to become a socially accepted or ideal person. The Vaishnava ideals are a proper guideline in this regard. Gandhi's Vaishnava family background oriented him towards the path of truth and nonviolence. Here the ideal can be shown to all person under supervision.

In fact the poem by Narasinha Mehta (1414-79) of Gujarat, Which gives the Vaishavaideal, became part of Gandhi's daily prayers:

"A true Vaishnava is he

Who is moved by other's sufferings:

Who helps people in distress,

And feels no pride for having done so.

Respectful to everyone in the world,

He speaks ill of none

Is self-controlled in action, speech and thought

Twice-blessed the mother who bore such a one.

He has an equal-seeing eye, and is free from all craving,

Another's wife is to him a mother;

His tongue utters no untruth,

And never his hand touches another's wealth,

Moha and Maya have no power over him

In his mind reigns abiding detachment;

He dances with rapture to Rama's name

No centre of pilgrimage but is present in his person.

A man he is without greed and cunning,

And purged of anger and desire;

Offering reverence to such a one, says Narasinyo

Will bring release to seventy one generation of one's forbearers".[15]

Satyagraha principles show a method to change. Due to the passage of time and the changes occurred in social system, the consequent changes also are to be made in the Satyagraha. Gandhi wrote;

"As far as the particular conditions of India were concerned, he had been of the opinion that Gandhi's own satyagraha and his major objective of freedom from British yoke were very much conditioned by the then situation but the conditions are different now. There is democracy and the people against whom we have to conduct satyagraha, are our own. Therefore instead of copying the forms of Gandhi's satyagraha, we have to examine the basic philosophy behind them and change their forms in the context of the prevailing conditions. Accordingly the following four principles were laid:

1. The form of Satyagraha should be positive, i.e., constructive, and not negative.
2. In case one form of Satyagraha proves ineffective, instead of adopting a more extreme form, one should take to a milder or gentler form.
3. It should be such that its very name does not create fear in others, but rather gladdens them.
4. It should permit the truth to assert itself, not the Satyagrahi. In the context of the present democratic conditions, internal problems should be solved by constitutional means, including change through the ballot box, persuasion and societal change through people's own efforts."[16]

The vision of Gandhi is amazing in the sense that the entire population involved in one or other form of Constructive programme with a common goal, resulting in social change:

"Let the reader mentally plan out the whole of the Constructive Programme and he will agree with me that if it could be successfully worked out, the end of it would be the independence, we want."[17]

Gandhi introduced the Constructive programmes, touching social political, educational, economic and cultural aspects of man's life. Gandhi from 1915 to 1945 was able to formulate a compact programme of total transformation of society. This Constructive Programme can also utilised as a tool for social rehabilitation of a person under supervision. In its final form in 1945, it covered the following items:

"1. Communal Harmony
2. Removal of untouchability
3. Prohibition
4. Khadi
5. Other village Industries
6. Village Sanitation
7. New or Basic education
8. Adult education
9. Women
10. Education in Health and Hygiene
11. Provincial Language
12. National Language
13. Economic Equality
14. Kisans (peasants)
15. Labour
16. Adivasis (Tribals)
17. Leprosy
18. Students
19. Improving of cattle
20. Nature cure."[18]

The role of women in propagating the Gandhian concept is enormous. As Gandhi himself wrote,

"I have suggested in these columns that a woman is the incarnation of ahimsa. Ahimsa means infinite love, which again means infinite capacity for suffering"[19]

Dealing with theft can be in a spiritual way as Gandhi wrote:

"You set this armed robber down as an ignorant brother: you intent to reason with him at a suitable opportunity: you argue that he is after all, a fellow man, you do not know what prompted him to steal. You, therefore, decide that, when, you can, you will *destroy the man's motive for stealing.* Whilst you are thus reasoning with yourself, the man comes again to steal. Instead of being angry with him you take pity on him. You think that this stealing habit must be a disease with him. Hence, you therefore keep your doors and windows open, you change your sleeping place, and you keep your things in a manner most accessible to him. The robber comes again and is confused, as all this is new to him: nevertheless he takes away your things. But his mind is agitated. He enquires about you in the village, he comes to learn about your broad and loving heart, he repents, he begs your pardon, returns you your things and leaves off the stealing habit. He becomes your servant, and you find for him an honorable employment."[20]

Gandhi tried innovative experiments in *family life* at phoenix and Sabarmay. Gandhi gave importance to spirituality in life and gave up his sexual life in his thirties. Harilal, one out of his four sons rebelled against him. About the role of parents, Gandhi wrote in a Letter to Harilal dated November 26, 1918,

> "I am very pleased to learn that you cook own food and you enjoy doing so. May be you will find this an instructive, experience, understand through of, the secret of life and repair past mistakes, bring light into your past."[21]

Gandhi wrote in Harijan 15-10-1938 (PP-287-88) about the *obscene* and erotic passages in textbook.

"It is for one thing to defend the liberty to read what one likes. But it is a wholly different thing to force on young minds acquaintance with literature that cannot but excite their animal passion, and an unhealthy curiosity about things which, in due course and to the extent necessary, they are bound to learn. The evil becomes accentuated when it comes in the guise of innocent literature bearing the imprimatur of great Universities."[22]

Gandhi gave importance to *individual freedom* and the omnipotence of conscience.

"The only tyrant I accept in that world is the still voice within… In matters of conscience the law of majority has no place"…"I do believe that, where there is only a choice between cowardice and violence, I would advice violence"… and to Gandhi the highest social good was "nothing but the extension of individual spirituality."[23]

Dr. Zakir Hussian the then President of India said,

"If the spare time of our students and young people could meaningfully divided between the play ground or gymnasium, library or reading room, and a Centre for creative art or a *Forum for social service,* student indiscipline and juvenile delinquency will be a thing of the past".[24]

Quoting Subbarao (1977) in the book "A Daniel comes to judgment, Amrita Bharati, Thiru. S. Muthuswamy former Chief Probation Superintend, Tamilnadu, wrote:

"During the nineteenth century, India was fortunate in having an ideal English Judge. Mr. Pennel an English man, was a Sessions Judge in Bengal. In 1899, Corbett an Englishman holding the post of Superintendent of Police of Chaapra District. A beat police constable Narasingh, an Indian as he refused to do forced labour to an English District Engineer, a friend of the Superintend of Police. Moreover the constable was prosecuted on false charges. Due to higher level of pressure, he was sentenced to imprisonment for two months by the magistrate on frivolous charges. The constable preferred an appeal to the District Court, which was admitted by Mr. Pannel, and the constable was acquitted. Mr.Pannel who was not 'race-ridden", pure and perfect an exemplary judge remarked. 'In this country the only people who will come forward to give evidence against officers are those who do not mind their house being burnt, their shops looted, their relatives turned out of Government employment, themselves and members of their families dragged upon false charges and send to Jail."[25]

Gandhi wrote in Harijan on 5-8-1933 about the relationship between the kind of *food one intake and his character.*

"There is a great deal of truth in the saying that man becomes what he eats. The grosser the food the grosser the body."[26]

The quality of food, its cooking, the quantity of intake, the time of intake are said to have an impact with digestion and health condition as well as the formation of behaviour and habits of the person.

Negative thoughts are the root cause of crimes. In Gita, while discussing about detachment we can classify the relevant passages of the Gita into three categories:

"(a) Those, which maintain that a detached person should not be a slave to his feelings, emotions, passions, etc.

(b) Those which state that a detached person should renounce the fruits of his actions and,

(c) Finally, statements which maintain that a detached person should renounce not the fruits of his action, but also the action and the desire for action. This does not mean that he becomes like a robot.

> The Gita continuously stresses the fact that a person should not be a slave to his passions, that he should not be ruled by his emotions, and that he, who is so swayed by his senses 'perishes'.

When a man meditates on the object of sense, attachment to them is produced, from attachment springs desire, from desire wrath arises, from wrath comes infatuation, from infatuation leads to anger, from anger leads one to loss of memory, from loss of memory to loss of mind, and from loss mind he perishes." [27]

Community Based Correctional method have the following Advantages:

"(a) Correctional scope is more than in Institutional set up (b) More humanistic; (c) Less costly; (D) Free from stigma; (E) Free from vices; (f) Community resources to be widely employed; and the Panchayaths Raj Institutions can play a greater role in the areas of:

(a) Voluntary Probation Officers
(b) Naya Panchayats
(c) Juvenile Youth Bureau (Quasi official basis) and
(d) Nehru Yuva Kendra." [28]

Reformation and rehabilitation of *dacoits* are to be undertaken by providing suitable employment opportunities and proper guidance is a means to ease out the rebellious attitude of dacoits, though a hindrance may arise due to the dual role of Prison.

"By keeping them (dacoits) in an open and clean set-up and by affording opportunities to them for reformation through self help and offering various forms of guidance, the Government hopes to enable them to shake by off their ill-feeling and their rebellious attitude towards society and turn into good civilians."[29]

During home visits the Probation Officer can organise various programmes so that useful or fruitful interaction takes place with the wards:

"Home visiting is time consuming and produces a relatively uncontrolled situation. Although the officer can arrange with his clients some structuring of the visit, provided. He is certain about its purpose and importance. It can be good casework to watch a television programme with a family, but the situation more often arises from officers inability to ask to the set to be switched off."[30]

House visits by Probation Officer are aimed to help the persons under supervision and the other members of his family.

"An officer who wishes to see people who belongs from the clients environment for two reasons: to gain information, or to work with them and the clients towards a solution of the client's and family's difficulties...Officers are visiting prisoners' wives and helping to come to a decision about the future"[31]

Probationers in India are, not allowed to mingle each other or to form group for fear that it become of the will lead to antisocial activities. But group experiences are often considered as proper technique of correction.

"The traditional method in probation has been individual meetings between officer and offender, but experiments are taking place in the use of groups. Especially since 1960 (HMSO, 1966)... groups are being formed either of probationers unknown to each other, or of those jointly charged or living together in a hostel. Others have provided various kinds of group experiences such as *Summer Camps, Weekend outings or Play groups*".[32]

"In *group work* the probation service may be able to learn from personal services, which use groups of various kinds, ranging from small therapy groups to large living groups."[33]

Poverty and grinding indigence, parental tyranny, deprived homes, evil of drink, and sub human living conditions have forced many children to the streets and to crimes. The role of Probation Officer in correcting them:

"The child and the Probation Officer should jointly arrive at a common understanding of the goal as the result of intimate heart to heart discussion but *over kindness is very often be mistaken for weakness* ...The Probation Officer should be a highly resourceful person directing his probationer".[34]

Dr. Walter C. Reckless, an expert appointed by the technical assistance administration of the United Nations in the year 1951-52 to India recommended the Central Government to consider a specialised technical assistance in the field of Probation and Aftercare.

"The Government of India should consider the need for specialised technical assistance in this field following as quickly as possible the termination of this mission.

(a) Technical assistance in the field of probation and after-care.

(b) Technical assistance in the field of special facilities for juvenile delinquents.

(c) Technical assistance in field of prison industries and vocational work programmes.

(d) Technical assistance in the field of agriculture programmes for prisons.

(e) Technical assistance in developing an adequate system of record keeping.

(f) Technical assistance to help establish the Advisory Bureau for Correctional Administration.

(g) Technical assistance to develop demonstration training centers".[35]

Instead of the present Inspector General of Prisons, he proposed to establish and integrated department for Prisons, Borstals, Probation and aftercare, headed by the Director.

"The large states of India should develop integrated departments of correctional administration and one minister, including jails, Borstals, revising boards, probation, and after-care. The Director of such a department should be the modern substitute for the present Inspector-General of Prisons. In the, meantime, there is no reason why the Inspector-General of Prisons' office cannot have a positive rather than a negative orientation".[36]

Vinoba started his Peace Mission in Chambal Valley from Agra on May 8, 1960 and furnished his tour on June, 7, 1960 at Gwalior. Vinoba covered 8 to 10 miles per day, sometimes even 13 to 14 miles in Ravine area. Vinoba and party had its camps at 26 such village which were associated with the names of notorious dacoits and their relations. Vinoba appealed to dacoits and their relations to give up wrong path and repent for their misdeeds. Peace Missionaries of Vinoba also tried to contact outlaws of Ravine area and convey the message of love... The outcome of Vinoba's Peace Mission was the surrender of 200 notorious dacoits of Chambal Valley which included Mansing Roopa gang."[37]

"The type of treatment depends upon the problems and circumstances of each child. It may be positive motivation, play therapy, group therapy, storytelling, or remedial teaching".[38]

Reformation of an individual can occur in the solitary Prison cells as beautifully described by Sri. Aurobindo, after his own solitary confinement as freedom fighter.

"God was having a game with me, through which he was giving, me a few necessary lessons. First, He showed me the state of mind in which prisoners condemned to solitary cells move towards insanity, and turned me wholly against the inhuman cruelty of the western prison administration, so that I might, to the best of my ability, turn my countrymen and the world form these barbarous ways to the path of more humane prison organisation. This was the first lesson I remembered, fifteen years back, after return home from England, I had written some bitterly critical articles in the 'Induprakash', of Bombay, against the petitionary ethics of the then Congress. Seeing that, these articles were influencing the minds of the young, the late *Mahadeo Govind Ranade* had told me, when I meet him, for nearly half an hour, that I should give up writing these articles, and advised me to take up some other Congress work. He was desirous of my taking up the work of prison reform. I was astonished and unhappy at the unexpected suggestion and had refused to undertake that work. I did not know then that this was a prelude to the distant future and that one day God himself would keep me in prison for a year and make me see the cruelty and futility of the system and the need for reform.

Now, I understand that in the present political atmosphere, there was no possibility of any reform of the prison system, but I resolved before my conscience to propagate and argue in its favour so that these hellish remnants of an alien order were not perpetuated in a self-determining India. I also understood his second purpose: it was to reveal and expose before my mind, its own weakness so that I might get rid of it forever. For one who seeks the yogic state, crowd and solitude should mean the same. I needed, the weakness dropped off within a very few days, and now it seems that the central poise would not be disturbed even by twenty years of solitude. In the dispensation of the All-Good (Mangalamaya) even out of evil comes good. The third purpose was to give me this lesson that my yoga practices would not be done by personal effort, but that a spirit of faith or reverence (Sraddha) and complete self-surrender (atma-samarpana) were the road to attain perfection in yoga, and whatever power or realisation that Lord would give out of his benignity, to accept and utilise these should be the only aim of my yogic endeavour. Since the day when the deep darkness of Ignorance began to lessen, I started to see the true nature of the All-Good Lord's amazing infinite goodness as I watched the different events in the ward."[39]

The reformation of an offender's behaviour involves inducing right behaviour by motivating him to develop his inherent good character traits. Understanding the process of developing a criminal behvariour and its disastrous consequences is a necessary quality required for a Probation Officer. He is to consider the following principles.

"(i) Treatment based on the consent of the probationer.

(ii) Treatment planned with the effective participation of the probationer, and

(iii) Treatment planned to re-structure the probationers thinking and emotions."[40]

Sri. Aurabindo describes his inner life and how he regained this mental strength through prayer, while he was imprisoned:

"Troubled by mental listlessness, I spent a few days in agony in this manner. One afternoon, as I was thinking, streams of thought began to flow endlessly and then suddenly these grew so uncontrolled and incoherent that I could feel that the mind's regulating power was about to cease. Afterwards when I came back to myself, I could recollect that though the power of mental control had ceased, the intelligence was not self lost or did not deviate for a moment, but it was, as if, the intelligence was watching quietly this marvelous phenomenon. But at that time, shaking with the terror of being overcome by insanity, I had not been able to notice that. I called upon God with eagerness and intensity and prayed to him to prevent my loss of intelligence. That very moment, there spread over my being such a gentle and cooling breeze, the heated brain become relaxed, easy and supremely blissful such as in all my life, I had never known before. Just as a child sleeps, secure and without fear, on the lap of his mother, so I remained on the lap of the World Mother. From that day all my trouble of prison life was over. Afterwards on many occasions, during the period of detention, inquietude, solitary imprisonment, and mental unease because of lack of activity, bodily trouble or disease, in the lean periods of yogic life, these have come, but that day, in a single moment God had given, my inner being such strength that these sorrows as they came and went, did not leave any trace or touch on the mind; relishing strength and delight in the sorrow itself, the mind was able to reject these subjective sufferings. The sufferings seemed as fragile as water drops on a lotus leaf. Then when the books came, their need had considerably lessened. I could have stayed on even if the books were not there. Though it is more the purpose of these articles to write a history of my inner life, still I could not but mention this fact. *From this one incident* it will be clear how it was possible to live happily during long solitary confinement. It was, for this reason that God had brought about this situation or experience. Without turning me mad, he had enacted in my mind the gradual process towards insanity that takes place in solitary confinement, keeping my intelligence as the unmoved spectator of the entire drama. *Out of this came strength* and I had an excess of kindness and sympathy for the victims of human cruelty and torture. *I also realised the extraordinary power and efficacy of prayer"*.[41]

Vinoba mentioned that there existed a nexus between Dacoits of Chambal and Police. A Chambal Peace Committee was formed which started cottage and village industries and reclaimed the wasteland in the ravines.

"While in Kashmir, Vinoba had received a letter from Tehsildar Singh, the son of the famous dacoit Man Singh, from the Central Prison at Naini, Allahabad, where he was under death sentence, expressing a desire for his darshan before being hanged. Vinoba deputed Yadunath Singh, a retired Major General who was In-Charge of his Kashmir trip, to meet him in the prison. After seeing him, Yadunath Singh went to the Chambal region and met several dacoits of Man Singh group. On return, he gave Vinoba his impression that some dacoits might surrender to him if he visited the area. Vinoba, therefore, expressed a desire to visit it and try for the conversion of the dacoits. The idea was welcomed by Chief Minister Dr. Kailash Nath Katju of Madhya Pradesh and, consequently, when Vinoba was at Agra, the Union Home Minister Pandit Govind Ballabh Pant and the Uttar Pradesh Chief Minister Shri. Sampurnanand met him and it was decided to lend support to him, in his peaceful efforts to make the dacoits surrender and give up their ways. The police authorities of the three concerned States of Uttar Pradesh, Madhya Pradesh and Rajasthan were instructed to help in the process.

Vinoba started on his mission on 7 May, and in his first day, post–prayer speech, he repeated the same idea about the criminals, which he had expressed in Dhulia Jail, some two years back. A few days later at Fatehabad, the first surrender of Ram Autar Singh took place promising that he would commit no more crimes. At that time, Vinoba said explaining to some police officers present there. 'No one is a born dacoit. It is a natural result of exploits2ation; miserliness, cruelty and callousness…If we love dacoits, show kindness to them, transform our village into a family, and the whole problem would be solved by itself. These dacoits are very simple, brave and fearless. *'If we change their line of action they will easily turn into saints'*. And he added: *'The police cannot solve this problem.* If they come to stay here, the dacoits will do likewise, and so also malice, hatred, aversion and animosity'.

After some time, a dacoit Lachhi Pandit with considerable sum on his head also came and placed himself and his family in Vinoba's hands. He had come from Bombay, having read about his missionary efforts in the papers. Thus the mission gradually gathered momentum, and on 19 May, eleven top dacoits led by Lokman alias Lukka, laid down arms at Vinoba's feet after the evening prayer meeting. Speaking on that day, Vinoba had said. *'The three, main causes of this (dacoit) problem are poverty, personal feuds and police. The fourth cause is party politics and elections. If these causes are eliminated, the problem will be solved by itself.'* On 22 May they took leave of Vinoba and went to the jail, where Vinoba also met them the next day.

All this was not liked by some police officers. Sometimes, there were revelations of the nexus between dacoits, on one hand and some police officers and politicians, on the other. This probably led to the statement by the then Inspector General of Police, Madhya Pradesh, that Vonoba's mission had 'delivered a blow to the morale of the police force'. He also alleged, that the dacoits were assured during negotiations of a lenient treatment. This was totally incorrect and to it Vinoba's reaction was: 'One sees God according to one's own light. It is incorrect to say that the dacoits who surrendered to me had been given any assurance. All along my tour, I have been publicly stating that it is for the law courts to decide whether they are to be acquitted or punished.' As regards human touch in dealing with such cases, he observed. 'The very fact that the President of India is empowered to commute death sentences is a positive proof that the Indian Constitution honors, kindness and compassion'.

To those, Sarvodaya workers who did not relish their being put in prison, Vinoba said that he did not want to do anything against law, which has its, limitations. All that, he could do was to see justice done to them, to provide legal aid to them and, if possible help to their families to lead a good life. He even did not want them to seek pardon, for none could escape the fruits of one's karma, action. The cases, however, did not take long, since they all pleaded guilty to genuine charges.

By the time Vinoba left the region, the number of surrendering dacoits was twenty. To utilise the changed climate generated there, the Sarva

Seva Sangh, under the guidance of Vinoba constituted, a Chambal Peace Committee. It helped in the expediting of the cases in the law courts of the three concerned States, collected funds for the reclamation of waste lands in the ravines and started a few cottage and village industries to train the dacoit families."[42]

During the period of Probation *Aftercare supervision,* the prisoner shall be under the supervision of the Probation Officer whose duty, it shall be to see that the conditions of release are not violated and to give the prisoner any protection, assistance or advice, that he may need. Rule 908 (2) IX of Kerala Prison Rules (1958) states that the Chief Welfare Officer,

"Shall manage and scrutinise the activities of welfare officers of each Prison in strict coordination with the Superintendent of the prison and see that the Welfare Officers are working in liaison with families of the prisoners, Probation Officers, and the Aftercare Agencies/Associations, with a view, to implement effective rehabilitation of prisoners."[43]

As per the rule 9 of the Kerala Prison Rules, a Bond executed by the prisoner at the time of release and it states that:

"That I will carry out such lawful directions as may from time to time be given by the said Probation Officer for the due observance of the conditions before mentioned".[44]

The Aftercare work started in England in the early 18th century. "The Aftercare is an execution of services already rendered in an institution. It is an effort to facilitate readjustment and re-assimilation of an ex-inmate of an institution with the community. Initially, John Howard (1728-1790) started aftercare work of the offender in England for ameliorating the conditions of prisoners both within and outside, the penal institutions.

After the death of Howard, the Quakers continued his work and took increasing interest on crime causation in England. They set up a society in 1808 for providing aids to released prisoners. This was the beginning of efforts for organised aftercare in Europe and America." [45]

The Quakers who had fought for the rights of offenders as well as victims used non-violent methods to create self awareness. One of their inspirations is an old Chinese saying.

"Go to the people

Live among them

Learn from them

Start with what they know
Build on what they have.
But of the best leaders
When their task is accomplished.
Their work is done
The people all remark
We have done it ourselves."[46]

In-service training to Probation Officer can be made effective by including various topics:

"Criminology, Penology such as theories of crime causation, philosophy of punishments, the present theories on therapeutic approaches to punishments and various correctional processes. Also psychology, sociology – and related field such as possibility of change in human behaviour, the relationship between behaviour and life experience, variety and complexity of human feelings, the nature and significance of family relationships, the ways in which one person may help another: to make adjustments and to cope with his problems more satisfactorily, and the many difficult and painful experience people may have, and the forces which sometimes press upon clients and Probation Officers. The trainees should be prepared through this theoretical training to think diagnostically, to assess and constantly review the needs of the client".[47]

Advance planning is required for the rehabilitation of habitual offenders, which grossly ignored in these days, though the All India Jail Manual Committee recommended in it's report during 1919-20.

"Stress should be given on the advance planning of Aftercare help for habitual offenders".[48]

The *Interview Dynamics*, which is one of the techniques used by Probation Officers for correction:

"Social investigation involves the Probation Officer's interviewing the juvenile as often as may be necessary, his paying visits to the collateral sources of information, and his interviewing the juvenile's parents and relatives, former school teachers and friends. The limiting factor of time sometimes acts as a brake on his enthusiasm to adopt a puristic casework approach, to get at the finer points in the juvenile's developmental history, or at the subtle nuances in his bahaviour. Unlike in a purely casework setting, where the caseworker – client relationship is allowed to be build up over a period of time through consciously planned, tension – free, informal interviews, in order to get at the more elusive and subtle aspects of the client's personality and behaviour, the Probation Officer is required to work in a formal setting the boundaries of which are determined by the requirements of law and the directives of the competent authority. In such a context, the Probation Officer, mindful of the limiting time-factor, can seldom afford to have an unlimited number of interviews for building up anything like a cordial relationship or rapport, which is regard to be the essential ingredient of the casework process".[49]

The probation supervision envisages permanent charges in the offender placed under supervision. So, the quality time spend between them becomes crucial, as wrote by Hilary Walker:

"A consumer survey by Nottingham Probation Officers reported that probation was generally described as, a five minute talk which was unrelated to the rest of their activities and which because or happened infrequently (although definitions of frequency varied, e.g., only once a month to only once a week) could not, therefore, have any impact."[50]

A primordial form of Community Service, was prevalent in Egypt during the year 1917, as in evident from the report of all India Jails Committee of 1919-20, which appends (Appendix XI) note by the Inspector General of Prisons in Egypt. It gives an account of an interesting experiment which has been made in that country in allowing persons, sentenced to imprisonment for non-payment of fine and persons sentenced to simple imprisonment for periods, not exceeding three months to *secure exemption from actual imprisonment by releasing instead to do six hours' work a day for a fixed number of days.* The statistics appended to that note show that in the City of Alexandria during the four years 1914-1917, an average number of 2,510 persons annually elected to work in lieu of undergoing imprisonment. Of this total 813 subsequently paid their fines and so released themselves from the obligation to labour."[51]

Involvements of Probation Officer in the community became very relevant in these days as wrote by Hilary Walker:

"Probation extracts from the offender, a contribution within the limits of his capacity, to the well being of others, whether it is through his usual employment in the community or through his participation in the life of the family, or other social group. In doing so, it minimises the economic and social disruption caused by the probationers offence... and seeks to avoid the harm to others, that follows, for example, the imprisonment of a bread winner". [52]

Rani Dhawan Shankardass Wrote about Community Service in England that:

"Community Service Officers visit these institutions regularly to ensure that there is proper coordination and that any problem encountered be resolved.

Once the trial Magistrate has ordered an offender, to perform certain number of hours of Community Service at a particular institution, a copy of the order is immediately forwarded to the head of the relevant institution. By the time, the offender presents himself to the institution for community service, the head of the institution will have made necessary arrangements for the offender to carry out his orders.

The fact that most people who perform Community Service are not likely to re-offend must surely be a good news for society".[53]

Vinoba opined that since the dacoity problem is a man made problem it may be solved nonviolently.

"The dacoits of Chambal ravines are simple and brave. They are not die hard. They may be persuaded to give up wrong path. If they are treated sympathetically, they may be turned into good citizens of India".[54]

Annual Report of the California Department of Corrections states the various types of substance abuse treatment services that are offered through these Centers include the following:

1. "Substance abuse assessment and treatment planning
2. Detoxification services
3. Day treatment services
4. Residential Substance Abuse treatment service
5. Outpatient treatment
6. Alcohol and Drug free housing
7. Alcohol and Drug education
8. Individual, group and family counseling
9. Social and recreational service
10. Transportation
11. Referral to other appropriate community Resources".[55]

Guidance, counseling and leadership training are techniques of correction. Psychological, sociological and even biological awareness is to be imparted. The aims and objectives of life, milestones of development and by helping to acquire self awareness in relation to one's role in the society in which he is a member. This awareness itself often results in the solution of many problems faced by a probationer.

"Guidance and leaderships do not mean moralising. Guidance and leaderships with parolees will probably be effective in direct ratio to the imagination and initiative powers of the social worker."[56]

Robert Mayer wrote about the child guidance clinics:

"The need for the application of modern science in industry and several other fields, is fully realised. In the field of juvenile delinquency, the most promising modern invention is the Child Guidance Clinic.

The particular service can render, and the one that has led to a call for a wide extension of it's scope, is its ability to cope with the problem child, if possible in the home, though many parents are unwilling, unsuitable or unable to help. Whether such a child becomes a delinquent depends entirely upon chance. If his unsatisfactory behaviour is noticed in time and suitably treated, he may quickly become a useful member of society.

If it so happens that the problem child's behaviour brings him into contact with the police very likely, he will either be place with foster parents lacking in the psychological training, that is particularly necessary in his case, or be sent to an approved school, where individual handling of maladjustment is difficult".[57]

The All India Jail Manual Committee 1957-59 recommended, on how to deal with adolescent offenders in Prisons, that:

"Prisons are not the places where delinquent children and adolescent offenders should be kept. Wherever this is being done, delinquent child and adolescent offenders should be taken out of prisons. Very high priority should be given to this question. Where the number of adolescent offenders in a State exceeds 200, separate institution for adolescents should be set up. Besides this, Central and District Prisons should have annexes for adolescent offenders. In states, where the number of adolescent offender is small, these offenders should be kept in annexes of Central and District Prisons. Institutions for adolescent offenders should be diversified, as per provisions of chapter XLI of the draft manual. More can be initially admitted and then classified in accordance with their training needs. Where this is not immediately practicable part of the institution, which has been earmarked for adolescent offenders, should be converted into a Reception Unit, where the study and understanding of the problems of adolescent offenders can be conducted on a scientific basis.

(xii) Adolescent offenders should be kept in Training Institutions as shown in chapter XLI of the draft manual, where major emphasis can be given on their training and treatment. Where possible, Semi-open and open Training Institutions for adolescent offenders may be set up, so that the impressionable groups of adolescent offenders can, to some extent be saved from getting institutionalised. Such institutions should however be organised, on the basis of experience gained in these fields and also in terms of available facilities and local conditions in each State.

(xiii) Adequate educational and technical staff should be posted at these institutions. Institutions for delinquent children and adolescent offenders should be properly equipped to conduct diversified training and treatment programmers". [58]

Manipulative Techniques, described by Elliot in the following way. The techniques of casework can be applied in the case of probation work also in order to improve the quality of correctional work. The importance of casework is that it considers the total personality of the individual. The techniques used by correctional workers are, mainly manipulative techniques:

"Manipulative techniques are extremely important with the offender groups. Sometimes that manipulative service apparently peripheral, is the first step in establishing a stable behaviour pattern, such as.

- Job finding
- Accommodation finding
- Betterment of community conditions and
- Removal of discrimination."[59]

Executive Techniques are the other category, which the Probation Officers can adopt to rehabilitate the words.

Probation officers have not much fund at their disposal for rehabilitation of wards under supervision. He can utilise the resources available in the community through referral service of the right wards under supervision to right places, in the right time.

"Of important to the parolee are such services as by referral as these:

- Job getting
- Education of children
- Medical care
- Public grants
- Housing Loans
- Institutional Placement
- Nursery care of children
- Legal aid
- Educational and vocational guidance
- Recreation
- Social agency help etc.

Executive services, however, do not amount to a fragmentation of various aspects of a case, whereas each to be treated in itself." [60]

The non-custodial punishments are mainly, Community Service in Africa. For this purpose, there exists National Committee, Provincial Committee, and District Committees. A Judge and members from Police, Social Welfare, Labour Health, University, and Non Governmental organisations, chair these Committees.

"There is a growing realisation in Africa and elsewhere that imprisonment is not the solution to offending behaviour and it is a very expensive option". [61]

The contents of Probation Officers enquiry, while analysing and interpreting information, which it is advisable to collect collaterally, some of the points, which may be profitably kept in mind, are listed below.

(a) "*Identifying Data:* The offenders' legal involvement, social antecedents, personal objective facts, etc.

(b) *Present Offence:* Abstract of the complaint, and description of the offence, and the parents reaction to the offence and their attitude towards the offender. This information must be given in a narrative style, detailing the time and place of offence, the circumstance in which the offence was committed, the nature of the offence, sequence of events, the part played by the offender and his associates, if any, in the commission of the offence; the role of the police and the versions of the offence.

(c) *Statement by the Offender:* The alleged offender's explanation of his conduct should be accepted as he gives it for recoding, without the probation officer embellishing it. Often, the Probation Officer comes up against a lot of resistance. Overcoming it, calls for interviewing skills for breaking down the offender's resistance and evasion. No experienced interviewer will attitudinise or moralise: and whenever he must, of necessity, do so, he should honestly label such characterisation as his own.

(d) *Mitigation of Aggravating Circumstances:* The investigation report must not merely be a factual recording of events and sequences. Rather, it must be an intelligent probing into the circumstance, which may have led the offender, step by step, into commission of the delinquent act. Was the offence premeditated or deliberate or accidental ? Was there resistance on his part to arrest, or repentance, or what deference was this to his first offence? If not, was it connected in any way with his earlier difficulty? Is his present offence against property or against person? Is sex factor operating in some way in the delinquent act? Has the act caused any physical damage to any other person? Is the offender's mental condition sound enough, so that he could comprehend the seriousness of his delinquent act?

(e) *Family background:*

1. *Parents:* Family attitudes and interrelationships can be important factors in assessing what reception or reaction, the offender may expect from the family, in the event of his being placed on probation, or in the event of his being committed to the institution and ultimately relapsed form the institution. The family attitude is the crux of the adjustment problem, in his discharge by the court, or by the institution, as the case may be.
2. *Brothers and Sisters:* The sibling relationship vis-a-vis with the offender. Their relationship with him and the psychopathological treads involved therein must be noted. Nothing is so as conducive to social adjustment as emotional adjustment with parents and siblings. Social adjustment in most cases begins at home.
3. *School and Extra-scholastic Activity:* A chronological record of achievements and disappointment at school, at work, in sports or in any other creative or constructive activity, should prove to be a dependable guide to measuring his improvability in behaviour. What factors were accountable for the gap between his aspirations and achievements? Were they remediable? Are they remediable now?"[62]

Regardless of the criminal background of the offender, the Probation Officer is to develop a non-judgmental and warm relationship with the offender. This good relationship can be used to, kindle the hope and confidence in the mind of the offender and help him to become a law abiding citizen. Training in soft skills would help in this regard.

"In correctional institutions caseworker keeps the relationship, a relative one, using the possible elements in the relationship to motivate and influence, the client towards a maximal solution of his problems. Thus in the correctional settings, the caseworkers activity, in respect to motivation is directed toward redirecting the strength of factor inhibiting the clients use of help, toward identifying and utilising the constructive motivating forces, that the client has hardy developed. This is for purpose of adaptation and mastery and reward, offering opportunities that may induce constructive motivation where it does not exist.

In correctional settings the social Caseworker attempts to establish a relationships, which, over a period of time, free the individual to express his feelings, master, his ego strength, change his antisocial values and become a law abiding citizen. Thus relationship is the core of social caseworkers contribution along, with the use of community resources. It means the caseworker accepts the client, understands and respects him. The client gradually develops feeling towards the caseworker, and shares his ideas, emotions and quarries. Then, through a bond of heart and support, changes are effected. The case worker is non-judgmental sensitive to the needs of the offender, and conveys a feeling of respect for the integrity and individuality of the offender regardless of his criminal conduct." [63]

Methods of treating offenders

The Probation Officer should possess academic qualifications and necessary skill to undertake activities of correction like.

"Some important methods are: (1) psychotherapy, (2) reality therapy (3) behaviour therapy (4) Activity therapy and (5) Motivation therapy. Punishment is not discussed as a treatment method because it is no longer viewed as a viable technique of treatment, though some, do feel that pain serves as a deterrent to further criminal action. Restrictions and reprimands can be effective supplements to the major treatment approach utilised but punishment cannot become an end in itself.

The two basic approaches, in dealing, with younger are the individual and the group methods of treatment. Of these, it is generally, the individual method, which is used, by psychologists, psychiatrists, sociologists and social workers, though psychologist, sometimes do use group methods as well. Sociologists usually take a 'Social engineering' approach to delinquency that, is they deal with the conditions of the social structure that breed delinquency, while psychologists treat the individual and emphasis interpersonal dynamics. Sociology is regarded as a theoretical discipline, reasoning the causes and effects of crime and delinquency. The Profession of social work is the 'practical' of the sociologists (Trohaniowizc, 1973: 229) as such the achieve-mentioned five therapeutic methods are generally utilised by psychologists, Phychiatrists and social workers".[64]

Through the effective and intelligent intervention of the Probation Officer as a correctional officer, an offender is being reformed into an enlightened and law abiding citizen:

"Probation is helping a criminal fit into a community, fitting him into their standards. Only skilled and competent persons can effectively serve both as Caseworkers and law-enforcement officers.

Through probation, a criminal is helped to be an enlightened citizen, and a reformed individual of a interdependent community. It is the most meaningful method or re-education a criminal. Hence, prison authorities should seriously consider the alternatives to imprisonment before starting the construction of more prisons in this country." [65]

The technique can be effective in the building and sustaining of morale. The approval and encouragement of the correctional Social Worker may keep up the courage and determination of a man, struggling through a difficult situation. The warmth and objective judgment of the Social Worker can create the willingness on the part of the individual to ask him for help in any situation.

"In Indian circumstance particularly with youthful offenders, the support and encouragement of the Social Worker can play an important role."[66]

"The Social Workers must remember at all times, in field that basically they will help people change only when they have aided them to eliminate certain compulsions, to resolve certain conflicts, so that they want to face reality in a stable sensible, and staying".[67]

"May need a crutch for a time, but he cannot grow if he used the Social Worker as a crutch forever"[68]

"The correctional caseworker would be making a mistake if he assumed that, the only way, he can help is to be, an instrument, in bringing about some radical change, in the individuals personality" [69]

The notable work of aftercare organisation is to help the released prisoner in removing the stigma attaching to conviction.

"Aftercare agencies in general, find, they have a role to play in removing prejudice and discrimination against former prisoners as concerns employment". [70]

Each probationer is a unique individual so that the supervision is to be different from case to case.

"The emphasis in casework varies from case to case, since the cause of maladjustment may lie primarily with the individual, or with the environment, or in some combination of these personal and social factors, the casework may be directed at strengthening the personality, in order to increase the capacity and understanding the offender. This is true, of instance in the case of those, who suffer from nervous and emotional disordered, from frustrations and conflicts, which prevent successful adjustment in any situation. In other cases, the emphasis may be directed, at a change or enrichment of the environment, to eliminate harmful conditions and make use of helpful resources. This is true for example, in the case of children who live under conditions in delinquency area where adjustment is difficult for even, the most normal types.

In attaining both immediate and ultimate goals, three fundamental processes are seen interplay at every point, the use of the resources, assisting the offender to understand his needs and possibilities: and helping him to develop the ability to work out his own social programme through the use of available resources. Therefore, casework is a joint action in which both the caseworker and the offender take part and in which they develop a definite relationship. (Page-129)

Aftercare work involves the development of socioeconomic, religious and spiritual aspects of the released prisoners' life. In the past, financial assistance was the chief contribution of aftercare agencies to released offenders."[71]

Instead of giving an amount, which has limited scope of money to them, the preference is being given to provide vocational training:

"In addition to assisting the individual, to obtain employment, the correctional Caseworker can serve effectively as a vocational counselor to the parolee".[72]

Visiting the employer of the released prisoner at the place of work during working hours by the Probation Officer often results, adverse, on the experience to those under supervision.

"Hence caseworker meeting with the parolee's employer will be advisable only when the latter knows the employee is on parolee".[73]

"The basic assumptions underlying the casework which are applicable in helping the offender are noted down as:

"(1) Every individual must be seen as a person of dignity and worth: (2) behaviour whether acceptable or unacceptable to the community, express a need of the individual: (3) an individual can and will change his behaviour if the right help is given at the right time and in the right amount: (4) if the offer of help is given before the problem becomes seriously aggravated, the response is likely to be better: and (5) the family is the most influential force, in the development of personality, in the crucial early years".[74]

The technique of supervision of juvenile delinquent, who is in need of care and protection but adult probationers are different. The Probation Officer is to help their family also, with an object of helping the ward to adjust him/her, to lead an honest and industrious life. Dealing with victims of crimes, is also necessary for the social justice:

"Supervision of victimised or exploited juveniles, especially adolescent girls, who come as victims of maltreatment, kidnapping or sex exploitation, call for deep insight by the Probation Officer into the psychology of traumatic experiences, undergone by the juveniles, and his discriminating use of the social, psychological and data available on them.

Social investigation invariably reveals the causative factors, which might have culminated in victimisation or exploitation. Laxity in parental control, at the critical age and stage of the juvenile's psycho-sexual development, curiosity of sex experience, during the upsurge of adolescence, titillating experience, transmission of sex life, patterns of sex, violence – crime films, or combination of any two or more of such factors may precipitate victimisation, or exploitation, or maltreatment of juveniles. Supervision, in such cases, calls for attitude, implantation therapy, patiently rearning away the juvenile from bad habits, gradually weeding out unhealthy, negative attitudes and implanting healthy, positive attitude in his mind towards, sex and its social moral and biological implications. Only trained experienced officers, should be entrusted with the delicate, sensitive job of supervising and guiding such juveniles on probation. Supervision of girl probationers should preferably be entrusted to lay probation officers."[75]

The three steps in a successful correctional treatment are:

1. *Discovering the cause:* For the correctional treatment, the Probation Officer must discover the causes of deviant behaviour of the criminal. The discovery of the underlying reasons of criminality is difficult: it requires intensive work with the criminal.
2. *Goal Oriented Relationship:* This cannot be accomplished unless the Probation Officer is able to establish, an understanding relationship with the individual probationer. The criminal must be able to know that the Probation Officer wants to understand and help. In his initial contact with a criminal on Probation, the Probation Officer needs to utilise all the skill at his disposal, then, in order to get the individual to understand, what he is there to do. If the Probation Officer is to be enabled to give correctional treatment, he has to build up a mutually satisfying relationship with the criminal.
3. *Achievement in relationship:* A relationship once begun, must continue to have meaning and value of the person who seek help, if it is, to last and yield fruits. The relationship can continue to grow and be productive if both the Probation Officer and the criminal understand, what that relationship does not mean. Both of them must know that correctional treatment in probation is for the rehabilitation of the offender in his community as a law abiding and constructive individual".[76]

The Indian Jail Reforms Committee recommended that the Probation Officer should not be given more cases than he can handle. An average number of supervision cases suggested are 60. And it is the duty of the Probation Officer, to report, to the court, in order to cancel, the supervision order. It is worth mentioning the observation of the Committee on these issues.

"Other points to which, attention must be directed, in the working of the probation system are as follows: It is essential that a Probation Officer should not be given more cases than he can look after properly. In England, sixty, has generally been accepted as a maximum, and if so large a number is given, they, must both be scattered over too extensive area. In the case of a voluntary probation worker, any, such number of cases as sixty would be quite out of the question, but it, might be feasible to entrust one or more cases to such a worker. Volunteer works are little, if at all, used in America where, the system of appointing paid Probation Officers has attained great development, and even in England, options differed a good deal, as to their value; but we see suitable persons if come forward, the plan might prove useful in this country. It was generally held in England that the volunteer should be placed under the paid officer, but this would be clearly inadvisable in India if the voluntary worker were an experienced missionary. It is generally useless to place a child on probation if its home is a thoroughly bad one, and in such a case, it is better to commit the young offender, at once, to suitable institution. The practice of placing a child on bond, a second or third or fourth time on probation, in spite of, his having several time released is also generally condemned and has brought discredit on the whole system. If a child who has been placed on probation willfully breaks the conditions on which he was discharged, refuses to follow the advice of the Probation Officer or in any way, seriously misconducts himselfm, it should be the duty of the Probation Officer to report the case promptly, to the magistrate who made the probation order and who will then be able to cancel the order and to take fresh measures."[77]

One of the techniques of correction used by the Probation Officer is casework. It enables the probationer to mend his ways because of the relationship created between them because the:

"Social case work is an art, in which, knowledge of the science of human relations and skill in relationship, are used to mobilise capacities in the individual and resources in the community appropriate for better adjustment between the client and all or any part of his total environments. So casework is the process of dealing with the individual case. It is concerned with the individual in relation to his social environment and aims at his successful adjustment.

A professional casework relationship is one that enables the client to express facts; attitudes and feelings, which guarantee that the workers' response, will be granted to the client's needs, not to the worker's need. The caseworker is responsible for facilitating communication verbal and non–verbal, without which, no relationship can be established and developed. This relationship is connected with the treatment process.

The two types of casework treatment currently used in correctional settings are the supportive treatment method and curative treatment. The former required the use of a number of techniques that help the client to improve his functioning within the framework of his established ego mechanism of defense. The latter requires the use of different techniques that help the client to improve this functioning through modification of selected ego mechanisms of defense. The outward form of the client's behaviour and selected internal process are modified".[78]

The workload of a Probation Officer is decisive, in the quality of supervision. Higher the number of cases, decreases the quality of supervision. *Training in case work* is very important, to enhance the responsibility:

"The service can never grow by diminishing, the sense of personal responsibility of individual officers and increasing their dependence but only by going, its utmost, to increase responsibility by developing an awareness of what is involved in good casework and by improving skills"[79].

The Probation Officer is being perceived with subsection with wards as he is an official "The Probation Officer has to play the double role an authority figure representing the court to the probationer and of a case worker trying to help him to resolve his personal problems".[80]

Group work often considers as essential to reach the offender for they reaming closed, otherwise. He can be, at ease, with his peers. Thus the main purposes of group work are:

1. The strengthening of the security of the individual in the framework of the groups that he does not feel alone and helpless, but also moves towards not being, wholly dependent on it.
2. The strengthening of the individual's independence by helping him to actually participate in group discussions, not to submit to the gang leader or a powerful sub-group.
3. The introduction of an adult, who represents the values of a society they often reject because of his accepting attitude represents adult security and love. The delinquent can meet this adult group, while still feeling the support of his contemporaries and relating in different degrees of intensity. It also provides an opportunity of gaining satisfaction, in the need for adventure and experimentation in various ways that are accepted by society.
4. An opportunity to gain inner resilience and status with the group through accomplishments in activities accepted by society."[81]

Some opines that *Group counseling* was found to be inadequate to meet the problems faced by the delinquents in several countries.

"Group counseling was introduced since long but their training has become difficult in view of the problems of today's delinquent".[82]

Group work in the correction of delinquents is a better method to some of the offender, is reacting with a group in the controlled conditions stipulated by the officer concerned.

"Social group work, is a method of rendering service to persons, through providing experience in groups. Development of the person towards his individual potential, improvement of relationship and social functioning competencies, and social action are recognised as purposes of social group work. The worker functions within a framework of ethical and social values. In social group work, the worker helps members and group to use their abilities and strengths. The worker uses himself is the different ways in relation with to specific objectives. The group member and the group are inextricably and the condition of each is bonded to affect to each other.

There can be three main reasons for the use of the group, in the treatment of the delinquent and the criminal. First, the dynamics of the offender himself. Second, the specific correctional setting in which he finds him. Thirdly, the specific purpose for which society has put him into the correctional setting".[83]

Group therapy, group counseling and specialised institutions were accepted and introduced as different forms of treatment in the 1950's in England.

"About the administrative scenario and cites newer directions in treatment like: midway institutions for mentally diseased, psychopathic personality. Group therapy as a technique has been experimented in institutions with exciting results. Group counseling differencing it for, professional group therapy is a fairly new concept in the correctional service particularly in institutions."[84]

Co-operative communities are the answer to the present day problems, which includes the increase in and Juvenile adult crimes.

"Despite anything science can do about it, mankind faces the bleak prospect of cities doomed to increasing congesting, increasing tension and anxiety, increasing water and air pollution and increasing change of subtler kind, also mental and spiritual change. Solutions must be found for mankind is rapidly losing faith in anything except what may and proceed with childish arrogance as "The great God, Ego".[85]

"The clients who come through the doors of probation officers are generally not, the kind of material that caseworkers are, looking for. They are reluctant conscripts to the treatment process, unmotivated towards introspection and used to expressing their feelings". [86]

With regard to the Aftercare and rehabilitation, the Committee recommended that the "Financial consideration should not in any way handicap programmes of care, welfare training and treatment of women offenders".[87]

Post Sentencing dispositions

The Competent authority shall have, at its disposal, a wide range of post sentencing alternatives, in order to avoid institutional and to assist offenders in their early reintegration society.

Post-sentencing dispositions include:

(a) Furlough and half-way houses

(b) Work or education release

(c) Various forms of parole:

(d) Remission

(e) Pardon."[88]

The All India Committee on Jail Reforms emphasises the proper implementation of aftercare service.

Aftercare services should include all kinds of help, which could result in the proper readjustment of the released prisoners in the society. They should be well equipped for all types of assistance including:

(a) Guidance and counseling to prisoners overcome their psychological and social problems:

(b) Educating prisoners about their role in the society as law abiding citizens

(c) Legal assistance to those whose land has been grabbed

(d) Securing cooperation of prisoners, families in accepting them back after release:

(e) Material assistance in the form of food, clothing and journey expenses enabling them, to reach a safe place, in the society after their release from the prison: and

(f) Distribution if printed literature to inmates, detailing after care facilities and programmes open for them, both from Government agencies and from voluntary organisations."[89]

The aftercare supervision under the Probation Officer is to become an integral part of institutional treatment, as recommended by the Jail Reforms Committee.

"The first thing we envisage in this regard, is that the process of aftercare and rehabilitation of the offender should be an integral part of the process of his institutional care and treatment. Delinking the two will lead us nowhere."[90]

The All India Committee on Jail Reforms, 1980-83 recommend the established aftercare organisation in such a way that:

"Efforts should be made to set up at least one voluntary organisation in each district. Till such Voluntary Organisation came forward aftercare work should be done by Probation Officers in the field and Head Quarters organisation of the department". [91]

The Probation Officer as the Aftercare Officers were personally duty bound to supervise and bring back before the court upon violation of conditions of bond executive upon releases.

Probation Officers are is to conduct inquiry and supervision of the offenders released by courts. Aftercare if person as form Juvenile Justice Homes, Borstal Schools, prisoners and matrimonial counseling.

Until 1948, an officer's name was inserted into each probation order and the officer was, and still is, responsible to the court for his handling of any probation supervision: he personally just bring back to court, probationers, who break the conditions of their order, and he does this not as an official of the probation service but in his own right as the supervising officer."[92]

Industrial units are to be established with the involvement of after care organisation.

"Small scale industries departments of State government/ Union Territory Administrations should formulate schemes of small production units, which could be run by ex-prisoners on cooperative basis, Cooperative could be organised in the field, carpentry, weaving, iron pipe furniture, steel furniture etc., which are jobs, commonly organised in Indian Prisons. These units can be financed by State Finance Corporations, Cooperative and other Banks under their Innovative banking schemes. Government departments should give preference to these units, in purchasing goods manufactured by them. The aftercare and follow-up

Units will have to play a vital and continued role in the establishment and efficient functioning of such cooperatives".[93]

The probation and the aftercare and follow-up service in India speak of a tragic story pointing out the disappointing state of affairs to which the juvenile offenders are allowed to drift in. Why does this happen is not a difficult question to answer.

"Our attention has so far been on developing institutions for juvenile offenders, the consequence of which has been that both non-institutional programmes and services have been badly neglected. The dearth of aftercare services has further been caused due to complete ignorance of the nature of problems, that the juveniles face, soon after their discharge from the institutions. There is no significant research on the subject. Prof. M.S. Gore's report is the only, worthwhile document that people rush to consult. The problems in the field of juvenile aftercare are enormous, but things can certainly be improved, if the action is initiated on the following lines:

1. The number of aftercare institutions and organisation should be so raised, as to make them adequate in terms of the nature and need of the problem.
2. Aftercare should be made an integral part of the process of institutional care and treatment. In fact, the planning for aftercare must begin soon after the inmate enters the institutions.
3. Aftercare organisation that exists in a moribund state should be revitalised and adequate financial aid be given to them by concerned governmental departments in order to make them work, effectively in the task of, reintegrating the ex-inmates of correctional institutions in the Community.
4. Aftercare of offenders discharged from juvenile correctional institutions should be, the statutory function of the correctional services.
5. There should be a properly staffed Aftercare and follow-up unit at the headquarter organisations of Correctional Services in each State/Union territory.
6. Efforts should be made to set up, at-least one voluntary organisation in each district to which the work of extending help, to released inmates of correctional institutions could be entrusted.
7. Voluntary workers engaged in aftercare and rehabilitation work should be given necessary encouragement, help and guidance from the officials of the concerned governmental department.

8. Both voluntary and governmental organisations departments concerned with aftercare and follow up work should be so equipped as to make them discharge their roles and responsibility effectively.
9. State governments should consider the desirability of taking suitable measures to ensure that the juveniles do not suffer any disability in finding employment after release from Correctional institutions.[94]

A comprehensive aftercare programme was initiated during the Second and Third Five Year Plans, at the instance of the Central Social Welfare Board. The Central Social Welfare Board appointed an Advisory Committee on Aftercare programmers in the year of 1954 under the Chairmanship of Prof. M.S. Gore of the Tata Institute of Social Sciences, Bombay. The Committee studied the nature and size of the problem of those adults and juveniles who were discharged from correctional institutions. Referring to the state of affairs in regard to aftercare programmers and services, the Committee observed with the exception of a few aftercare organisations, to meet the needs of persons discharged from custodial institutions, there was hardly any work, which had been done, is this field. Even these aftercare organisations for ex-convicts and juvenile delinquents had developed only in some of the districts of a few States.

The Crisis of Aftercare Organisation

"The genesis of the failure of aftercare organisation lies in the following.

1. Frustration, discouragement, lack of public appreciation and constant financial troubles.
2. Marked inadequacy of organisational resources at the command of organisations.
3. Lack of cooperation from the concerned Governmental departments.
4. Woeful inadequacy of grants-in-aid
5. Shortage of dedicated workers.
6. Loss of organisations' public credibility.
7. Public's unwillingness to accept ex-offenders as persons worthy of trust, confidence and help.
8. Little cooperation from the police, responsible citizenry and allied social service organisations."[95]

If the Society, Legislative, the Police, Judiciary, Correctional personnel and Human rights organisations in India *play their role properly,* Crime can be prevented controlled and reduced, to a greater extend?"[96]

"Now remand prisoners continue to be in custody for a period more than the maximum period of imprisonment prescribed for the offence committed". [97]

Aftercare supervision of inmates released from Borstal schools is valuable and the Committee suggests to introduce aftercare supervision in India also, that.

"The system of aftercare to be exercised over ex-inmates, both during the period, if any, spent on license and afterward, in one of the most important points connected with the scheme of Special Institutions. As far as we could judge, the provision for the aftercare of inmates discharged from the Borstal institutions of Great Britain is the most valuable feature of the English system. We wish to insist very strongly on the importance of developing in India some corresponding method for assisting and watching over adolescent offenders released form Special Institutions." [98]

Regarding Volunteers and Other Community Resources, the Tokyo rules says:

"Public participation should be regarded as an opportunity for members of the community to secure the protection of their society."[99]

"Government agencies, the private sector and the general public should get encouragement to support voluntary organisations that promote non-custodial measures. Conferences, seminars, symposia and other activities should be regularly organised to standardise of the need for public participation in the application of non – custodial measures.

All from of mass media should be, utilised to help, create a constructive public attitude leading to activities conducive to a broader application of non custodial treatment and the social integrate on of offenders.

Every effort should be made to inform the public of the importance of its role in the implementation non-custodial measures."[100]

"The probationer should not visit the probation officer at the appointed time merely to sign the concerned register and the papers, but should look forward to such opportunities to meet the Probation Officer who will happily discuss the probationer's problems and together with him evolve ways and means of effectively solving them.

The Probation Officer should be a highly resourceful person directing his probationer to agencies of medical, educational, vocational and recreational facilities, which will assist towards the probationer's homogeneous development. He must also be a trained social worker who should instead of being aseptic, have an absolute faith in the modern philosophy of correction."[101]

Boys scouts provides activities to inculcate good character in young minds. So the Boys clubs or Boy Scouts are to be adopted as an aid to probation work. Unfortunately such programmes are not being inducted into probation service in India so far.

"It is not necessary to attempt any detailed account of the methods to be followed in probation work. It was generally agreed that the boy's clubs or the Boy Scout organisations, as they found in Great Britain, are valuable aids, to the probation work, as providing a fresh outlet for energy a fresh source of interest". [102]

The author Kiran Bedi is, an IPS officer and recipient of Raman Magsaysay Award for social services. The present book '*As I see... it*', her sharing of experience with prisoners, their families, drug addicts, slum children and adolescents. The book gives public awareness about the issues behind the above said problems. In such a way the book analyses 68 cases in a simple and lucid way. The book helps one to perceive the social reality prevailing in India. This Awareness helps personel and social change in a positive way."[103]

The constructive programmes are, in other words, a technique for uniting the people, for the cause of freedom struggle at the same time leading to economic self-sufficiency to the people.

E.F. Schumacher, a Western economist who, perceived the importance of Gandhian economic remedies to solve unemployment, suggested his own remedies in the Gandhian model like:

(i) "Agro-based industries should be established in rural areas and small towns,

(ii) The means of such production should be simple and cheap and should be within the reach of an average individual,

(iii) Raw materials must be locally available for production and consumption, and

(iv) Quantum of production per man is not important but the main consideration is, maximum employment potentialities for the unemployed and the underemployed".[104]

The various types of *substance Abuse treatment* services that are offered through these contracts include the following, like:

- "Substance abuse assessment and treatment planning
- Detoxification Services
- Day Treatment Services
- Residential Substance abuse treatment
- Out patient treatment
- Alcohol and Drug free housing
- Alcohol a drug education
- Individual group and family counseling
- Social and recreational services
- Transportation
- Referred to other appropriate community resources."[105]

Exploring the Non-custodial punishments: Zimbabwe's Community Service Scheme, by, Paddington Garweand Andrew Msengezi:

> "there is growing realisation in Africa and elsewhere that imprisonment is not the solution to offending behaviour and it's a very expensive option."[106]

The World Cancer Research fund directory Guidelines to Lower Your Cancer Risks can be used for physical well being of the offender:

1. "Eat more vegetables, fruits, whole grain bread and cereals.
2. Cut down the amount of fat in your diet, both saturated and unsaturated from the current average of approximately 41 per cent to a level of 30 per cent of total calories.
3. Consume Salt-cured, salt-picked and smoked foods only in moderation
4. Drink alcohol in moderation if at all."[107]

The United Nations Guidelines for the Prevention of Juvenile delinquency states about *the role of education*:

1. "Governments are under an obligation to make public education accessible to all young persons. Education systems should, in addition to their academic and vocational training activities, devote particular attention to the following:

(a) Teaching of basic values and developing respect for the child's own cultural identity and patterns, for the social values of the country in which the child is living, for civilisations different from the child's own and for human rights and fundamental freedoms;

(b) Promotion and development of the personality, talents and mental and physical abilities of young people to their fullest potential;

(c) Involvement of young persons as active and effective participants in, rather than mere objects of, the educational process;

(d) Undertaking activities that foster, a sense of identity with and of belonging to the school and the community;

(e) Encouragement of young persons to understand and respect diverse views and opinions, as well as cultural and other difference;

(f) Provision of information and guidance regarding vocational training employment opportunities and career development;

(g) Provision of positive emotional support to young persons and the avoidance of psychological maltreatment;

(h) Avoidance of harsh disciplinary measures particularly corporal punishment:

2. Educational systems should seek to work together with parents, community organisations and agencies concerned with the activities of young persons.

3. Young persons and their families should be informed about the law and their rights and responsibilities under the law, as well as the universal value system, including United Nations instruments.

4. Educational systems should extend particular care and attention to young persons who are at social risk. Specialised prevention programmes and educational materials, curricula, approaches and tools should be developed and fully utilised.

5. Special attention should be given to comprehensive policies and strategies for the prevention of alcohol, drug and other substances abuse by young persons. Teachers and other professionals should be equipped and trained to prevent and deal with these problems, information on the use and abuse of drugs, including alcohol, should be made available to the student body.

6. Schools should serve as resource and referral centers, for the provision of medical, counseling and other services, to young persons, particularly those with special needs and suffering from abuse, neglect, victimisation and exploitation.

7. Through a variety of educational programmes teachers and other adults and the student body should be sensitised to the problems,

needs and perceptions of young persons, particularly those belonging to underprivileged, disadvantaged, ethnic or other minority and low-income groups.

8. School systems should attempt to meet and promote the highest professional and educational standards with respect to curricula, teaching and learning methods and approaches, and the recruitment and training of qualified teachers. Regular monitoring and assessment of performance by the appropriate professional organisations and authorities should be ensured."[108]

The guidelines with regard to the family of the young persons are as below:

"11. Every society should place a high priority on the needs and well-being of the family and of all its members.

12. Since the *family* is the central unit, responsible for the primary socialisation of children, governmental and social efforts to preserve the integrity of the family, including the extended family, should be pursued. The society has the responsibility, to assist the family in providing care and protection and in censuring the physical and mental well being of children. Adequate arrangements including *day-care* should be provided.

13. Governments should establish policies that are conducive, to the bringing up of children in stable and settled family environments. Families in needs of assistance, in the resolution of conditions of instability or conflict should be provided with requisite services.

14. Where a stable and settled family environment is lacking and when community efforts to assist parents, in this regard have failed and the extended family cannot fulfill this role, alternative placements, including *foster care* and *adoption*, should be considered. Such placement should replicate, to the extent possible, a stable and settled family environment. While, at the same time, establishing a sense of permanency for children, thus avoiding problems associated with 'foster drift'.

15. Special attention should be given to children of *families affected by problems,* brought about by rapid and uneven economic, social and, cultural change, in particular the children of indigenous, migrant and refugee families. As such changes may disrupt the social capacity of the family, to secure the traditional rearing and nurturing of children, often as a result of role and culture conflict, innovative and socially constructive modalities for the socialisation of children have to be designed.

16. Measures should be taken and programmes developed to provide families with the opportunity *to learn about parental roles* and obligations as regards child development and child care, promoting positive parent-child relationships, sensitising parents to the problems of children and young persons and encouraging their involvement in family and community – based activities.
17. Governments should take measures to promote family cohesion and harmony and to *discourage the separation of children* from their parents, unless circumstances affecting the welfare and future of the child leave no viable alternative.
18. It is important to emphasise the socialisation function of the family and extended family; it is also equally important to *recognise the future role*, responsibilities, participation and partnership of young persons in society.
19. In ensuring the right of the child to proper socialisation. Governments and other agencies should rely on existing social and legal agencies, but, whenever traditional institutions and customs are no longer effective, they should also provide and allow for innovative measures."[109]

The rule 10 states that,

"Emphasis should be placed on preventive policies, facilitating the successful socialisation and integration of all children and young persons, in particular, through the family, the community, peer group, schools, vocational training and the world of work, as well as through voluntary organisations. Due respect should be given to the proper personal development of children and young persons, and they should be accepted as full and equal partners socialisation and integration process."[110]

Rule 29 state that,

"School systems should plan, develop and implement extra-curricular activities of interest to young persons, in co-operation with community groups; rule 30 states, special assistance should be given to children and young persons who find it difficult to comply with attendance codes, and to 'dropouts'; rule 31 states that, Schools should promote policies and rules that are fair and just; students should be represented in school policy, including policy on disciplines, and decision-making."[111]

Industrial units are to be established with the involvement of After Care organisation with Small Scale Industries Department of State Governments/Union Territory Administrations should formulate schemes of small production units, which could be run by ex-prisoners, on a cooperative basis. These Cooperatives could be organised, in the field of carpet weaving, carpentry, iron pipe furniture, steel furniture etc., which are jobs, commonly organised in Indian Prisons. State Finance Corporations, Cooperative and other Banks under their innovative banking schemes can finance these units. The Government department should give preference to those units, in purchasing goods manufactured by them. The After-Care and Follow-up Units will have to play a vital and continued role in the establishment and efficient functioning of such cooperatives"[112]

The Probation Officer, Voluntary Probation officer and Aftercare officer are to exercise their knowledge, and skill in imparting the reformation and rehabilitation of the probationers under supervision. The Prison Reforms committees of India and United nations had proposed several useful and valid recommendations in this regard. Each probationer is different in his or her personal, educational, social, cultural and economic status. Hence, it is the educational qualification of the Probation Officer, Budgetary allocation for reformation and proper rehabilitation work and the public participation are the key factors, needs attention of all concerned.

Footnotes

1. United Nations (1951) *Probation and Related measures,* U.N. Publication, New York, p. 7.
2. *Story of Ungulimala* (2005) Pustak Mahal, New Delhi, p. 7.
3. United Nations – (1951) *Probation and related measures,* United Nations Publication Division, New York, p. 243.
4. United Nations – (1951), *Probation and related measures,* United Nations Publication Division, p. 242.
5. V.V. Devasia and Leelamma Devasia (1992) *Criminology Victimology and Corrections,* Ashish Publishing House, 8/81, Punjabi Bagh, New Delhi – 110026, p. 138.
6. Ram Ahuja (2000), *Criminology,* Rawat Publication, Satyam Apartments, sector – 3, Jawahar Nagar, Jaipur – 302004, p. 341.
7. Kum Kum Chadha (1983) *The Indian Jail – a contemporary document,* Vikas publishing house, Pvt. Ltd., 5 Ansari Road, New Delhi – 110002, p. 179.
8. Tim Newell (2000), *Forgiving Justice- Quaker Vision for Criminal Justice, Swarthmore Lecture 2000,* Quaker home service, friend's house, Euston Road, London NWI 2 BJ, p. 33.

9. Gene Sharp (June 1997), *Gandhiji wields the weapon of moral power,* Navajivan Publishing house, Ahmedabad – 380014, p. 176.

10. M.K. Gandhi, complied by H.M. Vyas (May 1996) *Gandhiji Expects,* Navajivan Publishing house, Ahmedabad – 380014, p. 185.

11. M.K. Gandhi (1969) *Collected works of Mahatma Gandhi,* Vol. 3, Publication Division Government of India, New Delhi, pp. 219-20.

12. M.K. Gandhi (2002) *Gandhi,* Navajivan publishing House, Ahmedabad–380014, p. 111.

13. M.K. Gandhi (2004), *Ramandma,* Navajivan Publishing House, Ahmedabad – 380024, p. 51.

14. Davis George (2000) *Dynamics of Power: The Gandhian perspective,* Frank Bros & Co (Publishers) Ltd., 4675 – A, Ansari Road, 21 Daryaganj, New Delhi – 110 002, pp. 148-49.

15. Davis George (200), *Dynamics of Power: The Gandhiyan Perspective,* Frank Bros and Co Publishers Ltd., 4675-A, Ansari Road, 21 Daryaganj, New Delhi – 110002, p. 28.

16. Vishvanath Tandon (1992) *Acharaya Vinoba Bhave,* Publication Division Government of India, New Delhi, p. 55.

17. M.K. Gandhi (1948) *Constructive Programme – Its meaning and place,* Navajivan Publishing House, Ahmedabad – 14, p. 7.

18. Anil Dutta Mishra (2002) *Rediscovering Gandhi,* Mittal Publications, A- 110, Mohan Garden, New Delhi -110059, pp. 138-9.

19. B.K. Ahuwalla (1970) *M.K. Gandhi – Selected Writings,* Sagar Publications, Ved Mansion, 72 Janpath, P.O. Box, 553, New Delhi – 1, p. 341.

20. Bharathan Kumarappa (January 1954), *M.K. Gandhi 'Sarvodaya'* Navajivan Publishing Trust, Ahmedabad – 14, p. 110.

21. CWMC, Vol. 15, (1969) p. 38; Kottukal Sreedhar Kurup (1999) *Gandhian Concept of Family system,* Southern Book Star. T.C. 13.1212, Kumarapuram, Medical College P.O., Thriruvananthapuram - 11 Kerala, p. 56.

22. M.K. Gandhi (May-2996) *Gandhi expects,* Navajivan Publishing House, Ahmedabad 380014, p. 99.

23. M.Y. Ghorpade (28 October 1969) *Memorial lecture on Gandhiyan– Concepts, Challenges to present day* G 346 K.G. 13146, Gandhi museum Library, Madurai 20, pp. 5-9.

24. N.K. Chakrabarti (1999), *Social Defense in the Administration of Criminal Justice,* Deep & Deep publications Pvt. Ltd., F – 159 Rajouri Gardens, New Delhi – 110027, p. 33.
25. S. Muthuswamy (Jan 2002), *Crime Control in India,* published in the *Social Defense,* Quarterly journal by National Institute of Social Defense, New Delhi, Vol. 53, No-151, p. 58.
26. M.K. Gandhi (January 2005) *The moral basis of vegetarianism,* Navajivan Publishing House, Ahemedabad 380014, p. 22.
27. *Gita,* Chapter II, from Stansas (62 & 63).
28. N.K. Chakrabarti (1999) *Social Defense in the Administration of Criminal Justice,* Deep and Deep Publications Pvt. Ltd., F-159 Rajouri Gardens, New Delhi – 110027, p. 48.
29. R.G. Singh (1985), *Sociology of Deviance,* Jainsons Publication, 4, Ajith Arcade, Kailash Colony, New Delhi, 110048, p. 129.
30. Phyllida Paresole (1967), *The Work of the Probation and Aftercare Officer,* Routledge and Kegan Pual Ltd., Broad way House, 68-74, Carter Lane, London, EC4, p. 42.
31. Phyllida Paresole (1967), *The Work of the Probation and Aftercare Officer,* Routledge and Kegan Pual Ltd., Broad way House, 68-74, Carter Lane, London, EC4, p. 37.
32. *Ibid.,* pp. 44-45.
33. *Ibid.,* pp. 50-51.
34. Dr. J. Visuvathas Jeyasingh (1987) *Deviant Children,* Published by Mr. Aiya swami, Proprietor Sri. Iyengar Industries, Madras, pp. 122-23.
35. W.C. Reckless (1952), *Jail Administration in India,* Government Press, Simla, p. 36.
36. Dr. W.C. Reckless (1952) *Jail Administration in India,* Govt. of India Publication, Simla, p. 36.
37. Sri. Krishna Datta Bhatta (1962)…*and they gave up dacoity,* A.B. Sarva Seva Prakasan, Rajghat Varanasi, p. 297.
38. Dr. J. Visuvathas Jeyasingh (1987) *Deviant Children,* Sri. Iyengar industries, Madras, p. 149.
39. Sri. Aurobindo (1997) *Tales of Prison life,* Sri. Aurobindo Ashram, Pondicherry, pp. 41-42.
40. V.V. Devasia and Leelamma (1992) *Criminology, Victimology and Corrections,* Ashish Publishing House, New Delhi 110026, p. 144.

41. Sri. Aurobindo (1997) *Tales of Prison life,* Sri Aurobindo Ashram, Pondicherry, pp. 42-44.

42. Vishvanath Tandon (February 1992) *Acharaya Vinoba Bhave,* Publication Division, Ministry of Information and Broadcasting, Patiala House, New Delhi – 110001, pp. 81-83.

43. *Kerala Prison Rules – 1958,* Government Press, Trivandrum-01, p. 33.

44. *Ibid.,* p. 6.

45. Dr. Sunil. K. Bhattacharya (2000) *Juvenile Justice – An India Scenario,* Regency Publications, 20/36-G, Old Market, West Patel Nagar, New Delhi – 110008, p. 147.

46. Tim Newell (2000) *Forgiving Justice – Quaker vision for Criminal Justice, Swarthmore Lecturer 2000,* Quaker Home Service, Friends House, Euston Road, London, NWI 2 BJ, p. 66.

47. Nirumal Kanti Chakraborti (October 1989) *Social Defense,* Vol. XX VIII No. 98, National Institute of Social Defense, New Delhi - 66 (Page – 48)

48. *All India Jail Manual Committee – 1957 – 59* Government of India Press, New Delhi, (Para 146), item IX, p. 86.

49. M.S. Sabins (1995) *Juvenile Justice and Juvenile Correction, Pride and Prudence,* Somaiya Publications Pvt. Ltd., New Delhi, p. 258.

50. Hilary Walker, Bill Beaumont (1981) *Probation Critical Theory and Socialist Practice,* Basil Blackwell Publisher limited, 108 Cowley Road, Oxford, OX4, IJF, England, p. 30.

51. *Report of the Indian Jails Committee 1919 -20,* Vol. I, Government of India Press, Simla, para-44 A, pp. 229-30.

52. Hillary walker and Bill Beaumont (1981) *Probation Critical Theory and Socialist Practice,* Basil Blackwell Publishers Ltd., Oxford, England, p. 25.

53. Rani Dhawan Shankaradas (Editor) (2000), *Punishment and the Prison Indian and International perspective,* Sage publication India Pvt. Ltd., 32 Market, Greater Kailash-1, New Delhi – 110048, p. 247.

54. Shrikrishna Datta Bhatta (1962) *...and they gave up dacoity,* A.B. Sarva Seva Sangh Prakashan, Rajghat, Varanasi, p. 298.

55. *California Department of Corrections an overview of substance*

Abuse programmes, (December 1999) Office of the substance abuse programmes, P.O. Box 942883, Saeramento CA 94283 – 001, p. 5.

56. Panakal. J.J. (1986) *Indian Prison and Correctional Service,* Indian journal of Criminology (14, 2, 1986).
57. Robert Mayer, (19460 *Young People in Trouble,* Victor Gallancy Ltd., London, pp. 54-55.
58. *All India Jail Manual Committee- 1957-59,* Government of India Press, New Delhi, pp. 80-81.
59. Studt, Elliot (1959) *Education for Social Workers In Correction Field,* Council of Social Work Education, New York, p. 175.
60. Devasia, V.V., and Leelamma Devasia (1988) *Prison as a Social System and Prisonisation in relation to Prison Administration.* The Indian Journal of Public Administration Vol. (xxxiv), New Delhi, pp. 144-153.
61. Rani Dhawan Shankar Dass (2000) *Punishment and Prison,* Sage publications India Pvt. Ltd., 32 maket, Greater Kailash – 1, New Delhi 110048, p. 243.
62. M.S. Sabins (1995) *Juvenile Justice and Juvenile Correction, Pride and Prudence,* Somaiya Publications, Pvt. Ltd., New Delhi, pp. 261-63.
63. V.V. Devasia and Leelamma Devasia (1992), (pp. 127-128); Ram Ahuja (2000) Criminology Rawat publications, Satyam apartments, sector 3, Jain Temple Road, Jawahar Nagar, Jaipur – 302004, p. 118.
64. Ram Ahuja (2000) *Criminology,* Rawat publications, Satyam Apartments, Sector 3, Jain Temple Road, Jawahar Nagar, Jaipur – 302004, p. 118.
65. V.V. Devasia and Leelamma Devasia (1992), p. 146.
66. Saxena, D.P., (1980) *Difficulties in Treatment in Modern Correctional Institutions,* Indian Journal of Criminology, pp. 52-54.
67. Bansal, S.L. (1980) *Discharged Prisoners Aid Societies: A case study of Navajeevan Mandals in Maharashtra,* Indian Journal of Criminology, pp. 67-70.
68. Khan, M.Z. (1983), *Crime Problem A Challenge to Social Scientist,*

Indian Journal of Criminology, pp. 77-87.

69. Boehm, Werner, W. (1956) *Objective of Social Curriculum of the Future,* Council of Social work Education. New York, p. 7.
70. Misra, L.S. and U.S. Agnihothri (1985) *The Community Practices informal Social Controls in Rural India,* Indian Journal of Criminology, pp. 96-102.
71. Roy Guha Ayatilak (1989), *New Dimensions in Criminal Justice Administration,* Indian Journal of Criminology, pp. 26-30.
72. Mohanty. S, (1985), *Understanding Human Factors for better Implementation of work Programme in Jails,* Indian Journal of Criminology, pp. 139-143.
73. Dias. S.M. (1981) "Criminal Justice System – Correctional process problem and possible Remedies", Indian Journal of Criminology, pp. 81-85.
74. V.V. Devasia and Leelamma Devasia (1992), p. 129.
75. M.S. Sabins (1995), pp. 266-77.
76. V.V. Devasia and Leelamma Devasia (1992), p. 142.
77. Report of Indian Jails Committee 1919-20, Vol. I, para–377, p. 200.
78. V.V. Devasia and Leelamma (1992), p. 127.
79. John. F.S., and King B.A. (1958) The Probation Service, p. 129.
80. *Ibid.,* p. 171.
81. V.V. Devasia and Leelamma (1992), p. 127.
82. Roger Hood (1965) Borstal Re-Assesses, Heinemann Educational Book L.T.D., 48 Charles Street, London W-1, p. 22.
83. V.V. Devasia and Leelamma, (1992), p. 130.
84. David Dressler (1959) *Practice and Theory of Probation and Parole* Columbia University Press, New York, pp. 205-07.
85. J. Donald Walters (2004) Hope for a better world, The Small Community Solution, New Age book A-44 Naraina phase – 1 New Delhi- 110028, p. 13.
86. Geoffrey Parkinson, 'I gave them money'. New Society, pp. 52-70.
87. All India Jail Manual Committee 1919-20 Para 132, p. 76
88. Tokyo Rules- 1990.

89. All India Committee on Jail Reforms – 1980-83, Vol. I & II, Ministry of Home Affairs, New Delhi, para- 22- 13.9.1, p. 266.
90. All India Committee on Jail Reforms – 1980-83, Vol. I & II, Ministry of Home Affairs, New Delhi, para- 22- 9, p. 264.
91. All India committee on Jail Reforms – 1980-83, Vol. I & II, Ministry of Home Affairs, New Delhi, para-22- 13.4, p. 276.
92. Phyllida Paresole (1967), *The work of the Probation and Aftercare Officer,* Routledge and Kegan Pual Ltd., Broad way House, 68-74, Carter Lane, London, ECH, pp. 6-7.
93. Indian Jails Committee – 1919 – 20, Vol. I, Government Press, Simla, para- 377, p. 267.
94. S.P. Srivasthav- 1989, pp. 116 – 118.
95. S.P. Srivastav, 1989, p. 115.
96. S. Muthuswamy (2002) Former Chief Probation Superintendent, Crime Control in India: Strategies for the Future, Social Defence – A Quarterly Journal By Nisd, New Delhi – 66 Vol. 53. No. 151. January 2002, p. 59.
97. *Ibid.,* p. 60.
98. Report of the Indian Jails Committee 1919-20, Government Central Press, Simla, Vol. I, para-413, p. 213.
99. The Tokyo Rules (1990).
100. The Tokyo Rules (1990), p. 177.
101. Dr. J. Vishvathas Jeyasingh (1987) Deviant Children, Published By: Mr. Aiya swamy Proprietor Sri. Iyengar Industries, Madras, pp. 122-3.
102. Report of the Indian Jails Committee. 1919-20, Government Central Press, Simla, Vol. I, Appendix IX, p. 482.
103. *Ibid.*
104. E.F. Schumacher, (1977) Small is Beautiful, Radha Krishan, Publications, New Delhi, pp. 160-74.
105. California Department of Corrections, *Overview of Substance Abuse Programmes* December 1999 Prepared By California Dept. of Corrections Office of the Substance Abuse Programmes P.O., Box. 942883, Sieramento, CA 94283 – 0001 (916) 3273707 Calnet 476-3707, p. 34.
106. Rani Dhawn, Shankar Dass (2000), *Punishment and the Prison,*

Indian and International perspective, Sage Publication India Pvt. Ltd., M-32 Market, 'Greater Kailash-1, New Delhi, p. 242.

107. *Dietary Guidelines to Lower Your Cancer Risk* (Published by), Vegetarian Society of Delhi, Ahimsa Sthal, Anuvrat Marg, Mehrauli, New Delhi – 110030, Tel – 011 664. 3248/49, p. 3.

108. The United Nations Guidelines for the Prevention of Juvenile Delinquency.

109. *United Nations Guidelines for the Prevention of Juvenile Delinquency– 1990,* UN Publication, New York, p. 5.

110. Police Research and Development: (July- September 1991) *United Nations Guidelines for the Prevention of Juvenile Delinquency - 1990,* p. 23.

111. United Nations Guidelines for the Prevention of Juvenile Delinquency – (1990).

112. *Indian Jails Committee – 1919* – 20- Vol. I (1920) Government Press, Simla, p. 267.

12

Case Laws on Probation

The Probation of Offenders Act was enacted on 16th May 1958 by the Parliament of India, is a social welfare legislation. Its objective is to mend the ways of selected offenders. It is the prime Act in the field of non-institutional treatment of offenders in India. If the provisions of the act are implemented intelligently, it will help many of the deviants to restore normal social life. The philosophy behind the Act can be observed from the writings of Mahatma Gandhi:

"All criminals should be treated as patients, and jails should be hospitals, admitting this class of patients for treatment and cure. No one commits the crime for the fun of it. It is the diseased mind. The cause of a particular disease should be investigated and removed. There need not be palatial buildings, when the jails become hospitals. No country can afford that, much less a poor country like India. But the outlook of the Jail staff should be, that of physicians and nurses in a hospital. The prisoners should feel that the officials are their friends. They are there to help them to regain their normal mental health, and not harass them anyway. The popular Governments have to issue necessary orders, but meanwhile the jail staff can do not a little, to humanise their administration".[1]

The object of the Probation of Offenders Act is to give, a uniform law and to prevent the offenders becoming harden criminals, due to their mingling with mature criminals in prisons, as stated in various Judgments of the Supreme Court of India, as well as High courts, as it is a non institutional form of correction ordered by the Court.

The important provisions of the Act are:

Section 3 of the Act gives power to the court to release certain first offenders on admonition after finding him guilty considering the age, circumstances of the case and character, the nature of the offence, gravity of the offence and antecedents of the offender. The offences under sections 379,380,382,404 and 420, Indian Penal Code 1860 and any other offence punishable with imprisonment for not more than two years or with fine or with both, will come under its purview and they can be ordered to be released by the judicial officer after due admonition. But the offenders will not be placed under supervision of a Probation officer.

Section 4 of the Probation of Offenders Act 1958, which is giving five sub-sections, is one of the cardinal sections and widely used. It states that any person, irrespective of his age or previous conviction and found guilty for an offence, which is not punishable with death or imprisonment for life can be considered for releasing on probation. Here also the court shall consider the circumstances in which the offence was committed: the nature of the offence; the reputation or character of the offender and the report of the Probation occupation. Then offender shall be placed under the supervision of the Probation Officer for a minimum period of one year; and a maximum period of three years under Sub Section (3) of section 4 of the Act. Under sub section (1) of section 4, he will be released on probation with or without sureties are having fixed place of abode after executing a Bond. The bond shall contain the conditions to be observed, like, the change of residence, occupation, abstention firm intoxicants or any other matter as the court may think fit. After explaining the conditions of the bond, the judge may given a copy each of the supervision order to the offenders, the sureties and to the Probation Officer. Thus it is a benevolent provision and by preventing a person becoming a hardened criminal, the society gains a lot materially and morally in the long run. But misplaced leniency should not be shown, for the sake of the society. The person placed under supervision of a Probation Officer is called a Probationer. The section also envisages that the Magistrate shall explain the conditions of the bond to him and give a copy to him. Copies may also be given to the Probation Officer concerned.

Section 5 states that upon release of an offender under section 3 or 4 of the act, the court may further order to pay compensation and costs as it thinks reasonable. That is there is no upper limit, prescribed for the amount to be awarded as compensation. The actual pecuniary loss or indirect pecuniary loss sustained, the value of their time, the expenses of the suit; mental sufferings, insults etc., will be considered for calculating the amount.

Section 6 of the Act, makes it mandatory, on the part of the court to satisfy itself considering the character of the offender, the circumstances of the case, the nature of the offence, whether it would be desirable to deal with under section 3 or section 4 of the Probation Offenders Act, in all the cases where the age of offender is below 21 years; and the offence not punishable with imprisonment of life. In case he is ordered for imprisonment, the court passes the order, stating the reasons, for not considering to call for the report on the offender from the Probation Officer.

This section specifically provides that it is mandatory on the of the court to call for the report of the Probation Officer and consider it, if any. if an offender is below 21 years.

Section 7 states that the report of the Probation Officer shall be confidential and only if the court considers it fit, the substance of the report may be divulged to the offender. This is to help the offender to produce evidence to defend himself.

Section 8 states that on the interest of the Probationer or Public; and upon the application of the Probation Officer, the court may order to vary the conditions of the bond; or, extending or diminishing the duration of the bond. In any case the duration shall not be extended to more than three years from the original order. Before making such an order the probationer and his sureties are to be given an opportunity to be heard.

Section 9 of the Probation of Offenders Act, stipulates the procedures to be taken, in case the probationer, under supervision fails to observe the conditions of the bond. Upon the report of the Probation Officer or otherwise the court which released him on probation may issue a warrant of arrest; and summons to his sureties, to appear before the court. Then the court may remand him or released him on bail till the case is concluded. When the court concludes that the probationer had failed to observe the conditions of his bond, it would sentence him for the original offence; or impose a penalty not exceeding Rupees fifty, if the failure is for the first time. But if such penalty is not paid then the court may sentence the probationer for the original offence. This section shows the importance to be given for the protection of the society, also that the probation is not a left off.

Section 11 states that if a person below 21 years is convicted by a court and declined to deal under section 3 or 4 of the Probation of Offenders Act, the higher court can call for and examine the records upon the application of the convicted person or the Probation Officer. The Appellate Court or High Court has the power of revision, in the case or a person dealt under section 3 or 4 of the Act.

Section 12 says that there will be no disqualification attached to conviction if the probationer satisfactorily completes the period under supervision, as per section 4 of, the Probation of Offenders Act.

Section 13 defines the Probation Officer:

(a) A person appointed to be a Probation Officer by the State Government or recognised as such by the State Government; or

(b) A person provided for this purpose by a society recognised in this behalf by the State Government; or

(c) In any exceptional case, any other person, who, in the opinion of the court, is fit to act as a Probation Officer in the special circumstance of the case.

The Probation Officer will be named in the supervision order and it can be changed at any time by the Court or by the District Magistrate.

Section 14 provides the duties of the Probation Officer as under.

(a) Inquire, in accordance with any directions of a court, into the circumstances or home surroundings of any person accused of an offence with a view to assist the court in determining the most suitable method in dealing with him and submit reports to the courts;

(b) Supervise probationers and other persons placed under his supervision, and, where necessary, endeavour to find them suitable employment;

(c) Dvise and assist offenders in the payment if compensation or costs ordered by the court;

(d) Advise and assist, in such cases and in such manner as may be prescribed, persons who have been released under Section 4; and the duties relating to other statutes are:

The Kerala Prison Rules were, as per the powers conferred under section 59 of the Prisons Act 1894 (Central Act IX of 1894).

The Rules with the duties and responsibilities of personnel in prisons; the procedures with regard to classification of prisoners, Daily routine, offences and punishments, remission system, Dietary, Cloths and bedding convict labour, jail industry; leave, transfer, release, Advisory Board, escapes, medical examination and Hospital management, sanitation, water supply, under trial prisoners, female prisoners, youthful prisoners, lunatics, lepers, TB, Welfare officer, etc.

Rule 905 (7) states that, the Welfare Officer shall work in liaison with the prisoners, their families, *Probation Officers,* and the Aftercare Agencies Associations, with a view to paving the way for the social rehabilitation of prisoners upon their discharge by arranging for any job, placement or by extending assistance to find means of livelihood. Sub rule (8) states;

"He shall make use of pre release programmes as a stepping stone for arranging the aftercare and rehabilitation of offenders". [2]

Immoral Traffic (Prevention) Act, 1986 is an Act in pursuance of the international convention signed at New York on the 9th day of may 1950 for prevention of immoral traffic. It defines prostitution as the sexual exploitation or abuse of persons for commercial purposes.

The Act envisages punishments as well as corrective measures to offenders, where the role of probation officers, comes as under.

Section 19 (3) states that, "The magistrate having jurisdiction may make an inquiry, including an inquiry by the Probation Officer into the personality, conditions of the home and the prospect of rehabilitation if the applicant make an order that the applicant be kept (i) in a Protective Home, or (ii) in a corrective institution or (iii) under supervision of a person for such period as may be prescribed in the order."[3].

Here the social inquiry by the magistrate can be ordered to be conducted through the Probation Officer concerned.

The Narcotic Drugs and Psychotropic Substances Act 1985 provides stringent punishment. But the Act has provision to release, an addict who is found guilty of possessing small quantity of drugs as said under section 27 of the Act. The offender will be considered for detoxification treatment. Upon successful competition of treatment he can be released on probation for one year. This is stated in section 39 of the Act. Again the section 33 states that a person who is under 18 years of age, can be released on Probation under section 360 of the Criminal Procedure Code of 1973. The section 360 of the Code ceases to operate, where the provisions of the Probation of Offenders Act 1958 are in force. In this way, probation can also be considered for persons below 18 years of age and also for drug addicts who possess small quantity of psychotropic substances or narcotic drugs for his personal consumption.[4]

The *Universal Declaration of Human Rights* adopted and proclaimed as General Assembly resolution 217 (a) (III) of 10, December 1948. It is meant to probation a common standard of achievement for all people of all Nations; to the end that every individual and every organ of society, keeping this Declaration constantly in mind, shall strive by teaching and education to promote respect for these rights and freedom and by progressive measures, national and international to serve their universal and effective recognition and observance both among the people union of member States themselves and among the people of union territories under their jurisdiction. The rights are relating to equality, freedom, justice, association, movement, and nondiscrimination etc. of all persons. Article 9: No one shall be subjected to arbitrary arrest, detention or exile. Article-11: Everyone charged with a penal offence has the right to be presumed innocent until proved guilty according to law in a public trial at which he has headed all the guarantees necessary for his defense". 9 (5) States: Anyone who has been a victim of unlawful arrest or detention shall have an enforceable right to compensation."[5]

International Covenant on Civil and Political Rights adopted and General Assembly resolution 2200 A (XXI) of 16 December 1966 enter into force: 23 March 1976, in a accordance with a total of 49 articles also envisages several rights to the citizens in the member countries.

The following are *the dictums* relating to Probation supervision from the judgments of the Higher Courts of India.

1. The Supreme Court observed in a case for smuggling of gold charged under section 135 (i) and (ii) of the Customs Act 1962 against an accused aged 24 years, that:

"It was not desirable to allow the benefit of probation law to such professional offenders and that these offences being injurious to the public at large need to be tackled sternly".[6]

2. Justices A.N. Grover and M.A, Being of the Supreme Court held, that the court should not lightly resort to the provision of Probation Offenders Act:

"*Adulteration of food* is a menace to public health. The Act has been enacted with the aim of eradicating that anti-social evil and for enduring purity in the articles of food. In view of the above object of the Act and the intention of the Legislature as revealed by the fact that a minimum sentence of imprisonment for a period of six months and a fine of Rupees one thousand has been prescribed, the court should not lightly resort to the provisions of the Probation Act, in the case of persons above 21 years of age found guilty of officers under the Act". [7]

3. Probation is not applicable to *Food Adulteration Act 1954,* as reiterated by justice V.R. Krishna Iyer, where the accused sold adulterated 'sugar' with prohibited sweetener 'saccharin' and 'cyclamate', that:

"The kindly application of probation principle is negated by the imperatives of social defence and the probabilities of moral proselytisation. No chance can be taken by society with a man whose antisocial operations guised as at respectable trade, which imperils numerous innocents. He is a, security risk, Secondary those economic offences committed by white-collar criminals are unlikely to be dissuaded by the gentle probationary process".[8]

4. In a case charged under section 376 IPC for the abduction of a teenage girl and forcing sexual submission the Supreme Court held, that:

"The probation offenders Act should not be extended to an abominable culprit who had shown sufficient expertise in the art of abduction, seduction and sale of girls. It is an insulting stultification of the amelioratory legislations like Probation of Offenders Act to extent its considerate provisions to such anti-special socialist criminal."[9]

5. Probation was not by the granted to a person of 22 years who committed rape of his neighbor's wife aged 24 years, by stating that:

"Despite the fact that the accused was young offender that he had no criminal record, he had committed the crime in a fit of momentary impulse and was repentant for his act, that he was related to victim's family who were ready to forgive the molester keeping in view of his relationship with them, no leniency can be shown to the accused in cases of such 'lust loaded criminality".[10]

6. Section 4 of the Probation of Offenders Act 1958, was not granted to a person who committed an offence under section 354 of the Indian Penal Code 1860, i.e., Outraging the modesty of a woman, by Justice Ramaswamy, of the Supreme Court.

"If the beneficial provisions of the act is extended to the offenders like one punishable under section 354 IPC outraging the modesty of teenaged girl and of like offenses on women, would not only encourage further escalation of the crime, but also would because, difficult to check or arrest the perpetration of those crimes, an imperil the modesty of several innocent girls.

The sentence of fine was confirmed and the sentence of imprisonment was modified as to undergo the sentence, for seven continuous working days by sitting during the entire working hours in the court so that he will be exposed to the public gaze and thereby it will not only be a deterrence to him from repeating the crime but also would act as an antidote upon persons having a similar propensity to crime desist there from". [11]

7. Section 12 of the Probation of Offenders Act is a beneficial provision and hence it does not contemplate automatic disqualification,

"The words 'attaching to conviction of an offence under such law" in section 12, refers to two contingencies: (i) that there must be a disqualification resulting from a conviction and (ii) that such disqualification must be provided by some law other than the Probation of Offenders Act. The Penal Code does not contain any such disqualification. Therefore it cannot be said that section 12 of the Act contemplates an automatic disqualification attaching to a conviction and obliteration of the criminal misconduct of the accused. Thus the conviction of a delinquent employee simplicit or without anything more will not result in his automatic dismissal or removal form service".[12]

8. The stigma attaching to conviction continues till the period of "supervision' is completed, as found in the Judgment by Justices V.R. Krishna Iyer, A.C. Gupta, and S. Mustafa Fazal Ali, that:

"The order of release on probation is merely in substitution of the sentence to be imposed by the court. This has been made permissible by the statute, with a humanistic point of view, in order to reform youthful offenders and to prevent from becoming hardened criminals. The provision of section 9(3) of the Act would clearly show, that the control of the offender is retained by the criminal court and where it is satisfied that the conditions of the bond, have been broken by the offender, who has been released in probation the court, can sentence the offender for the original offence. This clearly shows that the factum of guilt on the criminal charge is not swept away merely by passing the order, releasing the offender on probation. Under sections 3, 4 or 6 of the Act, the stigma continues and the finding of them is conduct resulting in conviction on must be treated to be conclusive Proof".[13]

9. The scope of section 11 of the Probation Of Offenders Act 1958, was laid down by Justice K.S. Sbubarao and K.C. Das Gupta of the Supreme Court of India, that:

"In considering the scope of such a provision we must adopt the rule of beneficial construction as enunciated by the modern trend of judicial opinion without doing violence to the provisions of the relevant section that the appellate court in appeal or the High Court in revision could in exercise of the power conferred under section 11, make an order under section 6 (1) thereof as the appellate court and High Court, agreeing with the magistrate found the accused guilty of the offenders for which he was charged".[14]

The Supreme Court remanded the matter to the High Court to make an order after complying with section 6 (1) and did not itself exercise powers under section 11 of the Probation of offenders Act.

10. Justices- Dighe and Kambli of Bombay High Court holds that, upon finding that the lower court has come to a conclusion without proper enquiry would cause waste of time both by the trial court and appellate court.

"Section 11 of the Act provides that where an order under section 3 or section 4 of the Act is made by any court trying the offenders (other) than a High Court, an appeal shall be to the court to which appeals ordinarily lie from the sentences of the former court. The order therefore passed under section 4 of the Act is obviously Appellate and if it is found by the appeal court that such an order is passed, without there being sufficient material on the record the same would be liable to beset aside. In that case, the order passed without proper enquiry would be in some cases liable to be revoked and this would naturally involve, waste of time both of the trial court as well as the Appellate court. We therefore feel it necessary to emphasise that calling for a report from the Probation Officer under sub section (2) of section 4 of the Act, though not mandatory is absolutely essential, save in exceptional cases where there is sufficient material on record justifying the use of discretion conferred by section 4 of the Act"[15].

11. The court declares that the services of the Probation Officers are to be utilised by the courts for better disposals of the case under section 4 Probation of Officers Act,

"The Probation Officer is an important officer, in the machinery for the implementation of the act. The post is created to assist the courts in the matter of probation. There is, therefore, no reason why his services should not be availed of, before the order for probation is passed. It is essential that his services should be utilised for otherwise important material relevant to be considered will not be, available to the courts at all. It is therefore very essential that the courts should not, in order to hasten up the disposal of the cases, be inclined to dispense with calling for a report and give the benefit of section 4 to the offenders, without there being sufficient material on the record before them".[16]

Thus calling for a report from the Probation Officer is absolutely necessary for the sake of probation. It will thus be seen the circumstances that no previous conviction is proved against the offender, would not, by itself be a sufficient reason for infecting, no penalty upon him.

But the court also says that in order to collect all relevant materials is essential to call for a probation report. "All that the words, 'the court shall take into consideration the report, if any, of the Probation Office', indicates is that if the report is called for, by the court and that report is received, the court has to take that report into consideration. These words are not preceded by a clause, 'the court shall call for the report from the Probation Officer', as is found in section 6 (2) of the Act. The absence of such a clause, in our view shows, that the legislature did not intend to make it obligatory on the part of the court to call for a report from the Probation Officer though it made obligatory on the court to consider the report if any, received from the Probation Officer after it was called for.

Though we are inclined to think that calling of a report from a Probation Officer under section 4 (1) of the Act is not a condition precedent for making an order under section-4 (1) of the Act, it is very essential that such a report should ordinarily be called for from a Probation Officer.

The court also holds that persons can be considered for Probation of Officer if there is adequate materials on the record, that:

"Section 4 of the Probation Officer Act, 1958 confers, the discretion on the court and that discretion it appears to us, the legislature does not intend to restrict, by making it mandatory on the part of a court to call for report from the Probation Officer in a case where there is already adequate material on the record."[17]

It is obligatory on the part of the court, to take into consideration the report from a Probation Officer in the case of an offender below 21 years of age, as stated by justices Dighe and Kambli "Subsection (2) of section 6 of the Act makes it obligatory for the court, not to sentence an offender to imprisonment when he is under twenty one years of age and has committed an offence punishable for life, with imprisonment but not with imprisonment unless it is satisfied having regard to the circumstances of the case including the nature of the offence and the character of the offender, that it would not be desirable to deal with him under section-3 or section-4 and if the court passes any sentence of imprisonment on the offender, it shall record its reasons for doing so. In consonance with the object of the section, Subsection (2) of section-6 makes it *obligatory* on the court to call for a report from the Probation Officer and consider the report if any. If we turn to the phraseology, used in subsection (2) of Section - 4 of the Act, it would appear that the legislature did not use the expression, "The court shall call for a report from a Probation Offender. "All that the sub-section says is that, before making any order under subsection (1), the court shall take into consideration the report, if any of the Probation Officer concerned in relation to the case. It is obvious that there is a difference in the phraseology used in the two sections. If the legislature would have intended to make it obligatory, on the court, to call for a report from the Probation Officer, even under section 4 of the Act, it is reasonable to presume that the Legislature would have employed the same phraseology in sub-section (2) of section - 4 of the Act. We are, therefore, inclined to take view that the Legislative would not intend to make it, incumbent on the court to call for a report from a Probation Officer before an order, section -4 (1) of the Act is passed. The scheme of two sections namely sections 4 and 6 of the Act is different. Section 6 deals with a person under twenty one years of age and impose a duty upon the court, not to impose a sentence of imprisonment for the offences mentioned in that section unless the court is satisfied having regard to the circumstances enumerated in the section that it would not be desirable to deal with the offender under section -3 or section -4 of the Act".[18]

12. Justice O.C. Reddy, High Court of Andhra Pradesh stated in a seminar held at Hyderabad in connection with the celebration of Probation Year – 1971, that,

"The magistrates need to acquaint themselves with the latest techniques of treatment of offenders in particular with the system of probation; and the Magistracy should have deeper insight into the problems relating to probation and the probationer".

During the inaugural address in Saturday 18th May 1971 at Vijyan Bhawan, New Delhi to celebrate the Probation year- 1971, by Justice S.M. Sikri, former Justice of the Supreme Court stated:

"Not only the Probation Officers should be convinced of the advantages of the probation but the judiciary and the Bar must become its votaries; unfortunately, at present very little serious attention is paid to this aspect by the judiciary or the Bar".[19]

13. The benefits of probation shall not be given to persons who deliberately flout the law given in the Verdict of Nabin Chandra Das Case during the year 1979:

"The benefit of probation should not be granted to educated and experienced men of the World who deliberately flout the law. If such persons were to be released on probation, the very object with which the Probation of Offenders Act would be defeated and an impression would create in the minds of the criminals that they could commit offenders with impunity. In the instant case the petitioner was a grown up man and a journalist. Not only he used abusive language but raised him shows to assault a public servant at public place. The provisions of the Probation Of Offender Act cannot be applied to such as case considering, the nature of the offence in the light of the further fact that, the offence was committed by one who was expected to have a greater sense of responsibility. More respectable and better educated a man is, the less temptation there should be to commit offence".[20]

14. The provisions of section 360 of the Criminal Procedure Code 1973 were made wholly, in applicable in the State of Kerala by an order of Justice U.L. Bhatt that:

"section 360 of the Criminal Procedure Code relates only to persons not under 21 years of age convicted for an offence punishable with fine only, or with imprisonment of seven years of less, to any person under 21 years of age or any women convicted of an offence not possible with sentence of death or imprisonment for life. Such persons can be considered for release on probation.

The scope of section-4 of the Act is much wider. It applies to any person found guilty of having committed an offence not punishable with death or life imprisonment.Section-360 does not provide for any role, for Probation Officers assisting the courts, in relation to supervision and other matters, while the Act does make such provisions. While section12 of the Act states that the person found guilty of an offence and dealt with under section-3 and 4 of the Act shall not suffer disqualification, if any, attached to conviction of an offence under such law. The Code does not contain any parallel provision. Two Statutes with such significant differences could not be intended to co-exist at the same time, in the same area. Such co-existence could lead to analogous results. The intention to retain the provision of section-360 of the Code and the provisions of the Act, as applicable at the same time in a given area cannot be gathered from the provisions of section-360 or any other provisions of the Code.

By virtue of Section -8 of the General Clause Act, I have to hold that the State of Kerala where the provision of the Act has been brought into force, the provisions of the section-360, Criminal Procedure Code is wholly inapplicable".[21]

The section 17 of the Probation of Offenders Act 1958, states that where ever the Act is made into force the provisions of the section 360 of the Criminal Procedure Code will cease to operate.

15. In Criminal Appeal No. 916 of 1977 Justices Doraiswamy Raju and Arijit Pasayat held that the benefit of section 4 of the Probation of Offenders Act 1958, is in applicable since undue sympathy would result in miscarriage of justice. The case was charged on the basis of forged mark sheets and securing admission to a medical college.[22]

16. In Criminal Appeal No.591 of 2001 Justices K.T. Thomas and R.P. Sethi decided on May 2, 2001 that section 3, of the Probation of Offenders Act 1958 can be exercised for a punishment for 3 months charged under section 10 (n) of the Central Reserve Police force Act, since:

"The Probation of Offences Act, 1958 has been enacted in view of the increasing emphasis on the reformation and rehabilitation of the offenders as useful and self-reliant members of society without subjecting them to deleterious effects of jail life.

The Respondent, who was a Constable of Indo-Tibetan Border Police, was found over drunk on 26-11-1992 and absent at the time of the roll- call. It was alleged that under the influence of liquor, he entered the house of the Commandant of the Battalion and thus committed the offence punishable under Section 16(2), of the Central Reserve Police Force Act, 1949 by which he was admittedly governed. Upon trial, the Commandant of the Battalion who was also having the powers of the

Magistrate of the First Class, convicted the Respondent under Section 10(n) of the Act and sentenced him to imprisonment for a period of three months. Aggrieved by the order of conviction and sentence, the respondent filed an appeal, which was disposed of by the XIIth Additional Sessions Judge, Bareilly upholding his conviction but modifying of the sentence to the extent of till, the rising of the court. The appellate court further directed the 'this order shall not adversely affect the service career of the accused'.

For an offence punishable under section 10 of the CRPF Act, the sentence provided is one year with fine entitling the respondent to claim the benefit of section 3 of the Probation of Offenders Act. Both the courts below, have thought it expedient to take a lenient view and instead of sending him to jail, opted to pass a sentence till the rising of the court and in this context directed that the order of conviction and sentence would not adversely affect the career of the accused. It is true that nobody can claim the benefit of sections 3 and 4 of the Probation of Offenders Act, as a matter of right and the court has to pass appropriate orders in the facts and circumstances of each case having regard to the nature of the offence, its general effect on the society and the character of the offender, etc. A case of trivial nature, as the respondent is stated to have committed and keeping in view of peculiar circumstances, is a fit case where powers under section 3 of the Probation of Offenders Act can be exercised."[23]

17. In Criminal Appeal No. 609 of 1999, Justices Arijit Pasayat and C.K. Thakker decided on September 20, 2004, that the High Court was not justified to interfere with the benefit, extended by the trial court under the Probation of Offenders Act 1958. Allowing the appeal filed by the accused the Supreme Court held:

"Section 11(4) of the Act makes the position clear that only the propriety of the order passed under Section 3 or 4, in respect of offenders can be dealt with by, the appellate court or the High Court, as the case may be. The Appellate Court or the High Court exercising revisional power may set aside such an order, being passed either under Section 3 or Section 4 and in lieu, thereof, pass sentence on such offender. Obviously the sentence can be imposed only in respect of the offence relating to which the order under Section 3 or Section 4 of the Act has been passed. There is no scope for altering nature of the offence and for directing that the accused be convicted, for another offence. The High Court was, therefore, not justified in directing conviction of the appellants, under

Section 326 of Indian Penal Code. The trial court had given adequate reasons for passing the order under section 4 of the Act. That being so, the High Court was not justified to interfere with the benefit extended by the trial court under the Act."[24]

18. P.N. Bhagawathi, C.J. and Ranganath Misra. J. delivered in the case filed by a social worker Sheela Bharse, that:

"We would like to direct that where a complaint is field or first information report is lodged against a child, below the age of 16 years for an offence punishable with imprisonment of not more than 7 years, the investigation shall be completed within a period of three months from the date of filling of the complaint or lodging of the First Information Report and if the investigation is not completed within this time, the case against the child must be treated closed. If within three months the charge sheet is filed against the child in the case of an offence punishable with imprisonment not more than 7 years, the case must be tried and disposed of within a further period of 6 months at the outside and this period should be inclusive of the time up in committal proceeding, if any. We have already held in Hussaiara Khatoon Vs. Home Secretary, State of Bihar (1979) 3 SCR 169, AIR 1979 SC 1360) that the right to speedy trial is a fundamental right implicit in Article 21 of the Constitution.[25]

18.Guideline in the matter of exercise of the discretion was, therefore considered by the aforesaid decision. It was observed:

"The policy of the law on that above, an offence is an overly heinous one, grant of probation is ruled out as a matter of law. The heinousness of the offence and its deleterious effect, the body politic is in the eye of law, if not fundamental or very relevant factor for the grant or refused of probation. I am in respectful agreement with the analysis of the section and the summing up of the legal position.

A distinction has to be made between crimes, which are committed on the impulse of the moment, not in part and parcel of an organised underworld set up. When in evidence of an, organised activity for commercial gain, the inflexible inference that, the offender is connected with, an organised racket can clearly be drawn. In that context, a plea that he is a first offender may not be an innocent one.

In Criminal Appeal No 1307 of 2002 Justice H.K. Sema and Tarun Chatterjee of the Supreme Court decided on September 8, 2005, that the benefit of probation does not apply in the case, where the Respondent was convicted under section 7 of the Prevention of Corruption Act, 1988.

The court decided the propriety of invoking section 360 of the Criminal Procedure Code, 1973:

"Held, provisions of the Probation of Officers Act 1958 and section 360 Criminal Procedure Code are not applicable to conviction under the Prevention of Corruption Act".[26]

19. In Criminal Appeal No.426 of 2000, Justice K.T. Thomas and Doraiswamy Raju decided on May 4, 2000 in a case causing death by rash and negligent driving charged under sections 304 A and 279 of Indian Penal Code 1860, that the provisions of the Probation of Offenders Act do not apply since it involves rash and negligent driving. The court shall form an opinion as to whether, it is expedient to release the offender on probation.

"Held, in view of the galloping rate of road accidents in India and its devastating consequences, leniency cannot be shown and the benevolent section 4 of Probation of Offenders Act. The Act cannot be treated as applicable to the offence under section 304-A Indian Penal Code, Further, held, when deciding the quantum of sentence, deterrence ought to be the prime consideration. Every driver should fear that, if convicted, the courts will not treat him leniently. The injuries were fatal for bus driver knocking down cyclist, in front of the office gate in town area. Trial court and appellate court both finding appellant guilty of, rash and negligent driving and convicting him under Section 279 and 304-A, Indian Penal Code. Held, High Court rightly dismissed the revision petition filed by appellant. Section 4 of Probation of Offenders Act not attracted to case of appellant".[27]

20. In Criminal Appeal No. 660 of 2005, Justices Ashok Bhan and Dr. A.R. Lakshmanan of the Supreme Court of India decided on April 29, 2005 that the report of the Probation Officer is a condition, precedent to release of accused. The court held. "Section 4, release of offender on probation of good conduct. Exercise of discretion by the court in relation to Mode of Relevant factors to be considered. Held, discretion has to be exercised having regard to the circumstances in which, the crime, was committed, the age, character and antecedents of the offender. Such exercise of direction needs, a sense of responsibility. Court/Magistrate should carefully take into account the attendant circumstances. Respondent (R) convicted and sentenced under sections 332 and 461, Delhi Municipal Corporation Act, 1957 for committing the offence of unauthorised construction. High Court granting him benefit of Section -4, without

giving opportunity to appellant (Municipal Corporation) to file counter affidavit and without calling for report of Probation Officer in relation to conduct of R who was a previous convict, under the said Act of 1957. – He is not disclosing the said fact to the High Court – offence in question involving large scale irregularly and unauthorised construction carried on by builders despite strict direction of the municipal authorises and the courts. R had not put in substantial period in custody as he had been in jail for only three days. In view of the above, order of High Court extending the benefit of probation to R on the ground, that he faced the agony of a trial for over 12 years and had undergone some period in custody, held, not sustainable and the matter remitted to the High Court for disposal afresh." [28]

21. Probation of Offender's Act, 1958, section 6 was considered for the time of conviction, is the material time for, reckoning the age of the accused. (Chettur Sankaram Nair, J) State of Kerala Vs. Parameswaran Nair, Radhakrishan Nair – ILR 1995 (I) Ker 124.

Ranji Missar and another Vs. State of Bihar AIR 1963 SC. 1088 – Relied on: Tarran Lal Vs. The Stare of Punjab AIR 1965 SC. 444, Abdul Quyum Vs. State of Bihar AIR 1972 SC. 214 Musakhan and others Vs. State of Maharashtra AIR 1976 SC. 2566.

22. Whether section 4, of the Probation of Offenders Act is applicable to Section 51 (a) of the Kerala Police Act to a convict, was considered in this case by Justice M.R Hariharan Nair:

"The object of the Probation offenders Act is to avoid imprisonment of the person convicted with the intent to reform him. Those who commit the offences involving religious matters, anti-social offences, sex offenders etc. are not usually considered for an extension of the benefit. Those who perpetrate well planned and reprehensible offences are not given the benefit. Those who commit the offences with the motive of monetary gain and white collar criminals and economic offenders are also not usually given the benefit."[29]

23. A.R. Lekhmanan; K. Narayana Kurup, JJ. Delivered that:

"Section 12 An employee convicted under S- 498-4 IPC, but released on probation under the Probation Of Offenders Act, can still be dismissed from service as the offence is one involving moral turpitude, as the offence was as per section 10(1) (b) (i) the Banking Regulation Act, 1949". [30]

24. On March 22, 2002·Justices, R.C. Lohati and P. Venkatarama Reddy decided in the non compoundable section 498-A of Indian penal Code, that the release on Probation under Probation of Offenders Act, is applicable since the accused is of 42 years of age and employed as a Safely Officer in Coal India Ltd.

"The appeal is partly allowed. The conviction of Appellants 1 and 2 under section 498 A Indian Penal Code is maintained, but the sentence of imprisonment passed on them for an offence under section 498 A is reduced to the period already undergone. In so far, as Appellant 3 is concerned, in our opinion, it will meet the ends of justice if he is dealt with under section 4 of the Probation of Offenders Act, 1958, and released on probation of good conduct. The sentence of imprisonment passed on Appellant 3 is set aside and it is directed that he shall be released on his entering on into, a bond with one surely in an amount of Rs.5000, to appear before the trial court and receive sentence on being called upon during a period of one year and in the meantime to keep the peace and be of food behaviour". [31]

25. On January 24, 2003, Justices S.N. Vairav and D.M. Dharmadhikari of the Supreme Court of India, denied the benefit of section 4, of the Probation of Offenders Act, 1958 to the accused causing death of the deceased due to neurogenic shock by kicking him in his private parts. The Court ordered that:

"The evidence establishes that when he saw neighbors coming, he stated to the deceased that he would not leave him alive and then kicked the deceased with his right knee on the private parts. The evidence of the doctor clearly shows, that the death was caused, due to neurogenic shock resulting from injury to the testicles and scrotum. Thus the death is directly due to the injury caused by the respondent to the deceased. The injury was such, that it was sufficient in the normal course to cause death. The High Court was, in error, in stating that there was no injury. The High Court noted that death resulted from neurogenic shock but failed to note that the neurogenic shock was a result of the injury, to the testicles and scrotum. The High Court omitted to note that such injury could be caused by a kick and was sufficient in normal course to cause immediate death. This was not a case wherein, a fit of anger or in a scuffle some act had taken place. The injury caused was not even a simple injury. Section 323 would be wholly inapplicable in such case. This was a case were the conviction should have been under section 302 Indian Penal Code."[32]

26. In Criminal Appeal No. 334 of 1997, Justices Doraiswamy Raju and Arijit Pasayat decided on November 13, 2003 that the provisions of section 4 of the Probation Of Offenders Act 1958, apply for an offence punishable under section 376, read with section 511 of the Indian Penal Code, 1860.

The victim and the accused are related to each other, the latter being the cousin brother of the former. A law was set in motion on 1-8-1989 on the accusation, that the accused committed rape on the victim. An investigation was undertaken and the accused faced trial. The trial Judge was of the view that commission of rape was not established. However, an attempt to do so was established unerringly. Three years custodial sentence and a fine of Rs.3000 were imposed. On appeal, the High Court upheld the conviction, but considering the relationship and the age of he accused, applied section 4 of the Probation of offenders Act. The Supreme Court held,

Where accused and victim were related, the incident happened over 14 years ago, accused was under 21 years of age and trial court convicted him for attempt to rape only and High Court upheld such conviction, held, High Court's application of section 4 and 6 of the Act to accuse not bad. Hence, no interference called for". [33]

27. Provision in Section 12 for removal of disqualification attaching to conviction was considered. It is applicable only to the disqualification attached under the law providing for the offence and its punishment and does not bar the raking into account the conviction, for the purpose of his dismissal from Government Service as held by S.P. Bharucha and V.N. Khare. J. J that:

"Section 12 of the Probation of Offenders Act would apply only in respect of a disqualification that goes with a conviction under the law which provides for the offence and its punishment. That is the plain meaning of the words 'disqualification, if any, attaching to a conviction of an offence under such law' therein. Where the law that provides for, an offence and its punishment also stipulates a disqualification, a person convicted of the offence but related on probation does not, by reason of section 12 suffer the disqualification. It cannot be held that, by reason of section 12 a conviction for an offences should not be taken into account for the purpose of dismissal of the person convicted from Government service."[34]

28. Justice S.M. Sikri, former Chief Justice of India quotes, from the Home Office (UK) report published in 1966 on the sentencing practices by Magistrates, that:

"Four factors which influence the use which is made of probation:

(a) The attitude of the justices towards the concept of probation as being useful for adult offenders

(b) The use made by the Magistrates of the service for adding to their knowledge of defendants.

(c) The belief that the officers are already overworked by the great load of cases from the Juvenile Court and with matrimonial cases

(d) The confidence, which justices have in the ability of the probation officers".[35]

29. The provisions of Probation Officer of Offenders Act, if applied intelligently can produce wonders in bringing back many deviants to normal social life and prevent many from becoming habitual offenders. Further the idea of human right is widely discussed in these days. Similarly, here a convicted person, gets a chance to mend his ways in concurrence with the modern trend in criminals Jurisprudence that the reformation and rehabilitation of the accused. Probation is to be used with much discretion for public safety as evident from the comment, by Justice V.R Krishna Iyer:

"Economic offences are subtle murders practiced on the community, sabotaging the national economy. They have to be tackled with a new seriousness"[36]

30. The rehabilitation measures under the probation of offender Act 1958 may not be effective in the case of, offenders charged under Foreign Exchange Regulation Act and Customers Act, as held by the Supreme Court:

"The offender did not deserve to be treated with the ameliorative and rehabilitative measures, since the offence being grave and committed as a result of deliberate and preplanning at the risk of the safely and moral well being of the community."[37]

31. Justice U.L. Bhatt, of the Kerala High Court observed with regards to a plea for probation, that:

"Of course Courts must always bear in mind, that the offences rendered punishable under the, Abkari Act, are serious offences, not only involving revenue of the State but also involving public health. This background must be present in the mind of the court when assessing whether probation treatment could be given to a particular offender". [38]

32. Here the accused aged 20 years charged under section 452 and 379, Indian Penal Code and convicted for imprisonment for 7 years was released on probation on appeal after accepting the report from the Probation Officer, that:

"Probation Officers report that the accused belongs to a middle class respectable family but fell into undesirable company and come under evil influence of criminals, which assimilated abnormal criminal propensity in him was accepted, and ordered the benefit of Probation of Offenders Act".[39]

33. The offence under the Abkari Act is similar, to the offenders under Food Adulteration Act as held by Justice P. Janakey Amma of the Honorable High Court of Kerala, that:

"Like Adulteration of food, the manufacture of liquor is also an offence which has an adverse impact on the society and on the economy of the state. Prohibition of the consumption of intoxicating liquor, except for medicinal purpose is included in the, Directive principles of State policy as will be seen from Article 47, of the Constitution. A deliberate and calculate move to, defy the provision of the Abkari Act and Excise Law prompted by profit motive, does not deserve sympathetic consideration. The salutary provisions contained, in the Probation of Offenders Act 1958 may not serve their purpose by indiscriminate application of its provisions. The facts that a minimum term of imprisonment is fixed for a particular offence itself, reveal the gravity of the offence. The provision reflects the social abhorrence towards the offence and the intention of the legislature that the offence of this kind should be stopped with a stern hand, while there is no prohibition in applying the principles of probation even in cases above referred. To it requires much circumspection in actual application to cases other than those coming under section 6 of Probation Offenders Act- 1958". [40]

34. In a case charged under the Abkari Act where, scores of person died due to the sale of spurious liquor, the Horrible High Court of Kerala, held:

"The areas and pattern of crime are fast changing, in our country, that the court must also play its own role in ensuring that, the course of Public Justice is nor abandoned". [41]

35. Removal of disqualification attaching to conviction. Applicable only to the disqualification attached under the law, providing for the offence and its punishment does not bar the taking into account, the conviction for the purpose of this dismissal from Government Service as provided in Art.311 (2) Second proviso (a) of the Constitution of India. S.P. Bharucha and V.N. Khare. JJ. held that:

"Section 12 of the Probation of Offenders Act, would apply only in respect of a disqualification that goes with a conviction, under the law which provides for the offence and its punishment. That is the plain meaning of the words 'disqualification, if any, attaching to a conviction of an offence under such law' therein. Where law the provides for an offence and its punishment also stipulates a disqualification, a person convicted of the offence but released on probation does not, by reason of Section12, suffer the disqualification. It cannot be held that, by reason of Section12, a conviction for an offence should not be taken into account for the purpose of dismissal of the person convicted from Government service."[42]

36. Guidelines for applying section 4, to offence under the Act are as observed by the Supreme Court.

"The submission of the petitioners was regarding, Section 369, of the Code of Criminal Procedure while considering that plea, the court must necessarily have an overtake view, if the facts of the case and matters pertinent to objects underlying the section" [43]

37. The kindly application of the probation principle cannot be invoked in the case of a man:

"'whose antisocial activities, disguised as a respectable trade, imperial numerous innocents'. It was noted 'economical offences committed by white collar criminals are unlikely to be, dissuaded by the general probationary process'. The Supreme Court noted that the 27 report of the Law Commission had recommended the exclusion of the Probation of offenders Act to social and economic offences by suitable amendments."[44]

The interpretation of sections 360 and 361 of the Criminal Procedure Code and the duty of the court in that context had been neatly analysed, by a bench decision of the Punjab High Court, where the questions appear to have been debated exhaustively and effectively in the context of a reference, made to the Division Bench on the correctness, of some of the earlier decisions of this court was doubted. The court observed.

"It is not as if section 360, of the Code, is an inflexible mandate to grant probation to eligible persons, but indeed casts, only a duty on the Court to consider the expediency or otherwise of the grant of Probation. There is no gainsaying, the fact that since section 361 of the Code requires a social reason for dealing it, in the case of a person eligible for, its benefit the broad rule would be the grant of the same and its refused would be for good reasons. It may be noticed that the regularly significant words in section 360(1) are: 'The court may instead of sentencing him at once to one punishment...' The word used herein again in 'may' and there is no reason to read it as 'shall' and it was not even remotely acquired before as that this should be so constructed. Again, the said, words expressly leave the offender, to the recurrence, of the magistrate by using the word 'instead' for the two alternatives of sentencing him to punishment or grant of Probation. It is thus manifesting that section 360, vests discretion in the sentencing court.

Guidelines in the matter of exercise of the discretions were therefore considered by the aforesaid decision. It was observed that 'the policy of the law is that where an offence, is an overly heinous one, grant of Probation is ruled out on a matter of law. The heinousness of the offence and its deleterious effect in the body politic is, in the eye of law, 'if not fundamental, a very relevant factor, for the grant or refusal of Probation' I am in respectful agreement with the analysis of the section and the supreme of the legal position.

A distinction has to be made between crimes, which are not committed on the impulse of the moment or by part and parcel, if an organised underworld set up. Where there is evidence of an organised activity for commercial gain, an inflexible inference that the offender is connected with an organised racket can safely be drawn. In that context, a plea that, he is a first offender may not be an innocent one."[45]

38. In this case, the Supreme Court delivered the judgment and laid down the object of Probation of Offenders Act by Justices P.N. Bhagwathi, V.R. Krishana Iyer and S. Murtaza Fazl Ali. It was observed:

"The object of the Probation of Offenders Act is to prevent the young offenders becoming hardens by their association with offenders, in the Prisons, where they would get an opportunity to intermingle. It is unfortunate that the judiciary is no utilising the benevolent provisions of the Probation of Offenders Act, though such a benevolent Act is in force for several years".[46]

39. The offence under section 149, of Indian Penal Code 1860, was considered that the mere innocent presence, if makes accused a member of unlawful assembly.

"A mere innocent presence in an assembly of persons, as for example a bystander, does not make the accused a member of an unlawful assembly, unless it is shown by direct or circumstantial evidence that the accused shared the common object of the assembly. Thus a court is not entitled to presume that any and every person, who is proved to have been present near a riotous mob, at any time or to have jointed or left it at any stage during its activities is in law guilty of every act committed by it from the beginning have anticipated and contemplated the nature of the illegal activities in which the assembly would subsequently indulged. In other words, it must be proved in each case that the person concerned was not only a member of the unlawful assembly at some stage, but at all the crucial stages and shared the common object of the assembly at all these stages.

Wherein, a riot case although all the incidents starting from the beginning to the end were parts of the same transaction but nevertheless they were separate incidents, and some accused were found to be one particular stage but not at another, in these circumstances, the accused who were not present or who did not share the common object of the unlawful assembly, at other stages could not be convicted for the activities of the assembly at those stages. So Probation was considered.[47]

40. The applicability of section 6 of the Probation of Offenders Act 1958, was considered in this case by Deshmukh and Agarwal. J. J.:

"The Probation of Offenders Act is a social legislation, which is meant to reform juvenile offenders so as to prevent them from becoming hardened criminals by providing an educative and reformative treatment to them by the government. Unfortunately, though the provisions of section 6, thereof are mandatory, the Courts do not appear to make wise use of these provisions, which is necessary to protect the younger generation from becoming professional criminals and therefore a menace to the society". [48]

41. Section 4 of the Probation of Offenders Act (20 of 1958) on forming of opinions required for conviction under section 325 IPC and held:

"It is necessary to distinguish the cases of accused no. 2 from the case of accused nos.4 and 5. Accused no.2 is obviously not below the age of 21. Section 6 of the Probation of Offenders Act is not attracted in his case. However, accused no. 2 is neither convicted, under an offence nor punishable with death or imprisonment for life. The provisions of section 4 of the Probation of Offenders Act, would thus be attracted. In that case, according to us, it was for the accused and his counsel to place before the court, the circumstances and induce the trial judge as well as the appellate court to give the benefit of the Probation of Offenders Act 1958. Mr. Nerlekar the counsel for the petitioners however argued that even under section 4 of the Probation of Offenders Act to the accused and after coming to that conclusion alone, a substantive sentence should be passed. He bases this argument upon the construction of the provision of section 4 (1) of the Probation of Offenders Act, which he canvassed before us. We are unable to see any such obligation upon the court and are not inclined to accept the interpretation of Mr. Nerlekar.

These observation amply, make it clear that, where the provisions of section 6, are attracted, it is the duty of the court to follow the procedure laid down by that section and on the basis of the material that will be available on the record after following that procedure, that the court has to deny the benefit of sections 3 and 4, to a particular accused, in spite of the fact that his age is below twenty one years."[49]

42. Criminal Trial sentencing policy necessity to award compensation to victims while passing judgment of conviction necessity to create a fund from which compensation can be paid to victims Criminal Procedure Code 1973, section 357 and section 5 of Probation of Offenders Act, 1958:

"The sentencing jurisprudence presents a broad spectrum. It must be deterrent, but not deterrent alone. Penal justice is not the sole component of sentencing jurisprudence. It companies penal justice and restrictive justice. The 42nd Report of the Law Commission (page 50) noticed that the concept of reparation to the victim had been receiving increased attention in recent times. Mere punishment of the offender, though it may exhaust the primary function of criminal law, is not the total fulfillment of its functions. Prisoners being put to work have, several advantages, according to John Louis Gillin, 'Criminology and Penology'.

Work alleviated tediousness of prison life. It will help repress criminal instincts. Production of economic commodities by this process will also decrease cost of support, while another part could go to the victim. A Scheme has been evolved to pay wages, to prisoners for the work, done by them in jail. This cannot be faulted. But a better sense of priorities, for the work done by them into the offender must be extended to the victim. The proper perspective would be, to put the victim first, in priority and the offender next. Construction of a work force by the State consisting of convicts could be thought of, as it has several advantages. It can ensure channeling of convicts could be thought of, as it has several advantages. It can ensure channeling of energy, in light directions and utilisation of human resources. Those who would otherwise be classified criminals could be upgraded as a work force, relenting the normal prison rigorous, assuring them the dignity of existence. Rights of the victim to receive compensation, and duty of the State and the offender to pay compensation, were recognised by law. Various legislations were enacted to translate this recognition, into an operational scheme. Naturally, the question of funding resources must receive attention. There could be cases, where the offender can pay compensation and where he cannot. A methodology must be found. The creation of a fund will be an answer. Such a fund is maintained in the Netherlands. Switzerland also maintains a fund from which compensation is paid to victims. An indemnification fund was maintained by Cuba (pre-revolution era). A fund could be set up by channeling the fines, imposed by courts into it. However, fines have now become another source of revenue for the Government. How a fund is to be created and operated, and how the State and the offenders are to pool the fund, are matters for the Executive and the Legislature to consider. In India, section 357 of the Code of Criminal Procedure and section 5, of the Probation of Offenders Act, are powerful legislative devices to ensure justice to victims. If these provisions are modulated with judicial craftsmanship, criminology will be a meaningful reality. Section 357, of the Code of Criminal Procedure; enable the Court to award compensation, in addition to fine, which in certain cases is limited.

Section 5, of the Probation of Offenders Act, whiles sparing the accused the agony of incarceration, provides for atonement of his wrong. Even where there is no direct victim (as in the case of Abkari Offenses), compensation can be ordered to the State. The attitudes of the courts must change. They must take inspiration from the law, declared in Hari Kishan (AIR 1988 SC 2127) Criminal justice system is not longer penal justice alone; it is recitatives justices, too."[50]

43. "Object of the Act explained object is to prevent youthful offenders into obdurate criminals". [51]

44. Section 18, of the Probation of Offenders Act expressly excludes the operation of its provisions in respect of offences under Prevention of Corruption Act and there is no such exclusion of the provisions in Prevention of Food Adulteration Act.[52]

44. A Government servant convicted for offences under Indian Penal Code by release on probation under section 4, conviction can be taken into account for removing him from service."[53]

45. **Discretion of Court:**

Under Section 4, the power in Releasing a person on probation of good conduct be exercised, if the court feels it expedient to release him. Nature of offence committed in relevant circumstance to be considered while forming such opinion.

"In the matter of release of a person convicted of an offence on probation of good conduct, the Parliament has made it clear that it has to be only if the court forms the opinion that it is expedient to release him on probation for his good conduct regard being had to the circumstances of the case. One of the circumstances, which cannot be sidelined in forming the said opinions is provided sufficient indication that releasing the convicted persons on probation, if good conduct must appear to the court to be expedient. The word 'Expedient' had been thoughtfully employed by the Parliament in the section so as to view. Here the word 'expedient' is used in section 4, of the Probation of Offenders Act, in the context casting a duty on the Court to take into account 'the circumstances of the case including the nature of the offence…'.This means Section 4, can be resorted to when the Court considers the circumstances of the case, particularly the nature of the offences, and the court forms its opinion that it is suitable and appropriate for accomplishing a specified object that the offender can be released on probation of good conduct."[54]

46. Section 4, Benefit of probation granted on appeal, the complaint against accused for offence of cheating. Accused without having any academic qualification practicing as an advocate for long period of 8 years. Character of accused reflects in modality, in which he was inveigling in noble profession duping everybody concerned. Crime committed by him should be dealt with deterrent. But ordered releasing him on probation. It was set aside accused sentenced on each count

under saying 419 and 420, Penal Code for six months Rigourous Imprisonment and a fine of Rs. 5,000/- on each count."[55]

47. **Section 3 Probation:**

The accused, a homeopath operating a pregnant lady to abort. Uterus getting perforated patient dying and thus it was ordered that the accused does not deserve the benefit of probation.

"If a homeopath takes to his head to operate a pregnant lady and perforate, her uterus by trying to abort and the patient dies, he does not deserve the benefit of probation. It would have been a different matter if a trained surgeon while carrying out the operation as would have committed some mistake of judgment resulting in the death of the patient." [56]

48. **Section 4:**

Offence under Section 307/34. 323 of Penal Code was discussed.

"One of accused inflicting Gandasa blows on head of injured and another accused inflicting iron lathi below on the shoulder of injured does not share common intention and hence liable to be convicted under section 323. Attempt to murder one of the accused giving only, one blow on shoulder injury caused was simple one accused released under section 4 on probation"[57]

49. Applicability petitioner for Special Leave to Supreme Court found guilty of abducting a teenage girl and forcing her to sexual submission with commercial object. Held "the provisions of the probation of Offender Act could not be extended to this abominable culprit".[58]

50. Section 4, applied to section 302 and 304 of Penal Code (45 of 1860), and benefit of probation considering the age of appellant which was less than 21 years on date of occurrence. Appellant directed to be released on probation.[59]

51. Removal of disqualification attaching to conviction envisaged in section, 12 of the Probation of Offenders Act was considered. The words 'disqualification, if any attaching to conviction of an offence under such law' under section 12, meaning of Government servant convicted for offense under Penal Code but released on probation under section 4 conviction can be taken into account for removing him from service.

Section 12, the Probation of Offenders Act would apply only in respect of a disqualification that goes with a conviction under the law which provides for the offence and its punishment. That is the plain meaning of the words 'disqualification, if any, attaching to a conviction of an offence under such law therein'. Where the law that provides for an offence and its punishment also stipulates a disqualification, a person convicted of the offence but released on probation does not, by reason of section 12, suffer the disqualification. It cannot be held that, by reason of section 12, a conviction for an offence should not be taken into account for the purposes of dismissal of the person convicted from Government service". [60]

52. Under section 12, Central Reserved Police Force Act (1949) the disqualification attached to conviction order of imprisonment passed against delinquent under section 12 of CRPF Act, substituted by order of Probation Act, does not obliterate effect of conviction altogether. It is open to the departmental authorities to take appropriate disciplinary action against the delinquent. The section 12 of Probation of Offenders Act does not intended to exonerate the person from departmental punishment."[61]

53. Section 12, Scope of release of offender on probation was considered. It does not obliterate stigma of conviction. Employee dismissed from service in view of conviction under section 10, of Central Reserve Police Force Act. Not entitled to reinstatement in service upon getting the benefit of probation of good conduct.

54. In criminal trial, the conviction is one thing and sentence is another. The departmental punishment for misconduct is yet, a third one. The court while invoking the provisions of section 3 or 4 of the Act does not deals with the sentence which the offender has to undergo, instead of sentencing the offender; the court releases him on probation of good conduct. The conviction however, remains untouched and the stigma of conviction is not obliterated. In the departmental proceedings the delinquent could be dismissed or removed or reduced in rank on the ground of conduct which had led to his conviction on a criminal charge: Section 12 of the Act does not preclude the department from taking action for misconduct leading to the offence or to his conviction thereon as per law. The section was not intended to exonerate the person from Departmental punishment.

However, the Supreme Court altered the penalty of dismissal from service into removal from service following".[62]

55. Section 18, of the Probation of Offenders act was considered for an offence under Section 43, Defense of India Act (1962).

"Provisions of sections 3,4 and 6 of the Probation of Offenders Act, being inconsistent with provisions of Rule 126 P (2) (iii), D.I Act See Defense of India Act (1962) the court held not applicable."[63]

There are thus court cases in relation to most of the relevant section of the Probation of offenders Act 1958. It is also noted that there is no recent cases reported indicating the sparing use of the Act by the courts.

Footnotes

1. Mahatma Gandhi, Harijan, 1946: 5th May, Harijan.
2. *Kerala Prison Rules – 1958,* G.O (MS) No. 925 dt. Trivandrum 26-7-1958 Government of Kerala, Government Press, Thiruvananthapuram, p. 54.
3. *The Immoral Traffic (Prevention) Act, 1986* (Act No.104 Of 1956 As Amended Up To Act No.44 Of 1986) Allahabad Law Agency, University Road, Allahabad-211002, p. 4.
4. *The Narcotic Drugs and Psychotropic Substances Act 1985,* Allahabad Law Agency, 9 University Road, Allahabad-211002, p. 7.
5. *United Nations (1948) Universal Declaration of Human Rights,* New York, p. 10.
6. *State of Maharastra Vs Kapoor Chand and Kesarmal Jain* (AIR, 1981, SC, 927).
7. *Ram Prakash Vs State of Haryana,* (AIR, 1973, Supreme Court Cases 780).
8. *Pyarali. K. Tejani Vs. M.R. Dange* (AIR, 1974, SC, 288).
9. Smt. Devaki. Vs State Of Haryana (AIR, 1979, SC, 1948).
10. Phul Singh. Vs. State of Haryana (AIR, 1980; SC, 249).
11. Ippili Trinodha Rao Vs State of Andhra Pradesh (1984) Crl. L.J. 1254).
12. AIR, (1975), SC-2216.
13. Southern Railway and another Vs T.R. Chellappan (AIR, 1975, SC, 2216).
14. Rattan Lal Vs State Of Punjab (AIR (1965) S.C. 444 (V.52 C.72).
15. State of Maharastra, appellant Vs Body a Raniji Patil, Respondent, (1978) Crl. L.J. 411.
16. State of Maharastra Vs Body a Raniji Patil (1978), Crl. L.J-411.
17. State of Maharastra Vs Bodhya Ramji Patil, (1978, Crl. L.J-411.
18. State of Maharastra Vs Bodhya Ramji Patil, (1978, Crl. L.J-411.

19. Social Defence, Quarterly Vol VII No. 25 (July 1971) Central Bureau of Correctional Service, New Delhi (6-7).
20. Nabin Chandra Das Vs State of West Bengal (1979) 48 Cut L.T, 466-468.
21. State of Kerala Vs Chellappan George and others (1983, KLT, 811).
22. A.S. Krishnan and other Vs State of Kerala (2004), 11 Supreme Court Cases 576.
23. Commandant, 20th Battalion, ITB Police Vs Sanjay Binjola, (2001) 5, Supreme Court Cases 317 Para-9).
24. Prithv Raj and others Vs Kamalesh Kumar and others, (2004) 8 Supreme Court cases 303.
25. Sheela Barse and Another Vs Union of India, AIR 1986, SC, 1773.
26. State of Tamilnadu Vs Kaliaperumal (2005) 12 Supreme Court Case 473.
27. Dalbir Singh Vs State of Haryana (2000), 5, Supreme Court Cases 82.
28. MCD Vs State of Delhi and Another, (2005) 4 Supreme Court cases 605.
29. Joy Vs State of Kerala, 2002 (2) KLT SN 175: 2002 (1) 813. Dt. 14/06/2006.
30. Vincent Varghese Vs. State Bank of India, 1999 (1) KLT 602: ILR 1999 (2) Ker. 443. Dt. 20/01/1999.
31. Ramachadra Singh and other, Vs State of Bihar and Another, (2003) 10 Supreme Court Cases 234.
32. State of Karnataka Vs Muhammed Nazeer alias Babu (2003) Supreme Court cases 444.
33. State of Himachal Pradesh Dharampal (2004) I, Supreme Court Case 681.
34. Harichand Vs Director of School Education 1998 (1) KLT SN. 74 P.74: 1998 (2) SCC 383.
35. Social Defence, Quarterly Vol. VII, No 25 July 1971, Published by the Central Bureau of Correctional Administration, New Delhi, p. 8.
36. V.R. Krishna Iyer (1975), Law Freedom and Social Change, Orient Longman New Delhi, p. 88.
37. 1979 Crl. LJ, No.70.
38. Ammini Vs State of Kerala, 1981 KLT No. 28 Case No. 58.
39. 1983 Cr. LJ, 1043.

40. Mathai John Vs State of Kerala, 1978 KLT, 154.
41. Chandrasenan Vs State of Kerala (1983 KLT 911).
42. Harichand Vs Director of School Education 1988 (1) KLT SN. 74: 1998 (2) SCC 383].
43. Pyarati K Tejar Vs Mahadeo Ramachandran Dange AIR 1974 SC-228.
44. Prem Vs Dehli Administration, AIR 1977 SC 56; Joginder Singh Vs State of Punjab, 1980 Crl LJ 1218.
45. AIR, 1976, Supreme Court 2566.
46. Mushakhan and others Vs State of Maharastra, Criminal appeal No. 305 of 1971, dt. 11-10-1976.
47. Criminal appeal No 737 of 1970. Dated 5-11-1971 (Bombay).
48. Chandrakant Laxman Brate and others Vs. The State of Maharastra, 1978 CRl. L. J. 72 (Bombay High Court Criminal Appln, No. 3136 of 1976 D/- 30-3-1977.
49. State of Kerala Vs. Ashraf (1993) 1 KLT 501.
50. AIR 1988 SC 2127, (1991) Crl. L.R.841.
51. Judgal Kishore Prasad Vs State of Bihar. AIR 1972 SC 2522:1973 Cri LJ 23: (1972): 2SCC633: (1972) SCWR 452:1973 (SC) 307: 1972 Cri App R (SC) 382.
52. Ishwer Das Vs State of Punjab. AIR 1972 SC 1295: 1972 Cri LJ 874: (1973) 2 SCC 63 : (1973) I SCJ 571:1972 Cri LR App R (SC) 102.
53. AIR 1998 SC 788: 1988 AIR SCW 504: 1998 Cri LJ 1106.
54. Dalbir Singh Vs State of Haryana. AIR 2000 SC 1677: 2000CriLJ 2283: 2000(5)JT SCW 1653:2000 Cri LJ2283(5)JT463:2000 (3) Supreme 749:2000 (4) Scale 323: 2000 (5) SCC 82.
55. Nilgiri Bar Association Vs T.K. Mahalingam AIR SCW 398 : 1997 AIR SCW 4386: 1998 Cri LJ 675: 1997 (10) Supreme 262: 1998 (1) S CC 550: 1997 (7) Scale 472: 1998 Cri LR (SC) 247.
56. Dr. Jacob George Vs State of Kerala. 1994 AIR SCW 2282 : 1994 LJ 3851: 1994 Cri App R (SC) 430: 1994 (3) SCC 430: 1994 (3) JT 225: 1994 Cri LR (SC) 332.
57. 1994 AIR SCW 1451: 1994 Cri LJ 2201.
58. Smt. Devki Vs State of Haryana. AIR 1979 SC 1948: 1979 Cri LJ 1309. (1979) 3 SCC 760: 1979 UJ (SC) 594: 1979 Cri LR (SC) 573: 1979 Cri App R (SC) 259.

59. Mohammad alias Billiya Vs State of Rajastan,1999 AIR SCW 2215: 1999 Cri LJ 3509: 1999 Cri L.R (SC) 8.
60. Harichad Vs The Director of School Education AIR 1998 SC 788: 1998 AIR SCW 504 : 1998 Cri LJ 1106 : 1998 (1) JT 124 : 1998 (2) SCC 383: 1998 (1) Scale 136 : 1998 (1) Supreme 274.
61. Additional D.I.G of Police, Hyderabad Vs P.R. Mohan, 1998 SCC (L & S) 245: 1997 (11) SCC 571.
62. AIR 1990 SC 987: 1990 Cri :LJ 1013 : 1990 Lab IC 806 : 1990 (2) SCC 426 : 1990 (1) JT 339.
63. AIR 1976 SC 1271: 1979 Cri LJ 862.